THE UNWANTED SYMBOL

The Unwanted Symbol

AMERICAN FOREIGN POLICY, THE COLD WAR, AND KOREA, 1945-1950

Charles M. Dobbs

THE   KENT   STATE   UNIVERSITY   PRESS

Library of Congress Cataloging in Publication Data

Dobbs, Charles M.
  The unwanted symbol.

  Bibliography: p.
  Includes index.
  1. United States—Foreign relations—Korea. 2. Korea
—Foreign relations—United States. 3. United States—
Foreign relations—1945-1953. 4. Korean War, 1950-1953
—Causes. 5. World politics—1945-1955. I. Title.
E183.8.K7D597   327.730519   81-6261
ISBN 0-87338-258-7   AACR2

In Memory of my Father, Harry N. Dobbs

Contents

Preface

KOREA occupies a curious place in any account of the cold war in the 1940s. Ignored as relations between the Soviet Union and the United States developed into a grand hostility, Korea became an enduring symbol of the superpower confrontation with the outbreak of war in June 1950. American responses to the situation within and surrounding Korea in the five years after 1945 helped define much of American policy in East Asia in the years since 1950.

From the Second World War until the eve of the Korean War, Korea increased from a minor problem to a major concern—to a nearly total preoccupation of American foreign policy. The process by which Korea came to occupy a steadily more important place within American strategic interests illustrates the modern phenomenon of symbol creation. In Korea, American officials reacted to a difficult and confusing situation by avoiding reality, simplifying complexity, and creating a symbol of postwar contention. In time this unwanted symbolism became very powerful; by 1950 it can—and will—be argued that the symbol as much dominated the policy of the U.S. government as policy controlled the symbol. The government in Washington and its representatives abroad turned a repressive, undemocratic regime in the south, tinged by charges of wartime collaboration with the Japanese, unrestricted use of terror against opponents, and lack of "koreanness" (that it was an outside elite imposed on native nationalists) into "a beacon of light in Northeast Asia," "a continuing challenge in a communist sea," and the like. Having failed to bring about unification or rule by native and not expatriate Koreans, the Truman administration sought to withdraw. However, by 1950 it was trapped by its rhetoric and found it easier to remain in Korea. Knowledge of wartime and postwar diplomacy over Korea makes Truman's decision to intervene in June 1950 less surprising than had he chosen to avoid the conflict. The symbol, in part, became mightier than reality.

Korea also had an interesting relationship within the larger Soviet-American confrontation. Many scholars have detailed how the emerging cold war affected individual situations; few people know to what extent events in Korea during the 1940s may have determined the course of Soviet-U.S. relations. While Korea mattered little to most American officials, it may well have had great significance to the Soviets, Chinese (Nationalists and Communists), and Japanese. It occupies a critical area—"the fulcrum of power in Northeast Asia"—between China's resource-rich Northeast Provinces, Soviet Maritime Province, and Japan. History has demonstrated that the power which controls the Korean peninsula has a preeminent position in Northeast Asia. It is as important an area as Poland once was to Germany and Russia. Korea also bore similarities to the situation in postwar Germany, at least to Soviet leaders. Each area was divided into occupation zones where Soviet and American troops confronted one another; in each country, American actions might suggest that the United States would replace Germany and/or Japan as a threat to Soviet security. At times Soviet leaders may have sought to use Korea to establish a policy precedent for Germany. Korea also provides an example of how American officials submerged the problem of leftwing, Asian nationalism within the superpower confrontation.

American policy in Korea during the 1940s foreshadowed future policy in East Asia in the 1950s and 1960s. Attitudes, rhetoric, and policies would reappear as the government in Washington sought to impose a free world/communist world model in Asian lands wrestling with the last vestiges of colonialism. Having "lost" China, the U.S. government seemed determined to demonstrate its commitment and recover lost prestige through the backing of corrupt, inefficient Asian dictatorships. In the 1940s the American government sought to impress the Soviet Union with its determination and strength of purpose; in the 1950s and 1960s it sought to impress similarly the Chinese communists. American officials engaged in rhetorical overkill and sublimated a dislike of repressive regimes in favor of staunch anticommunist credentials. They avoided facing the powerful force of Asian nationalism. They did not perceive the bankruptcy of imperialism, the way many Asians viewed Western capitalism, and the longstanding national, ethnic, religious hatreds of the region. Avoiding reality, they failed to understand it. They concentrated on a political inclination—communists, democrats, conservatives—which did not always have relevancy. The result was and is tragic. The United States would emerge from its Korean experience a backer of old and discredited leaders, beliefs, regimes and allow its major adversaries the chance to appear champions of the underprivileged. The record also suggests that in creating a series of symbols beginning with Korea and later in other Asian lands, the government in Washington may have lost control over events. Clever Asian leaders and determined conservative politicians (and magazine editors and academics) in America may have learned how to maneuver successive administrations by using symbolism to promote continued U.S. involvement in Asian regimes.

I find the interwar period and Korea fascinating and I owe my interest to Professor John E. Wiltz of Indiana University's History Department. Professor Wiltz suggested I write a seminar paper about diplomacy and Korea and my interest developed. Wiltz exemplifies the best in a graduate school professor: concerned, demanding, encouraging. I owe him much for his many kindnesses as do many former graduate students and colleagues. I owe a larger debt of gratitude to my thesis supervisor, Professor Robert H. Ferrell, also of I.U.'s History Department. He helped explain the mysteries of research, the basics of good writing, the essentials of sound analysis to a hesitant, uncertain doctoral candidate. Many people have written in praise of the "Ferrell treatment" and I too attest to its beneficial effects. Professor Bernard W. Sheehan helped me to think, no small accomplishment. I owe my colleagues at Metropolitan State College a large measure of thanks for their constant encouragement and willingness to serve as sounding boards for my more imaginative flights of fancy. MSC is a teaching-oriented institution and their support helped make many long nights and weekends at the typewriter more bearable. The staff of the Kent State University Press helped turn an unsolicited and unrevised dissertation into a publishable manuscript with patience, wit, and the ability to find excellent outside readers. The willingness to read revision after revision kept me going. Lisle A. Rose of the State Department's Historical Office was kind enough to read a copy of the manuscript and suggest—with brutal honesty—the many places that required change, improvement, and expansion. Professor John Lewis Gaddis read a revised copy of the manuscript and forced me to place Korea in a broader policy context. Historian for the Strategic Air Command, Daniel Harrington, shared the fruits of his research into the Berlin situation and commented on the relevant chapter of the manuscript. Nancy Tucker of Colgate University and Howard Schonberger of the University of Maine allowed me to question them about their research when we participated on a panel about the United States and East Asia. Gary Clifford and Edmund S. Wehrle of the University of Connecticut offered valuable comments and encouragement on a version of chapters seven and eight. I must also thank the librarians and archivists who made the task of research a pleasurable hunt.

My family is wonderful and deserves a moment in print. My mother and father instilled a love of knowledge and a joy of learning in my sister Debra and I; they shared my triumphs and commiserated in my failures. All of my family has been supportive and none more so than my aunt, Miss Rose Dobbs, who, as a former senior editor, guided me and encouraged me all my life and helped me see this project to completion. My wife, Ann, is the greatest and in no way can I express all that I owe her. She has made my life complete. Last, but not least, Hannah Elizabeth arrived July 6, 1981, to make us a threesome.

Wartime Diplomacy and Korea

MODERN American involvement in Korea began during the Second World War as the State Department considered the question of the peninsula's postwar status. The Korea question touched on many issues of far greater importance: the future of Japan and its empire, the position of China, the influence of the Soviet Union in Northeast Asia, the status of European colonial empires, and the role of the United States in postwar Asia. It was a complex situation and American diplomats sought to postpone discussion until a postwar conference. Unfortunately it was not to be. In the early years of the Pacific war, the Nationalist government in Chungking had emerged as a self-styled protector of Korean nationalists, and when the United States entered the war in December 1941, Chiang Kai-shek's regime sought American support for Korean independence and the expatriate Koreans it supported. As long as China remained important in American military plans for the war against Japan, diplomats worried over Chiang's Korean policy, rivalry between Korean groups in China and the United States, and the effect early recognition might have on other, more sensitive areas. As China's importance lessened in 1944, American officials pondered the then-unstated role of Russia in postwar Northeast Asia. Would Stalin demand Korea? Would the desired Russian intervention against Japanese positions in Asia mean Soviet control over the peninsula? Would Soviet leaders attempt to revive tsarist dreams of hegemony in the East?

In the early part of the war, the Chinese government wished to reestablish its former influence over its neighbors, and in the case of Korea, it supported an exile organization in Chungking led by Kim Koo. Chiang wanted to secure Chinese influence over a future Korean government, and when the Japanese began a long-feared attack on China in the 1930s, many Korean exiles looked to the Chinese for help. During that decade the Nationalist government and the so-called Korean government-in-exile worked together in opposing Japanese aggression. In that struggle, the Chungking Koreans tied themselves closely to the illusion of Chinese power. It was an awkward arrangement because they were engaged in a rivalry with the "Korean Commission" led by Syngman Rhee, domiciled in Washington. Since his early days as a Korean revolutionary in the first decades of the twentieth century, Rhee had looked to the United States for help in overthrowing Japanese control of his homeland. As Japan and the United States moved closer to war, Rhee had increased his efforts to secure American support for Korean independence. By 1941 the aging nationalist uneasily watched his rivals in Chungking while he pressed the State Department for recognition.

As events lessened China's importance in the great task of defeating Japan—it no longer figured in invasion plans—the United States confronted Soviet power over the Korean issue. The fortunes of war, eventually favoring the USSR, reawakened Russian ambition in Northeast Asia. American strategy favored the European theater of operations over the Pacific. It would become apparent that Soviet help was necessary to defeat Japan since the atomic bomb was an unknown factor in the years 1943-44. Soviet assistance meant concessions to the Soviet government. As American leaders waited for Stalin's regime to declare its intentions in the Pacific war, they recognized the difficulty of prematurely supporting any Korean group and delayed planning for the future of the peninsula. Stalin's price for entering the war against Japan did not explicitly include Korea, but by the war's end Korea clearly lay within Russia's grasp.

I

The Korean expatriate organizations in Chungking and Washington had rejoiced at news of the Pearl Harbor attack and, convinced of an eventual American victory, they awaited the destruction of Japan's empire and Korea's return after thirty-five years of Japanese control to the family of sovereign states. The expatriates had a simplistic view of the world and were hopelessly cut off from the changing political climate within the peninsula. Nonetheless, they were confident of their ability to govern. Kim with his Chungking followers and Rhee with his American friends soon began to badger the government in Washington for recognition of Korea's independence and the legitimacy of their respective exile groups.

The Chinese also had hailed American entry into the war against Japan, and Chiang Kai-shek almost at once sought to use America's friendship to renew dreams of Chinese hegemony in East Asia, ignoring the problems of internal reform and reconstruction that awaited the war's end. In the mid-1930s, Chiang had abandoned the last remaining vestiges of Sun Yat-sen's "Three People's Principles" with its mild leftwing orientation and substituted a fascist-inspired revival of Confucian socio-political society. In addition to rebuilding China along centuries-old Confucian principles, Chiang hoped to resurrect China's traditional influence along its periphery. Chinese dynasties had prized control over the Korean peninsula, and Chiang recognized Korea's strategic location between three great Asian powers. Hundreds of years of on-again, off-again Japanese interest, tsarist attempts to gain Korea, and thirty-five years of Japanese rule all combined to make Chinese control over a future Korean government seem of great importance. Chiang would not, perhaps could not, see that times had changed, that the nationalism awakened by the May Fourth Movement (the May 4, 1919 response of Chinese students to the Paris Peace Accords awarding the Shantung Peninsula to Japan) and nurtured by Mao's forces would not be satisfied with a revival of Confucian orthodoxy, that his communist opponents were gaining public favor by seizing the mantle of nationalism, and that the depressed plight of the peasantry cried out for reform. Central to his illusion of power both within and outside China was control over a newly independent Korea. The Kuomintang championed Kim Koo's organization in Chungking, fearing the appearance of a Russian-sponsored Korean exile group in Siberia. It sought to enlist American support, contending that the alternative to Kim Koo (and Chiang) would be a Soviet-run Northeast Asia.

The State Department hestitated to accept Chinese suggestions, for Korea was an uncertain area, its potential leaders in prison or abroad. The problem of Korea seemed best ignored until a postwar conference, a meeting at which the Allies might arrange Korea's future. The department initially had found relations between Chiang, Kim, and Rhee confusing. From the outset, the Russian concern over Korea was clearly visible. When the Chungking exiles and Rhee both appealed for support, the State Department in a press release of December 10, 1941, expressed a "sympathetic interest" in exile organizations, guerrilla groups, and other resistance movements. Wishing to remain informed of their activities, the department would not, however, "extend any form of recognition to them, formal or informal."[1]

In ensuing months, the Koreans did their best to advance their cause, although it was a difficult time for the Allied war effort. Rhee arranged for the provisional government in Chungking to send him a formal declaration of war against Japan, to present to President Franklin D. Roosevelt. He felt confident that American recognition would follow. But the Americans continued to treat Rhee cautiously. While the director of the State Department's Office of Far Eastern Affairs, Stanley K. Hornbeck, received him with "careful circumspection," Ambassador Clarence E. Gauss in China was cabled soon after Pearl Harbor to "make very discreet inquiries . . . in regard to the so-called Provisional Government of the Republic of Korea, claiming to have its seat in Chungking." Far Eastern experts wanted to know the exile group's strength, its contacts with guerrillas in Korea and Manchuria (were there Korean guerrillas?), and its relations with the Chinese government.[2] As the State Department waited to learn the nature of Rhee's organization and its ability to help the Allied war effort against Japan, its leader continued his lobbying. His secretary, Chang Kee-young, had written in late December 1941 to Senator Guy Gillette, with whom Rhee was on friendly terms, asking for help. The senator replied that while he had discussed recognition of the provisional government with the State Department, and although the department was sympathetic, it hesitated to do anything that might arouse resentment toward those Americans still within the Japanese empire or about to be captured. A visit by Rhee to Gillette did not change the senator's mind, for Gillette would not help Rhee if, as the department believed, the Japanese might retaliate against Americans under their control.[3] It was the opening in what developed into a virtual war of words and nerves between the State Department and Rhee. An ardent nationalist who had lost touch with events within Korea after his exile well before the First World War, a Confucian who did not understand the change in Asian nationalism and whose hatred of anything Russian colored his outlook, Rhee continued to seek recognition. The department, realizing the factious nature of the expatriate Korean political scene, the lack of knowledge about events in Korea, and the danger of a hasty decision on a problem affecting relations with such powers as China and Russia, dealt with him cautiously.

Meanwhile, the embassy in China sent the department information about the Korean provisional government in Chungking and its links with Chiang's regime. Ambassador Gauss noted that, despite appeals of the provisional government's members for recognition and military aid, the exile group showed little strength (fewer than a thousand expatriates in the Chinese wartime capital), little organization, and little contact with the homeland. The embassy had learned that during the past decade the Chinese government had given Kim a great deal of assistance, doubtless in hope of reestablishing its traditional influence over Korea.[4]

With this and subsequent information, though preoccupied with the enormous complexity of wartime issues, the State Department slowly developed a policy with respect to Korea. Acting Secretary of State Sumner Welles cabled the embassy in London in February 1942 to tell the British Foreign Office that despite appeals of groups in China and the United States, the department would not recognize any organization of expatriates as "the primary movement for Korean opposition to Japanese oppression or make any commitment as to future recognition of Korea."[5] As Welles meanwhile had cabled Gauss, Japan's victorious advance in the Pacific momentarily made recognition by the United States "unlikely to arouse a response on any effective scale among Koreans generally in areas under Japanese control."[6] When the tide should turn against Japan, "a well-timed declaration might produce results."[7] The American government remained sympathetic. As early as February 9, 1942, Attorney General Francis Biddle issued a statement exempting Koreans in the United States from restrictions placed on enemy aliens since they had "never been sympathetic to the government imposed upon their homeland by military conquest."[8] Korean exiles received courteous treatment from most Americans, but they were unable to translate such sympathy into action favoring a future Korean independence.

The exiles continued to appeal to the United States for recognition, and the politics of expatriate Koreans remained a confusing affair; but it gradually became apparent that Rhee, rather than Kim Koo and the Chungking exiles, had the inside track with the American government, perhaps because Rhee was almost more of an American than a Korean. He had left Korea for the United States forty years before, and after receiving a Ph.D. at Princeton, with Woodrow Wilson as his thesis director, he had founded his own exile organization. From Wilson's presidency until the late 1930s he relied on that tenuous relationship and ties with American missionaries to plead Korea's cause. During the 1930s, Kim Koo had challenged Rhee for leadership of the exiles, and for a while he had used his reputation as an assassin of highly placed Japanese in Korea and his close ties with the Chinese to supplant Rhee as leader of the exiles. He reputedly accepted large bribes from Chinese officials. Then Rhee's star began to rise again. American entry in the Pacific war in 1941 bolstered Rhee's prestige within the independence movement, and Americans began to regard Rhee, who was head of what he described as the Korean Commission, as the George Washington of Korea.

Rhee's rise to influence with the government of the United States did not come without a great deal of effort. Rhee did his best to gain attention from the Americans, but it was difficult work and for months he could not be sure of the result. He wrote letters incessantly. To President Roosevelt he wrote that the provisional government of the Republic of Korea was "the sole representative of the Korean people."[9] He made every effort to increase his prestige and often exaggerated his role, perhaps believing that the State Department's reluctance to deal with him stemmed from a feeling of his unimportance. In fact, Hornbeck had remarked privately that the provisional government was a "self-constituted club with limited membership among a group of expatriates." Rhee took advantage of every opportunity. He arranged for two of his American admirers, John Staggers and Jay Jerome Williams, to get in touch with American missionaries driven out of Korea by the Japanese in 1940–41 to ask whom the Korean people believed to be their leader. Many years before, Rhee had become a convert to Christianity, and this act of conscience or perhaps politics enlarged his chances of leadership among the exiles. The missionaries apparently could not consider any non-Christian Korean as representative of the people, and answered that, at least for them, Rhee was the man. Hornbeck read the replies, and shelved the report.[10] Rhee again marshalled his American supporters. On March 6, 1942, the Reverend Frederick Brown Harris, minister of the Foundry Methodist Church in Washington, who along with Staggers and Williams was a trustee of the Korean-American Council, addressed a long letter to President Roosevelt arguing for immediate recognition of the provisional government. He asked also for military aid to train and arm the exiles. There was no answer. At the outset, it thus was discouraging work.

The Chinese government now attempted an obtuse strategy to lead the United States to recognize Kim Koo's organization and at the same time demonstrate China's greatness. A United Press report of March 23, 1942, published in the *Washington Post*, quoted an article in the official *Central Daily News* signed by Sun Fo, son of Sun Yat-sen, and president of the Chinese Legislative Yuan (one of the five branches of government under the Nationalist Chinese system), which urged the Chinese government to recognize the Korean government immediately. Acting Secretary Welles urgently cabled the embassy in Chungking for its

views, and Gauss replied that the embassy believed Sun Fo had
acted on his own.[11] This was difficult to believe. During the
1930s, the Chinese government had become Chiang Kai-shek,
and vice versa. Chiang would not have permitted Sun Fo to urge
the government into action unless it had his approval and suited
his purpose. If American officials followed the example of
Chinese recognition or even failed to discourage it, perhaps it
would bolster Chiang's declining prestige, cover up his domestic
difficulties, and demonstrate to Asians that China, once again,
was a great power.

In the effort to advance Kim Koo rather than give support
to the exile leadership of Rhee, the Chinese would not let the
Americans rest. Gauss cabled that a meeting of the Supreme
National Defense Council had heard a proposal for immediate
recognition of the Chungking exiles and after a three-hour discussion had sent it to the Generalissimo for a decision. "Please
inform the Chinese Vice-Minister urgently," Welles reacted, "that
we hope that, before the Chinese Government takes any defin-
itive action with regard to the question of recognition of a provisional government of Korea, it will be so good as to make
available to us its views and conclusions in this matter." The
Americans seemingly could not make clear to the Chinese their
unwillingness to recognize a provisional government domiciled
in the remote wartime captial of Nationalist China. Four days
later, Gauss informed Welles that the Chinese government would
keep the United States informed of any contemplated action.[12]

This maneuvering formed a part of what seems to have been
Chiang's plan to gain leadership of the expatriates. The president of China repeatedly confronted the State Department with
the Korean issue, sometimes appearing to give in to department
views, sometimes challenging them. Chiang, it was announced,
had decided to recognize the provisional government "without
delay," dispelling any suspicion that China had territorial ambitions in such Japanese-occupied areas as Korea, Thailand, and
Burma. It would prove China's adherence to the principles of
the Atlantic Charter. Chiang duly informed the Americans of his
views, desiring an early reply. Such a request was inconvenient,
to say the least. Secretary of State Cordell Hull wrote the presi-

dent on April 20, 1942, enclosing a draft reply to the Chinese. The letter called attention to Soviet interest in the question of Korea, and Hull concluded that "this whole question of Korean independence and recognition of a Korean government has many complicated and delicate aspects." He did not wish to dictate to the Chinese, he told FDR, but felt it would be appropriate for the United States to lay before the Chinese government an exposition of its views. With presidential approval, the secretary of state cabled Ambassador Gauss with a formal note for the Chinese. It mentioned the difference between "advocating independence for Korea and according recognition of any particular group of Koreans as the Provisional Government," and recalled the lack of unity among Korean expatriate groups and their lack of association with the Korean populace. Underlying the tone of concern was a strong disapproval of precipitate Chinese action. Shortly thereafter, Gauss was able to cable Washington that the Chinese had agreed to delay recognition, and thereby the case of Kim Koo, until some "more favorable time."[13]

At this early juncture the Koreans and Chinese did not hesitate to raise the specter of Russians hordes overrunning the Korean peninsula. For Rhee as well as Kim Koo, the devil had returned to Earth as a Russian bear. In January 1943, Rhee wrote Hull concerning Russia's ambitions in Korea. Failure to recognize the provisional government would "inevitably result in the creation of a communist state." In May of that year, he wrote the president that "now we have reports indicating Russia's aim to establish a Soviet Republic of Korea. . . . At the same time it should be borne in mind that the danger of Russian expansion in the Far East, so feared and dreaded by the United States forty years ago, has not entirely disappeared." In December 1943, Rhee claimed that Russia would use Korean divisions trained as part of Soviet Far Eastern forces to invade Korea and set up a communist republic. The evidence does suggest that Soviet leaders used such troops at Stalingrad and perhaps elsewhere along their western front in their desperate attempt to halt the German advance. Rhee's solution was recognition of the provisional government with himself as its head.[14] The Chinese likewise warned against the Russians. They desired the American government to equip an army of fifty thousand Koreans to counter the Soviet-armed Koreans in Siberia.[15]

Unwilling to confront the Russians on this issue when the war was hardly won, after the Soviets had defeated a German army at Stalingrad while the Anglo-American forces had not yet launched a cross-channel invasion of Europe, and with many issues of greater importance, State Department planners continued to move cautiously. The position of the Soviet Union as a neutral in the Pacific war also called for postponement of any decision on Korea until Soviet intentions in the Far East became more clear. If the United States supported Chiang's plans for Korea, that action (together with the embarrassing delay in the Anglo-American invasion of the continent) might have unforeseen consequences. Perhaps the growing perception that Chinese military weakness demanded Soviet help in the war against Japan also influenced the diplomats' decision to move cautiously.

In addition, the question of Korean independence and recognition of the provisional government meant a precedent-setting action regarding the European colonial empires of South and Southeast Asia. Gauss had cabled Secretary Hull in March 1942 that "the subject of Korea is not entirely unrelated to the problem of the independence aspirations of other Asiatic peoples including the Indians." The department agreed that recognition of an exile Korean government, whether under Rhee or Kim, without some statement on the future governance of other colonial areas, would be inopportune. Taking advantage of German military success in Europe, following the defeat of France and the Netherlands and continued threats to Great Britain, Japan overran most of the European colonial empires in Asia and the Pacific (as well as the American-occupied Philippine Islands). This action dealt the colonialism of white caucasians a mortal blow, though this fact would not become clear until the new wave of Asian nationalism after the war.

As the Japanese temporarily destroyed much of the colonial framework in Asia and threatened to dismantle what remained, President Roosevelt apparently was moving to ensure that when Japan finally was defeated those European empires would become history. Walter LaFeber notes that the president wanted to replace colonialism in Asia with a Chinese-backed (and American-dominated) system of trusteeships. Christopher Thorne writes that "Roosevelt did not consider France worthy, in the light of her colonial record, of receiving back Indochina after the war," and "he emphasized that no binding promises had been or could be made over Indochina." As other articles suggest, the president felt that colonialists had forfeited the right to rule. He viewed the French in Indochina with distaste, believed the British in the Indian subcontinent not much better, and had little good to say about the Dutch in the East Indies. Obviously, the manner in which the powers severed Korea from Japan's Inner Empire via early recognition would become a model for the remaining Asian empires. Since the State Department had less faith in the Nationalist Chinese, viewed the British more favorably, and recognized the importance of a hasty decision in Korea, and since the president wavered, there was more reason to delay consideration of Chinese and Korean requests for Korean independence.[16]

The issue of Korea as a precedent came to the forefront when the British failed to resolve their crisis in India. The British had a problem in India, for Mohandas K. Gandhi, having discovered a sense of "Indianness" as a result of discrimination in South Africa, represented a mounting threat to British control. Gandhi saw the attitude of European whites toward Africans and the so-called coloureds in which he was grouped. Perhaps the views of South Africans were extreme, but it caused Gandhi to return to the subcontinent; and by the 1940s he had aroused the latent nationalism of the Indian peoples at an inopportune time. The Japanese in Burma were threatening to invade India and possibly link up with German forces coming through the Suez Canal; Britain afforded that theater little materiel and men and feared a Japanese-inspired nationalist revolt. Some of Gandhi's supporters, in fact, viewed the Japanese with favor and looked forward to a British defeat. Throughout 1942, department officials, sensitive to the British problem in India, used it as a reason for inaction whenever the Koreans or Chinese raised the matter of recognition. The Roosevelt administration also was moving to resolve the ambiguities in its attitude toward colonial empires. The president made a distinction between "good" and "bad" colonialists and considered the British "good" (no doubt a result of his warm relations with Churchill) and the French as "bad." Given the additional complexities, department officers concluded that caution on Korea, which mattered little for its own sake, was essential. Under Secretary Welles believed that members of the Pacific War Council, which was an interallied group including not merely the British but other Pacific and Commonwealth nations, were willing to recognize a Korean government-in-exile and to help organize and equip a military force of Korean exiles only after a successful conclusion to the then-current negotiations of the British government with Indian nationalists. Sir Stafford Cripps was attempting to reach agreement over a form of self-government. He worried over the future of the empire; Gandhi and his followers were impatient. The negotiations failed, the problem of Indian independence continued and with it the hesitation of the American government to make any public decision over Korea.[17]

By the summer of 1943, diplomacy on the Korean issue almost had reached an impasse. The chairman of the House Committee on Foreign Affairs, Sol Bloom, sent the department on April 15, 1943, several copies of House Joint Resolution 109, "To provide for the recognition of the Republic of Korea." Clearly this was the result of Rhee's persistent lobbying efforts. Hull rebuked such congressional initiative, telling Bloom unceremoniously that "no useful purpose could be served by passage at this time of this resolution and that, on the contrary, passage by the Congress of this . . . could not but create confusion, misunderstanding, and embarrassment in the conduct of this country's foreign relations."[18]

In the autumn of 1943, the United States government arranged for the Cairo Conference between Roosevelt, Winston Churchill, and Chiang Kai-shek just before the Big Three meeting with Stalin at Teheran. Roosevelt seemed to want the conference in Cairo to prop up the prestige of Chiang's faltering regime.[19] Chiang needed a diplomatic success to cover his weak performance in the war. At the ensuing meeting in the shadow of the pyramids, the Western Allies pledged themselves to help

China regain all of the territory lost to Japan since the late nine-teenth century, including Formosa (Taiwan), the Pescadores, and Manchuria. Once again, China appeared a great power. Many Chinese saw this meeting of 1943 as their country's greatest dip-lomatic success, the final step to overthrowing the hated impe-rialist system. The Western Allies finally gave up their extraterritorial rights in China gained from the dying Ch'ing empire in the 1800s, and the United States once again, after a hiatus of some sixty years, permitted Chinese emigration. In some ways it was a great success, though it would prove illusory.

At Chinese insistence, the Cairo Conference proclaimed its support for Korean independence. Chinese sources indicate that Chiang had persuaded Roosevelt to resist Sir Alexander Cado-gan's appeal to avoid the Korean issue. Cadogan wanted it as a bargaining point with Japan while Chiang wanted to appear as the benefactor of a new Korean republic. Roosevelt had little difficulty siding with Chiang, and the conference endorsed the Chinese proposal.[20] However, the Americans at Cairo remained cautious about any involvement in the political problems of Ko-rea. On the issue of Korean independence, they accepted the wording suggested by the British delegation, which included a careful phrase, "in due course." The American draft of the con-ference communiqué, composed by Harry Hopkins, remarked that "we are mindful of the treacherous enslavement of the peo-ple of Korea by Japan and are determined that that country, at the proper moment after the downfall of Japan, shall become a free and independent country." The British draft, written in Churchill's hand, stated that "the aforesaid three great powers, mindful of the enslavement of the people of Korea, are deter-mined that in due course Korea shall become free and indepen-dent." The American proposal promised Koreans independence within a reasonable time; the British one seemed to anticipate using Korea as a bargaining point in postwar negotiations among the great powers. The Americans adopted the British version (which Stalin, too, later accepted).[21]

Perhaps the Americans made a mistake with the commu-niqué, for it angered the Koreans. In his memoirs, Cordell Hull later wrote that Roosevelt did not ask State Department advice in this matter. Hull, to be sure, was not present at Cairo, nor was he to be present in Teheran. In retrospect and at the time, he considered the Cairo statement on independence unwise. "The Koreans wanted their independence immediately after Korea was liberated and not in due course. . . . They feared their country would be placed under the control of China."[22] The Korean response had been immediate.[23] Syngman Rhee and Kim Koo denounced the communiqué; the expatriate publication, *The Voice of Korea*, editorialized against it; Korean organizations in the United States and Hawaii protested to Congress. More importantly, the exiles in China subverted it. The Chungking Koreans translated the English phrase "in due course" as "immediately" or "within a few days," for there was no Korean equivalent. Copies smuggled in from China flooded the peninsula. Knowledge of this erroneous translation, which raised Korean hopes unduly, did not reach the State Department until the first American forces landed in Korea almost two years later.

For the Chinese, the Cairo Conference proved only a temporary success as the tide of war in the Pacific reduced China's importance. In its last great campaign of November 1944, the Japanese army in China seized airfields used by the United States Army Air Force to bomb Japanese-held Chinese cities and even Japan itself, overran Chinese positions, and pushed Nationalist troops deeper into the interior of the country. With its best forces facing the communists to the north or awaiting the end of the deadly three-sided conflict, Chiang's government could do little to assist proposed American landings on the China coast. The American military thenceforth dropped the Chinese from their calculations. As a corollary to this situation, Chinese influence on Korean policy no longer concerned American officials.[24]

Yet one could foresee trouble looming over the Siberian landscape. The long-dormant Russian bear, its appetite whetted by colossal sacrifices against the Nazis and the coming power vacuum in Northeast Asia, threatened potential American plans. And as China's role lessened, Russia's importance increased in the great task of defeating Japan and liberating lands occupied by Japanese forces. Thus, American diplomats, having resisted Chinese lobbying for recognition of the Korean provisional government, now had to contend with the decidedly more powerful Soviet Union and its undeclared plans for postwar Korea (and Northeast Asia).

II

With victory beginning to appear certain in 1944, American officials took a new look at the Korean problem and found new areas of concern. The military needed guidance for a possible postwar occupation of the peninsula; the government in Washington pondered the effect that Soviet entry into the Pacific war would have on postwar East Asia; and Syngman Rhee replaced the Chungking exiles and the Nationalist Chinese government in asking embarrassing questions about Korea's postwar status. This complicated situation would continue until—with surprising speed—the war against Japan ended and caught American officials unprepared on the question of Korea.

Based on a series of papers by the Interdivisional Area Committee on the Far East, the State Department soon was drawing the outline of a postwar policy. The War and Navy Departments had asked the State Department for advice about military government. Planners wanted to know the extent of military responsibility for civil affairs in Korea in the event of an American occupation. Undecided about what nations would participate in any forthcoming occupation of Korea, the State Department looked forward to central, not zonal, administration. In the future occupation forces, it seemed "politically advisable" to include contingents from China, the United States, Great Britain or one of the Dominions, and (if it had entered the Pacific war) the Soviet Union. There should be "substantial representation" for the United States, but under no circumstances should America undertake to handle the Korean occupation by itself. (It is curious that the State Department recommended different roles for the United States in Korea, a part of Japan's Inner Empire, and the Japanese home islands without considering the relationship between Korea and Japan.) The army of occupation should be organized quickly, integrating the four commands. The department warned that a military government might have to rule

Korea for a "considerable duration." At this early juncture, planning was more theoretical than practical, based more on wishful thinking than on actual knowledge of the Korean situation.[25]

This theoretical plan set forth by the State Department was not without flaw. Unfortunately, few officials in the American government understood Korea's relationship with Japan. Was Korea a loyal part of the Inner Empire as evidenced by the presence of Korean units in the Japanese military (especially prison camp guards)? Were Koreans seething with unrest against their Japanese oppressors and ready to revolt against economic, social, and political tyrannies? The point was critical, but most American officials overlooked or missed its importance. It would become more clear in time over the difficulty of retaining Japanese technicians in Korea after liberation of the country. The lack of trained Korean nationals, which was the deliberate result of Japanese economic policies, meant that the Korean economy would be shaky and perhaps in danger of collapse. Officials sought to balance this problem against the intense hatred felt by the Korean exiles (and possibly by all Koreans) for the Japanese. The Department of State concluded unwisely that the "politically undesirable results" of retaining Japanese technicians would have to yield to the practical needs of Korean industry and government.[26]

More importantly, the department did not consider the position of the Soviet Union at the war's end. The Russian government already had given indications of being anxious to fulfill the old tsarist dreams for East Asia, replacing the rising sun with the hammer and sickle. Given the determination of American leaders to bring the Soviet Union into the war against Japan, few officials considered its postwar implications and remained content to wait for a conference after the war to settle outstanding issues. Without Soviet participation or with a delayed entrance into the war, meetings among Western Allies and China had to contend with an empty chair. The very closeness of Soviet power to the Korean peninsula, the common border with Siberia, and Korea's position at the fulcrum of power in Northeast Asia (astride China, Japan, and the Soviet Maritime Province) would threaten an American-imposed solution. Planners in the

State Department hardly knew what to do, for many combined a feeling of Korea's unimportance to American security with a general lack of appreciation for geopolitical realities. In a memorandum of May 4, 1944, the department's Interdivisional Area Committee on the Far East summarized the dilemma of the United States over Korea: an independent but weak Korea would again become subject to international pressure and intrigue, making it highly desirable that some form of interim supervisory organ be established.[27]

The year 1944 passed awkwardly, and then came the Yalta Conference in early February 1945 when President Roosevelt faced Soviet power openly in Europe, imminently in Asia (during the Moscow Conference of Foreign Ministers in October 1943, Stalin had promised Secretary Hull that Russia eventually would enter the Pacific war). FDR offered Stalin concessions in the Far East in exchange for a promise to enter the Asian war and relieve the United States of a longer, more costly struggle against Japan. Roosevelt, of course, gave away little at Yalta that Stalin could not seize. To obtain participation in the final assault on Japan, he offered the Russian leader a return to the position in East Asia that his nation had held prior to the Russo-Japanese War of 1904-5; economic concessions in Manchuria, warm-water ports at Dairen and Port Arthur, retrocession of all of Sakhalin, and (an extra concession) the Kuriles.

Debate would arise over Roosevelt's handling of the Korean question at Yalta. While Korea received little attention at the conference, Stalin's price seemed to include some form of hegemony over that nation. Power in Manchuria appeared to presume power in Korea.[28] Daniel Yergin, in *The Shattered Peace* (1977), argues that Roosevelt understood Russia would dominate northeastern Asia, perhaps a situation similar to the buffer states in Eastern Europe that FDR was conceding to help establish a "friendly" relationship with the Soviet dictator. Some State Department officials felt that the president had ignored a briefing paper on Korea which called for detailed agreement on a trusteeship. Roosevelt, however, was not seeking detailed agreements; he wanted to create a genuine friendship with Stalin and from that build a Soviet-American alliance, or at least an understanding. Scholars afterward were to discern a mistaken policy over Korea at Yalta. Cho Soon-sung, author of *Korea in World Politics, 1940-1950*, published in 1967, would fault Roosevelt for not obtaining some sort of Soviet commitment to Korean independence. But that was not possible given the president's view of the Yalta meeting and the indeterminate nature of final military positions in the Far East. Would an agreement appear silly if Russia occupied the entire peninsula, or if America did? E. Grant Meade, who wrote of his experiences as a Civil Affairs officer in Korea in 1945-46, recalled the wartime policy as "vague, ambiguous, and poorly thought out" and observed that Yalta was the proper time for an arrangement: "Months before that conference, the remaining Axis powers had ceased to constitute a serious offensive threat." Meade also ignored the purpose of the meeting. As long as American military strategists wanted the Soviets to defeat the Japanese on the mainland, how would Stalin interpret an American demand for all or part of the Korean peninsula? Leland M. Goodrich, in *Korea: A Study of US Policy in the United Nations* (1966), reflected that "while the 'Terms of Entry of the Soviet Union into the War Against Japan' did not mention Korea, they did provide for the recognition of Russia's pre-1905 rights in Manchuria, and consequently, must have strongly suggested by analogy that the Soviet Union would later assert the historical Russian interest in the future of Korea as well." Lisle A. Rose, in his study *Roots of Tragedy* (1976), does not offer an interpretation of Roosevelt's (lack of) Korean policy at Yalta. As with many other scholars who have studied American planning for postwar Asia, he notes that at that time there had been little planning; most American officials expected the war to continue for a few years. Such members of the so-called New Left school as the Kolkos, while not mentioning Korea, do agree that Roosevelt was seeking an accommodation with Stalin and thus seem to suggest he would have given the strategic peninsula to the Russians.[29]

Given the importance of Korea to American policy, it does seem that President Roosevelt practiced a shrewd diplomacy at Yalta. The proximity of Soviet power to the Korean peninsula argued, he appears to have realized, for a Soviet-dominated occupation. There was no reason to incur Stalin's anger over Korea and thus jeopardize an *entente cordiale* or more important objectives in Eastern Europe, Germany, or Japan. If Roosevelt made a mistake, it was in adhering too closely to traditional American diplomacy. In previous wars, the nation's leaders often postponed consideration of a postwar world—practical issues, not idealistic notions—until the war's end; perhaps it is an American tradition. In that respect, Roosevelt's handling of the Korean issue at Yalta was representative of much of American diplomcy in eastern Asia during the 1940s.

The expatriate Koreans seemed to be vastly unhappy about Yalta, and accused the United States government of secretly handing Korea over to the Soviet Union. Rhee believed he had seen the work of three decades brushed aside by a foolhardy attempt to buy Soviet friendship. Shortly after Harry S. Truman became president, Rhee telegraphed Senators Owen Brewster and Walter F. George and Congressman Clare E. Hoffman that Truman had learned of a secret agreement at Yalta ceding Korea to Russia. The agreement, allegedly signed by the United States, Great Britain, and the Soviet Union, declared that Korea would remain under Soviet influence after the war's end. It supposedly was made at Stalin's request. Secretary of State Edward R. Stettinius, Jr., Rhee said, refused to discuss the issue and was stalling. He concluded that "freedom-loving Americans" should urge Truman to speak out. When the three legislators made no reply, Rhee called a press conference and reiterated his charge. Since there was no large news stories at the time, the press gave the accusation wide coverage.[30] Rhee also directly addressed the president, repeating his charge: "The recent discovery of a secret agreement at Yalta contrary to the Cairo Declaration regarding Korea was doubtlessly just as startling to your Excellency as it was to me. This was not the first time that Korea was made a victim of secret diplomacy." Noting the forthcoming United Nations Conference at San Francisco, he asked Truman to prove there was no secret agreement by standing behind the government-in-exile's request for United Nations observer status. "Your Excellency's instructions alone can open the door for us," he concluded.[31]

The secrecy surrounding the Yalta negotiations helped Rhee raise an embarrassing protest; but the Department of State vigorously denied his claims. The letter to Truman went to the acting director of the Office of Far Eastern Affairs, Frank P. Lockhart, who answered on behalf of Acting Secretary of State Joseph C. Grew (by this time Stettinius was attending the San Francisco Conference). Lockhart, displaying the department's irritation with the persistent Korean, carefully urged Rhee to cease annoying the government. Lockhart pointed out that in Chungking a spokesperson of the provisional government had issued a statement to the Central News Agency denouncing as "groundless rumor" the talk of a secret agreement at Yalta about Korea's position after the war. Lockhart asked Rhee if this denial did not answer his charges. He reiterated the American position on the government-in-exile:

> The United Nations which are represented at the San Francisco Conference all have legally constituted governing authorities, whereas the "Korean Provisional Government" . . . has never had administrative authority over any part of Korea nor can it be considered representative of the Korean people of today. Its following among exile Koreans is limited. [We will not] . . . compromise the right of the Korean people to choose the ultimate form and personnel of the government which they may wish to establish. . . . This carries no implication whatsoever of a lack of sympathy for the people of Korea and their aspirations for freedom.

The harsh letter was directed more against Rhee than the Chungking exiles, for he had caused the department to spend considerable time answering charges over such a minor issue. Lockhart concluded the letter by referring to "you and other individuals interested in the welfare of Korea," pointedly ignoring Rhee's claim to official status.[32]

The Korean patriot tried once more, in a letter of July 25, 1945, in which he graciously thanked Lockhart for the "kind letter" and repeated his claim of a secret agreement. He said that "an American of unimpeachable reputation" had been his source, that Soviet authorities had remained "ominously silent," that Churchill had declared that not all the topics discussed at Yalta were for public consideration, and that Korea for decades had been the victim of secret diplomacy. Seeking to refute Lock-hart's charge (and the department's belief) that the provisional government was unrepresentative, Rhee contended that it had the support of the Korean people, that it represented many shades of opinion, and that it enjoyed de facto recognition from both China and France. He feared, he said, that his last chance to lead the Korean people to independence might fail.[33]

The Korean issue did not easily fade, if only because the tireless Rhee was agitating it. The United Nations Conference at San Francisco, lasting from April until June, presented another opportunity for appeal. The minister of foreign affairs of the Korean provisional government, Tjo So-wang, residing in Chungking, opened the new confrontation. In February 1945, the American chargé in Chungking, George Atcheson, related that during a visit to the embassy Tjo had added to his usual list of requests and asked that his "government" be invited to the San Francisco Conference. Rhee's Korean Commission, Tjo said, would supply additional representatives. Atcheson asked Stettinius for instructions. Grew replied that by agreement among the conference's sponsoring powers, meaning the United States, Great Britain, the Republic of China, and the Soviet Union, invitations had gone to nations which had joined the anti-Axis alliance as of March 1, 1945. The department had made no provisions for observers.[34] Rhee now wrote and repeated Tjo's request and received a reply from the secretary of state reiterating Grew's comments to Atcheson. Unwilling to cease his arduous efforts, Rhee sought to convince the department to change its views:

> The inclusion of Argentina, Syria, and Lebanon to the United Nations Conference since March 1 prompts me to ask whether or not the official delegation of the Korean Provisional Government might not be permitted to participate in the San Francisco Conference. If the department remains adamant, may I be permitted to respectfully request that, because of the admission of those nations, that nations participating in the San Francisco Conference be permitted to receive the request of the Republic of Korea for inclusion in their number and, through democratic processes (i.e., a vote) record their wishes on this vital subject.[35]

This letter of March 1945 went unanswered.

The State Department could hardly allow the Koreans to attend the UN Conference. Favorable action on Korea's case might create a precedent for policy toward colonial peoples— India, as mentioned, being the obvious case. It might also prove to be a precedent for other provisional governments, and the department wished to avoid precedents for recognizing (or not recognizing) the Soviet-dominated satellite states in Eastern Europe. There was a possible difficulty of a precedent applying even to the governments of northern Europe. During a May 30 meeting of the United States delegation in San Francisco, the members discussed whether the Chinese delegation might request Korean participation if Norway raised the question of Denmark's status in the world organization. Superficially, there were similarities between the wartime (and postwar) status of Denmark and Korea. Were they unwilling victims of aggression, Nazi and Japanese? Was Denmark's failure to resist Hitler's legions and Korea's place within the Inner Empire a sign that they were in the enemy's camp or, at the very least, not a member of the Allied nations making war on totalitarianism? It was confusing, and many other issues seemed more important. The American delegation wished to avoid a decision on Korea that might have unforeseen effects on the situation in Europe and in the colonial world. Secretary Stettinius reminded those present that the Korean question was an extremely private matter for many reasons, and that no word of its discussion should leave the delegation meeting. The Korean issue, he felt, was too complex for public display. Recognizing Korea meant recognizing Rhee and Kim Koo; this could precipitate a Soviet-American confrontation, for the Soviets might create a Korean government of their own.[36]

One complication after another seemed to arise over the postwar government of Korea. Particular points were the unrepresentative character of the Korean exiles, and their lack of connection with the homeland. The department knew what the exiles would not, perhaps could not, admit: that the expatriates had lost touch with the political climate in Korea, one which increasingly called for a radical solution to the problems of postwar reconstruction. In a letter discussing general postwar conditions in Asia, Grew explained to Secretary of War Henry L. Stimson that "there will undoubtedly be considerable confusion and chaos in Korea when Japanese rule ends . . . with the liberation, tenant farmers will undoubtedly expect sweeping agrarian reforms and may take definite steps to destroy control of the landlords." The exiles, he said, did not represent such radical views.[37] The Korean situation demanded radical reform; the people were almost desperate. As Gregory Henderson makes clear in his excellent book, *Korea: Politics of the Vortex*, published in 1968, three out of four Korean farmers were tenants on farms of three or four acres. Between one-third and three-quarters of their produce went to the landlord; with the remainder, the farmer paid his expenses, including taxes and irrigation costs. By late winter to early spring of each year, whole communities of peasants were reduced to eating root and bark. Many landlords and merchants were in league with the Japanese.

Rhee's intense nationalism and hatred of Japan and Russia rested on a foundation of Confucian thought and belief in an ordered society. He wanted to turn back the clock to the era of the Yi Dynasty: happy peasants would toil on small plots, supporting a native elite that would revitalize Korean culture and politics. Neither he nor Kim Koo, likewise a conservative, was capable of grasping the need for radical change, for drastically remaking Korean society. This need was felt especially in the countryside, for, as in China, landlords and industrialists had compromised themselves by cooperating with the Japanese oppressors. Neither Rhee nor Kim Koo could see the international ramifications of the issue. American officials, however, did understand the relation between societal upheaval and Soviet power. Grew had written Stimson that the economic and political situation in Korea was conducive to adoption of communist ideology even though most Koreans feared Russia. "The activities of a Russian-sponsored socialist regime in Korea might easily receive popular support."[38]

As Stettinius was speaking to the San Francisco delegation about the complexity of the Korean problem, he might have been thinking of the need for Russian help in the Pacific war, seemingly crucial to limit casualties in an assault against the Japanese home islands. General George C. Marshall was saying in these months that "our objective should be to get the Russians to deal with the Japanese in Manchuria and Korea." General Douglas MacArthur supported this judgment and "emphatically stated" that no attempt to invade Japan proper should occur until the Russians went into action in Manchuria. MacArthur realized that the Russians might demand all of Manchuria, Korea, and possibly part of north China, but he thought the taking of such territory by the Soviet Union was probably inevitable.[39]

As the time approached for the Russians to fulfill their Yalta agreement to enter the Pacific war, the American government belatedly sought some understanding over Korea, and the idea of trusteeship seemed the best device to prevent Soviet domination. Previously, the State Department had considered trusteeships only in theory: now Truman told Grew, Ambassador Averell Harriman, and Charles E. (Chip) Bohlen in mid-May that the government needed to clarify the question of a Korean trusteeship.[40] From Moscow, Harry Hopkins reported Stalin's approval of some form of trusteeship.[41] Assuming that the Soviets wished an agreement, the department prepared a series of briefing papers for the forthcoming Potsdam Conference. The Cairo Declaration, to which the Soviets had agreed in 1943, might not prevent the Russians from setting up a "friendly" regime in Korea. The department concluded that a written understanding was necessary to create an "interim international supervisory administration." In the event of Soviet intransigence or differing views, no one considered the alternatives; American leaders saw no reason for disagreement among wartime Allies over postwar objectives.[42]

As Truman made preparations for his first summit conference, he received some disquieting news about Russian policy. Harriman cabled the results of the Soong-Stalin talks, in which a Chinese delegation led by Chiang's brother-in-law, T.V. Soong, had offered to grant Russia's former position along the long Sino-Soviet border in exchange for support in the Kuomintang's dealings with the communists in Yenan. Harriman, an anti-Soviet hardliner, agreed with Soong's judgment that despite Stalin's desire for a "detailed understanding" over a Korean trusteeship, the Russians might deploy their Korean divisions and dominate Korean affairs even if there was a four-power trusteeship. Stalin's behavior with Soong made it seem wise, Harriman said, that American troops accept the Japanese surrender at least on the Kwantung Peninsula and in Korea. "I cannot see that we are under any obligation to the Soviets to respect any zone of Soviet military operation." A letter to Truman from Stimson two weeks later seconded Harriman's fears. "This is the Polish question transplanted to the Far East," the secretary of war concluded. He believed that "at least a token force of American soldiers or marines should be stationed in Korea during the trusteeship." Truman's personal representative on postwar reparations, former oilman and Democratic party figure Edwin W. Pauley, also wrote that "discussions on reparations and other matters convinced me that our forces should quickly occupy as much of the industrial areas of Korea and Manchuria as we can."[43]

At the Potsdam Conference in July-August 1945, military considerations dominated the discussion, and the Western Allies avoided Russian attempts to talk about Korean policies. Both Stalin and Molotov tried without success to reach an understanding over Korea with the British and Americans. Stalin on July 22 remarked that "there are other mandates. . . . We could exchange views on the question of Korea." Churchill interrupted: "We can exchange views on any subject but at the end we have had only an interesting discussion." Later that day Molotov tried to raise the question of Korea, with similar lack of result.[44]

But the no-discussion policy in fact gave the appearance of offering Korea to the Soviet Union. An exchange between General Marshall and the Soviet chief of staff, General Alexei E. Antonov, was illustrative. It took place during a tripartite military meeting on Tuesday, July 24, and the two men easily agreed on areas of operation for the respective naval and air forces. Antonov asked if American land forces would operate along the shores of Korea in coordination with Russian ground forces attacking from across the Yalu and Tumen Rivers. Marshall said no, that such an operation would expose American shipping to Japanese suicide attacks and require assault ships already planned for three landings on Kyushu. While Korea was of obvious importance to Soviet operations, American forces had the reduction of Japan as their principal objective.[45]

Whatever could be read into the Marshall-Antonov conversation, it is certain that from the meetings of military officials at Potsdam came the idea of the 38th parallel as a line of division between American and Soviet occupying troops in Korea. While at Potsdam, Marshall had called in Lieutenant General John E. Hull, then the army's chief of operations, and told him to prepare a plan to move troops to Korea. General Hull and some of his assistants studied a map of Korea and decided that the American zone should contain at least two major ports, including Pusan on the southeast tip of the peninsula. This led to the drawing of a line north of Seoul to include the port of Inchon along the 38th parallel. Later in Washington, a meeting on the night of August 10-11 confirmed the 38th parallel as the basis for zonal occupation. The imminent Japanese surrender forced an emergency consideration of orders for General MacArthur and arrangements with other Allied governments to liberate Korea. Staff members of the State-War-Navy Coordinating Committee (SWNCC) met in the office of Assistant Secretary of War John J. McCloy. The State Department wanted a line as far north as practicable. The military lacked troops for Korea. Nearby were several hundred thousand Soviet troops. McCloy asked Colonel Charles H. Bonesteel, III, and Colonel Dean Rusk to retire to an adjoining room to make a proposal. They recommended the 38th parallel "even though it was further north than could be realistically reached by U.S. forces in event of Soviet disagreement," but did so "because we felt it important to include the capital in the American zone." In recounting the events some years later, Rusk expressed surprise that the Soviets had accepted his proposal.[46]

Concerning the decision to draw a line at the 38th parallel, a conflicting story would appear in John M. Allison's autobiography, *Ambassador from the Prairie*, published in 1973. Allison, ambassador to Japan in the 1950s, wrote that Brigadier General George (Abe) Lincoln, one of Marshall's aides, had drawn the line, albeit in a manner reminiscent of Rusk's story. "Perhaps both Lincoln and Rusk were in the room and made the decision together." According to Allison, when the draft reached officers of the American navy in the predawn hours of August 11, Admiral M. B. Gardner suggested moving the surrender line north to the 39th parellel, believing that Secretary of the Navy James V. Forrestal favored such a recommendation. Gardner pointed out that the 39th parallel would place much of southern Manchuria with its warm-water ports and Japanese-built industry in the American zone. Lincoln felt, however, that the Russians would hardly accept a surrender line that barred them from Dairen and other parts of the Liaotung Peninsula and that in any case American units would have great difficulty reaching Dairen ahead of the Russians. He phoned Assistant Secretary of State James Dunn, who agreed, remarking that Korea was more important politically to the United States than Dairen, and that the new secretary of state, James F. Byrnes, would concur.[47]

In such a manner, whether by Bonesteel and Rusk or by Lincoln, the fateful line was drawn, and years later President Truman and other officials would characterize it as a convenient allocation of responsibility for acceptance of the Japanese surrender, a practical solution, "a military division that became a political one."[48] But historians have raised difficult questions about the drawing of the boundary at the 38th parallel. Why did Stalin accept a line that did not represent the limit of Russian military capability? Why did America seemingly challenge Russia for part of Korea? Most writers have answered the first question by saying that Stalin probably felt that some moderation was necessary. In the cables of the time, Stalin himself offered a reason for accepting the parallel, for as soon as he received Truman's message on Korea he replied with a request for permission to accept the Japanese surrender on Hokkaido. He was playing for a higher stake—control over part of Japan. If he could neutralize the Soviet Union's traditional enemy in East Asia, he could accept a temporary American presence in southern Korea. Soviet troops meanwhile would strip Manchuria of its Japanese-built industry and cart it off to Russia. But as early as 1943, the United States government had decided to handle the Japanese occupation alone, and, although the Russians persisted in their protests, American resolve in this regard never weakened.

As to the second question, the American decision to occupy part of Korea, a recent scholar has seen the 38th parallel as an "explicit testing of Soviet intentions. Korea was a prime index of Soviet plans for Asia, just as Poland for Europe." According to this view, the United States was challenging the security needs of the Soviet Union. But the theory does seem complicated. Considering the relative contributions of America and Russia to the war in the Pacific and the Korean peninsula's historic importance to Japan and China as well as to the Soviet Union, the American desire for the 38th parallel was within the bounds of political reasonableness. Ceding the entire peninsula might mean Soviet dominance in East Asia and threaten American plans for the United Nations and, thereby, for fulfillment of the Atlantic Charter.[49]

Wartime diplomacy over Korea set several important patterns. Given circumstances, American policy for Korea throughout the 1940s would develop logically from the Second World War. The confusions of wartime diplomacy would continue; the hasty and sometimes incomplete decision-making process would reoccur. American officials still would find Korea of little strategic significance; they would be surprised to find that the politics of Korea often influenced affairs in areas of great importance, as the issue had affected India, Indochina, and Japan during the war. Of course, as the confusion continued, policymaking vacillated, and the situation would worsen or suddenly change. Similar to the hasty decision to occupy Korea at the 38th parallel without consideration of likely consequences, the internal situation in Korea, or the attitude of Soviet leaders, American officials would continue merely to react to the situation. They would never control the situation, and in time they would realize their defenselessness. Having allowed policy to drift and the situation to worsen, they would turn in the future to making Korea into a false symbol of American values.

Wartime policy toward Korea indicated the nature of American crisis diplomacy. Clearly, Korea was not as important as Japan, or Germany, or the Soviet Union. Day-to-day attention remained at a minimum. Officials reacted when the situation demanded action. The sudden end to the war caught Far Eastern experts unprepared and luckily the Soviets did not choose to make an issue of the hastily chosen occupation lines. The Korean example was (and is) probably not unique. Throughout the 1940s, Korea would gain the attention of the harried men and women in Washington only when it seized the headlines through strikes, violence, or some other dramatic gesture. In almost every case, policy would be made only for the short-term. Events unfolding in and about Korea would demonstrate that the Soviets deserved the lion's share of the blame for the ensuing controversy; but the U.S. government also deserves criticism for its failure to gain control of the situation, to plan ahead, to be prepared to act when the moment called for action. American officials should have recognized that, given the surprising number of ways Korea affected other, more important situations during wartime, the peninsula would demand not just idle musings but serious, step-by-step planning. America would enter a disintegrating, chaotic situation with little idea of what to do.

The First Four Months

AMERICAN forces in Korea would confront a difficult situation in their initial four months of occupation, from September through December 1945, because the United States government had done almost nothing to prepare the army for its task. Men of the occupying forces hardly knew what to expect when they set foot on this little-known part of the Asian mainland. To the troops everything appeared so strange, so out of keeping with the parts of the United States they had known and even those areas of the western and southwestern Pacific they had encountered in their long and difficult struggle against the Japanese. As for the American officers in charge of the occupation troops, Lieutenant General John R. Hodge and his assistants could hardly guess their role when they and their men appeared in Korea. The State Department had not briefed them, nor had there been much advice from army headquarters in the War Department. They were as innocent, and perhaps one might have said as ignorant, as the first Americans who visited the Hermit Kingdom in the nineteenth century.

To their intense dismay, the occupying troops soon found that they were in the midst of a sullen and even hostile population. The Koreans did not at all care for their new supervisors who reminded them of nothing so much as the Japanese. Almost from the outset, the Koreans in the American zone of occupation demonstrated that they would be pleased if the Americans went home.

The forces of the United States in South Korea (as that part of the peninsula became known) came to sense another source of hostility as well: the Russian occupation troops in the north.

The Soviet Union evidently had been contemplating some sort of occupation of Korea, for reasons perhaps as much political as military. For whatever reason, the Soviets were ready for the problems of a Korean occupation and put their zone in order according to their political tastes. The Soviet administration then proceeded to undermine the authority of the bewildered American troops in the southern zone.

I

During the war years there had been an almost complete lack of planning by the United States for any occupation of the Korean peninsula. Burdened by the complexities of Asian diplomacy, oriented toward Europe, possessing limited amounts of people, resources, and time, State Department officials had delayed decision on the Korean issue; and by the summer of 1945, the planners had done little beyond theoretical musings on trusteeship. An official in the department, George McCune, later wrote that, judging from documents which passed through his hands, "almost no thought at all was given to Korea as a nation of more than 26 million persons located at an important Far Eastern crossroads."[1]

Japan's relatively sudden surrender had surprised the individuals responsible for postwar planning. American strategists had calculated that the army leaders who controlled the Japanese government would continue to fight. In August, the war was over. The Americans barely knew how to handle affairs for Japan, and they had thought almost nothing about Korea. They had talked vaguely about a trusteeship, presumably of the four major Allied powers, which implied a temporary period of military occupation. But Rodney C. Loehr, a historical officer for the Joint Chiefs of Staff, "stated that the chiefs never once discussed Japanese, much less Korean, occupation policy." A myriad of other questions remained unsolved. Notably, they had never decided whether they were liberating a captive people or occupying part of Japan's Inner Empire, nor had they fully contemplated Korea's postwar status, given its strategic location.[2]

The American occupation of Korea began, perhaps not unnaturally, with considerable confusion as to who would command the troops. On the evening of August 11, the commander of the Tenth Army, General Joseph W. Stilwell, learned that his forces would occupy the American zone in Korea according to BLACKLIST, the army's plan for the peaceful occupation of Japan and Korea. As his troops celebrated the war's end, Stilwell began to assemble men with experience in Korea from among the Pacific commands. His staff meanwhile advanced the opinion that the Russians had moved so rapidly in Korea that there might not be an American occupation. Within twenty-four hours, however, Stilwell learned that he would not be supervising any occupation of Japan and Korea. MacArthur informed him that Generalissimo Chiang Kai-shek opposed placing him in a command on China's Manchurian flank. Chiang would refuse to cooperate with American forces in China if Stilwell were in command of the Korean occupation. Rather than delay the American entry into Korea while he settled a political problem, and deeply concerned about the occupation of the Japanese home islands which was then underway, MacArthur dropped Stilwell. "Vinegar Joe" was bitter: "so they cut my throat once more." During the war Stilwell had been chief of staff to Chiang, among other duties, and had become so disgusted with Chinese inefficiency, the tortuous and complicated wartime politics of China, and his limited powers that he privately had called the Chinese leader a "little peanut."[3]

Stilwell's successor in China, Lieutenant General Albert C. Wedemeyer, was subsequently designated as the Korean commander. Troops from Wedemeyer's China command were to undertake the occupation. However, the rapid deterioration of conditions in north China made his experience in that area too valuable to lose, and Wedemeyer was also passed over. Because of the acute shortage of shipping in the Far East, it was deemed easier to take Korean occupation troops from Okinawa. As Supreme Commander Allied Powers (SCAP), MacArthur was demanding all available ships for his occupation in Japan. Haste was necessary. The Soviet Red Army had begun entering Korea on August 12 and had made rapid progress against the demoralized Kwantung Army (once the pride of the Japanese Imperial

Army but decimated and replaced with inadequately trained, second-line conscripts to meet the American advance across the Pacific). The closest large American units were in Okinawa, six hundred miles away. The XXIV Corps was designated as the appropriate unit to occupy Korea. The commanding general of XXIV Corps, Lieutenant General John R. Hodge, was designated Korean commander, and thus "went along with the package."[4]

Hodge had had an interesting career in the army. Of Illinois farmer stock, he had risen from the ranks without benefit of a West Point education. He had done well in the Pacific fighting of the Second World War. As commander of XXIV Corps, formed during 1944 for amphibious operations against Japanese-held islands, he had proved himself a battle-wise soldier and led his men through a series of bloody campaigns, from the Palau Islands and Leyte up to Okinawa in April 1945. He was a tough and courageous leader who shared hardships with his men. His no-nonsense attitude, his combat abilities, his resiliency in difficult situations earned him the respect and adoration of troops under his command. He had received the sobriquet of a "soldier's soldier."[5] But Hodge would walk blindly into Korea. Although he was a good and honorable man, his appointment to the Korean occupation command had been something of an accident. Perhaps he was "the first man to gain executive power over a nation of twenty million based on shipping time," i.e., the hours and days needed to transport his troops to Korea.[6] He had lived too long in a world of "we" and "they," good and bad, and would find the complexities of the peninsula outside his political experience and administrative competency.

Having chosen Hodge, the army's Pacific leadership proceeded to complicate its task even before the troops arrived. Despite a late wartime decision to treat Korea as a friendly nation, one of MacArthur's first proclamations threatened with death anyone who violated Hodge's directives. The supreme commander's staff had clearly drawn it up with Japan in mind. Proclamation Number 1 noted that "the purpose of the Occupation is to enforce the Instrument of Surrender and protect them [the Korean people] in their personal and religious rights" and did "establish military control over Korea south of 38 degrees north latitude and the inhabitants thereof." Proclamation Number 2 seemed designed for such enemy countries as Japan and Germany. Koreans who committed acts "hostile to the Allied Forces" would "suffer death or other such punishment as the Court may determine." While the announcement was hardly conducive to good relations, it also indicated the failure of American policymakers to view the Korean occupation independently of the situation in Japan. It would further the administrative confusion and exacerbate problems in intercultural relations. Hodge and the Korean population held differing views of the nature and purpose of the occupation.

Hodge himself showed considerable naiveté in a statement to his troops while they were en route to Korea. He viewed his function primarily as maintaining law and order, and told his men that

> the native people . . . are in effect 'a liberated people' and are not to be viewed and treated as Japanese. However, there are several hundred thousand Japanese residents of the area and we must watch our step on matters of security at all times. Take no chances, be wary of Oriental favors and on the alert for the double cross. Further, be careful of what you say. There are several political factions . . . 'on the make.'[7]

This was true, and yet it spoke of "Oriental favors," a phrase reflecting that ancient (Western) cliché, the inscrutable oriental mind. Hodge would enter Korea full of suspicion, regarding Koreans as a strange and alien people. His sole contact with East Asians had been warfare against the Japanese in the Pacific.

On the eve of the arrival of American troops, Korea was a study in chaos. Thirty-five years of Japanese rule with its social oppression, police despotism, economic exploitation, and cultural stagnation weighed heavily. Its effect was clear. It had destroyed societal patterns and undermined all established authority. Japanese forces prevented a total breakdown of society by their stern rule, but their withdrawal threatened to precipitate an anarchic and chaotic period. Industry had depended on Japanese technical assistance and indeed on the continued presence of Japanese engineers and technicians, and was now in a state of collapse. Korea had supplied Japan with large quantities of semimanufactured goods, and without further access to Japanese markets, the economy ground to a halt. In towns and cities, workers took prolonged holidays. Demonstrations occurred everywhere, and nearly all work ceased. In the countryside, tenants threatened landlords, peasants ignored the hated police and seized the land they worked. The peasants, to be sure, had many reasons for such action. Conditions in farming areas on the eve of liberation were "a virtually unrelieved picture of poverty, oppression, and degradation . . . in general, and in land relations in particular."[8] Whatever occupation authority (temporarily) replaced Japan, it would need purpose and force to help Korea through its coming time of troubles.

To maintain order and protect Japanese lives and property, the Japanese commander, Governor General Abe Nobuyuki hastily gave the Koreans considerable political freedom. While the Japanese awaited the arrival of Soviet troops, Abe had authorized formation of a Committee for the Preparation of Korean Independence (CPKI), which had a slight leftwing orientation to please the coming Soviet occupiers. At this time, the Japanese did not know that the Americans would occupy southern Korea and, apparently, favored Koreans the Soviets might accept. Under leadership of a moderate-left Korean nationalist, Lyuh Woonhyung, the CPKI soon exceeded the limited function which the Japanese had envisioned. It organized administrative units throughout the peninsula, and in the provinces it became the sole source of authority. When Abe belatedly learned that American troops would occupy the more populous south, including Seoul (and his command), he sought to restrict Lyuh's powers, but it was too late.[9]

When Soviet forces overran northern Korea, they had given the impression of cooperating with local nationalists. On August 9, the day after Russia's declaration of war against Japan, the Red Army went into action in Manchuria and north Korea; within five days it had moved far inside the Soviet-Korean border. Soviet forces numbered approximately two hundred thousand men plus some thirty thousand Korean exiles from Siberia. They were not the Red Army's finest troops. Discipline was lax, and in the ranks were many former prisoners from the Siberian frontier regions. Although they had freed Korea from the Japanese, these troops nearly dissipated the resultant goodwill in an orgy of rapes, lootings, and petty crimes. Their behavior was consistent with the Soviet practice of letting troops live off the land. Red Army advances (deliberately?) created a flood of refugees including Japanese, wealthy Korean collaborators, Christians, and Koreans abused by Soviet troops. People fled south ahead of the Russians and, along with Korean nationals which MacArthur had returned from Japan, furthered the chaotic conditions and endangered the limited food supply in the already overpopulated southern zone (and easing problems in the northern, Soviet zone). Either better informed of Korean feelings than their American counterparts or having a better idea of their objectives regardless of Korean desires, the Soviets used such Korean exiles as Kim Il-sung, together with native communists and patriotic organizations, as a front behind which they sought to control all aspects of Korean life.[10]

At the outset of the occupation, both in the Soviet and the American zones, the CPKI, which rapidly had overthrown Japanese control, became the creature of a communist minority. Within a week after the group's formation, CPKI headquarters in Seoul came under communist control. In the capital, the well-organized Korean communist party, a native (and not expatriate) group led by Pak Hun-yung that had formed the backbone of anti-Japanese resistance during the Pacific war, emerged from hiding. While Korean moderate and rightist factions organized local committees to keep order and help protect Japanese lives and property during this transition, the local communists infiltrated the Seoul CPKI headquarters. They seized key offices while maintaining a nominal unity of all Korean factions—conservative, moderate, and leftist—behind a facade of meaningless posts for aging provisional government officials. The Korean expatriates meanwhile were thousands of miles away in China and the United States and unable to influence the rapid-moving events. By the time American troops reached Korea, the communists were ready to confront General Hodge with a fait accompli. In a meeting of September 6, three days before Hodge and his men landed at Inchon, leftists arranged for CPKI head-quarters in Seoul to proclaim a national government backed by the power of the local committees. The CPKI, having become a communist front, then changed its name to the People's Republic and awaited the American arrival.[11]

Hodge and his troops finally did arrive on September 9-10. Forty-one ships, including seventeen transports, spread out in columns, had steamed through the Yellow Sea to Inchon. Most of the men were anxious about their new task of occupation. No one seemed sure that Japanese leaders in Korea would honor (or believe) the emperor's decision to surrender; and to protect their forces from any surprise action, Hodge's staff decided to treat the land operation as an "invasion without gunfire."[12] Staff officers prepared a military landing as at Okinawa and worried whether their troops, so recently in combat and having begun preparations for an invasion of Japan, would act properly with Korean civilians and the surrendering Japanese. After the rigors of the Pacific fighting, the kamikaze attacks, and previous Japanese troop surrenders where hidden grenades, land mines, and explosives took many American lives, it was understandable that XXIV Corps planners were suspicious of Japanese peaceful overtures.

As the troops landed, Hodge's troubles began. Initially, the seventy thousand soldiers met an orderly Japanese soldiery. To facilitate landing operations, Hodge had directed all Korean civilians to stay at home. When the Koreans nonetheless and not unnaturally appeared along the wharfs to watch the instrument of their country's liberation, Japanese troops fired on them, and several Koreans were killed. A near riot followed.[13]

Hodge then found himself in increasing difficulty, with one confusion after another swirling down upon him and little guidance from an overburdened government at home. Perhaps he was relieved that the Japanese had fired on civilians and not his troops. He praised the Japanese for maintaining order during the landing operation, for the Koreans, he said, had blocked the landing area. It was not an auspicious beginning. Hodge committed the politically awkward yet economically necessary act of retaining Japanese technical and administrative personnel, including Governor General Abe and his staff. The Korean reaction was immediate and predictable. Demonstrations broke out; workers went on strike. Exiles in the United States protested to the State Department. President Truman and the State Department acted through General MacArthur (Korea was within his area of command) and ordered Hodge to remove from office all senior Japanese administrators and replace technicians as quickly as possible with Americans or Koreans. The State Department conveniently forgot its wartime analysis that had recommended retaining qualified Japanese (owing to a shortage of qualified Koreans), overlooked its lack of explicit directives about the occupation, and condemned the general's action. MacArthur ordered Hodge to replace the Japanese "as quickly as practicable." Hodge found himself without support from his superiors and forced to back down before a stubborn and proud people. He nevertheless defended his use of Japanese personnel and predicted "great difficulty operating with any sweeping removal of Japanese unless we are willing to accept chaos. All utilities, communications, etc., are Japanese-operated and government-controlled. My military government is entirely inadequate to cope with this situation."[14]

The American general received a rude introduction to the task of occupying Korea, and his initial mistakes may have ensured the failure of the operation. In the eyes of Koreans, he lost face; his administration had shown weakness. The impression, perhaps, was harsh, but it lasted. Koreans feared that the Americans would institute a colonial-type administration, using former enemy personnel as officials of the new government. Hodge's initial, remarkably friendly gestures toward the Japanese made the view plausible. Resistance seemed the only method of expressing indigenous dissatisfaction. If Gregory Henderson's analysis in *Korea: The Politics of the Vortex* is correct, the government in Washington committed a crucial error by reprimanding Hodge and thus appearing responsive to Korean public opinion. If Korea was a society on the verge of a violent collapse after its harsh introduction to industrialized, modern society, it was still held together by the glue of authoritarian rule and the attendant use of force, violence, and repressive measures. Expecting a continuation of such rule, Koreans found Hodge weak and unde-serving of the kind of respect they had accorded Japanese commanders. This swift collapse of the Japanese system would doom the occupation and make its chances for success problematical.

II

The Americans created a contradictory regime in Korea. It retained the Japanese system of central administration without understanding Japan's philosophy of governing. The United States military government adopted the Japanese system because it was more logical to continue an existing structure than to create on a moment's notice an entirely different system. Per-haps the ideally decentralized structure of a true "people's re-public" granting much autonomy to local village groups would have lessened the number of Americans needed to staff a rigidly centralized structure with all decisions coming from Seoul. This would have served American goals better. Unfortunately, the occupation followed thirty-five years of Japanese control. Japan ruled by terror: a well-staffed central government, wealthy col-laborators, paid informants, a cruel police, secret files, and tor-ture. Allowing Koreans no role in their own governance or welfare, the Government-General taught the masses that secrecy, disobedience, and violence ensured survival. When Hodge adopted this administrative structure, Koreans expected a con-tinuation of dictatorship. They interpreted Hodge's moderate policy as the weakness of an occupier rather than the kindliness of a liberator. The American way of government, including med-ical care and the distribution of food, mystified them.[15] Koreans reacted to what they perceived as a new and perhaps ineffective oppressor.

The American commander thus became a symbol of both authority and impotence. At first General Hodge received the respect due a traditional leader; he was the personification of authority in a society based upon the centuries-old Chinese im-perial model. Japanese officials also raised in an "Oriental" tra-dition understood the importance of a ruler actually ruling, an injunction based on Confucius' attempt to rectify names and positions. American occupation authorities, however, inherited the Western, not Chinese, tradition and failed to see how Koreans would perceive them. The politics behind the removal of Japanese from government in the first week of occupation seriously undercut Hodge's position. Military authority had bowed to Korean public opinion. Koreans learned they could circumvent Hodge and appeal to his superiors. During Japan's rule, this situation never would have occurred: violence met more violence, force opposed force.

From the beginning, the communist-dominated Korean regime in Seoul challenged American authority. As American units spread through the lower part of the peninsula in mid-September 1945, they faced a de facto government supported by most Koreans and moving toward a radical, perhaps Soviet, ideology.[16] In the provinces, the Americans were too weak to contest the well-organized liberation committees. Seventy thousand troops had to staff a zone-wide bureaucracy, provide security, and disarm and repatriate Japanese troops and technicians. The strength of the so-called People's Republic grew. "People's Committees" maintained order and resisted demands to disband.

But within weeks, the early image of strength of the people's committees proved illusory. The People's Republic in Seoul collapsed when moderate and rightist factions learned that American forces and not Soviet troops would occupy the southern and more populated half of the peninsula. As Hodge's men made their way inland from Inchon, moderate and rightist politicians which hitherto had quietly acquiesced in the leftward move of the CPKI deserted that organization. While their defection ensured the downfall of the People's Republic in the capital, local committees continued to dominate life in the countryside. When American units reached the isolated villages and hamlets of southern Korea, people's committees moved rightward politically to curry favor with the occupying troops. By mid-October the early union of Korean political factions had come to an end, and this early attempt at Korean self-government collapsed.[17]

Having eliminated the People's Republic, the Americans at first put nothing in its place. Except for the obvious tasks of maintaining order and repatriating the Japanese, officers of the military government had little idea of what to do. Civil Affairs teams arrived five weeks late and were trained for Japan (an obvious enemy) or the Philippines (an obvious friend). Their personnel were often below standard. Many members of the teams believed that Koreans were an inferior people, and so often antagonized them. Were Koreans a captive people or willing participants in Japan's desperate gamble for hegemony in Eastern Asia? Civil Affairs teams were unable to distinguish the two peoples and might have recalled the brutality and cruelty of Korean guards on the Bataan Death March. The most talented civil administrators in the War Department had gone to Japan or Germany. The remainder, carrying the chip of Pearl Harbor on their shoulder, went to Korea.

The English-language skills of some Koreans became a sign of worthiness to American occupiers. Ignoring those nationalists who had fought Japanese oppression, who usually were poor and radical, American officials found friends among conservatives with fine houses and cultivated tastes. At that time, wealth usually meant collaboration with the Japanese. In an unpublished Ph.D. dissertation, Lee Won-sul details his assertion that the military government never punished the former collaborators who retained positions of prominence: Korean members of the police, small industrialists, and middle-level government officials. Instead, these people found themselves highly valued by the Americans. Perhaps this was the greatest error of the American occupation. While the military government superficially favored no political group, its affinity for wealthy elements, that is, Koreans believing in hierarchy, order, and the status quo, damaged its supposed neutrality.[18] Within weeks, Koreans would express dismay that their liberators socialized with the very people upon whom the Japanese had depended to enforce their oppressive rule. But what did they expect? With no direction from the government in Washington, American officers and men found themselves in a strange and alien land and responded to friendly overtures from English-speaking Koreans. Guerrilla leaders were too proud to approach the occupation troops, could not bridge the linguistic and cultural gap that existed, and thus found themselves ignored.

The military government looked to SCAP headquarters in Japan for guidance, but there was none. MacArthur knew little about Korea. He was ruling a conquered people in Tokyo and used the Japanese bureaucracy to lessen his burdens and calm fears; he could not empathize with Hodge. The supreme commander was nominally in charge of the Korean occupation, but he never visited Hodge. MacArthur was a politically minded general and felt that his primary task was to remake Japan. Perhaps he deliberately avoided the confusing situation in Korea, where there was little chance for political gain. Japan was a prize worth one's full attention. MacArthur did not answer Hodge's requests for detailed policy but made sure that all communications, supplies, and men passed through the SCAP command. He remained aware of the situation in Korea and exerted the force of his personality on the easily impressed Hodge. But MacArthur would not risk his prestige or his energies on an area of lesser importance than Japan.

Indicative of the manner in which the State Department likewise failed to provide Hodge with an appreciation of Korea's internal problems was the appointment of H. Merrill Benninghoff, a low-ranking department official, to advise the general.[19] The department was undergoing a tremendous expansion immediately after the war, and Korea stood low on the list of priorities for the few highly qualified Foreign Service personnel. Benninghoff had participated in many discussions about the future of Japan's empire and had some idea of the problems in Korea. He was familiar with the exile groups in the United States and China. But from experience in earlier posts in China and Japan he had learned to hate communism. He feared, and quite possibly did not understand the need for, the very sort of agrarian revolution that southern Korea required. In one of his first cables to the department, Benninghoff noted only two political factions—the left and the right—and felt "fortunate" that there were "several hundred conservatives among the older and better educated Koreans," noting that they were "probably the largest single group."[20] Given this prejudice, he would be of little help to Hodge in understanding the dynamics of Korean society and politics. Neither he nor Hodge could grasp the requirements of a proper ruler for such a society as in southern Korea on the edge of collapse. Hodge and Benninghoff turned about in confusion. In a report to the State Department in mid-September, Benninghoff raised questions: "Headquarters has no information . . . of future policy of the United States or its allies as to the future of Korea. What is going to happen to the nation and what will . . . be our general policies beyond immediate necessity?"[21]

Benninghoff's appointment illustrated one of the many problems that afflicted U.S. Korean policy just after the war's end. There was, first, the question of means. Given domestic political realities, the United States in 1945 and 1946 (and really until NSC-68 in 1950) could not devote sufficient resources to all its new worldwide responsibilities. Korea was the tail end of a long line of supplicants. The number of troops in Korea was insufficient for the many tasks; the occupation represented a commitment larger than the U.S. Army could afford. There was little time for reflection; there was little money to rebuild Korean society. "For want of a nail" might well characterize the American experiences in Korea until early 1950 when a changing set of realities would alter American foreign policy and provide the resources to back it.

The Department of State in Washington, therefore, was of little assistance. In the department, the assistant secretary of state for occupied areas was Major General John Hilldring, whose interests focused on such enemy states as Germany and Japan. His staff knew nothing about Korea and even placed it in an "occupied" rather than "liberated" category. It was a recurring problem in American policy for Korea. Hilldring and his overworked staff did not wrestle with its subtlety. As they faced the momentous task of leading Germany and Japan back to democracy after long interludes with Nazis and militarists at the helm, they paid Korea little attention. Hilldring outranked the department's experienced director of the Office of Far Eastern Affairs, John Carter Vincent. In any event, the civil war in China increasingly occupied Vincent, who was a China specialist. In

1945, as Henderson notes, the Korean desk consisted of a former army lieutenant who knew little about Korea.[22]

Hodge wanted detailed advice on policy and received generalities. In mid-October, the State Department cabled SWNCC 176/8, "an initial directive for Korea," but it did not tell him what to do beyond administering the area south of the 38th parallel, ensuring the health of the people, preparing Koreans for democracy, and readying the occupation area for trusteeship. It did not advise Hodge how to deal with former collaborators, leftwing nationalists, impatient farmers, and the myriad other groups complicating the political scene in southern Korea.[23]

Cast adrift by a distant, preoccupied leadership in Tokyo and Washington, Hodge, in a series of local moves designed to gain Korean confidence and cooperation, only managed to antagonize further Korean opinion. Benninghoff informed Secretary of State James F. Byrnes that Major General A.V. Arnold on October 11 had appointed an "advisory council composed of eleven carefully chosen prominent Koreans . . . leaders of two leading political groups . . . to build up in the consciousness of the Koreans the feeling that they are beginning to participate in their government." The Koreans did not understand the appointments to mean what the Americans understood them to mean. Many of the appointees were well-known collaborators, nearly all were wealthy. Most Koreans felt that the council represented the beginnings of "indefinite trusteeship." Meanwhile, the military government had established a 7:00 P.M. curfew rigidly enforced by arrogant troops. Soon a popular Korean comment was that the "only real difference between the former overlord and the present one was in skin pigmentation."[24] A Civil Affairs officer in Korea later summed up the effect of these ill-conceived actions:

> By suppressing the people's republic and identifying themselves with a minority group, the Americans distressed and antagonized the people; by providing a highly centralized government, they classified themselves with the Japanese; by arrogance and a patronizing attitude, they insulted and disillusioned those who had long held America in esteem; by failure to recognize Korean goals and the intensity of the people with respect to them, American prestige suffered severely in the eyes of the Koreans.[25]

By mid-autumn, Hodge was ready to apply his own intuition to the solution of Korean politics, and the resultant recommendation was one which favored conservatives. Hodge's background, to be sure, did not lend itself to understanding the complicated Korean scene. The general nonetheless believed that he had mastered the issues. Agreeing with Benninghoff's analysis, he saw an undesirable faction in Korean politics: the radical left. The Soviets dominated the left, or so Hodge (and Benninghoff) thought. And there was no middle group. What he called "conservative patriots," essentially rightist Koreans, some of whom were tainted by collaboration with the Japanese, were believed to share American goals. He accepted their explanation of local events, that Korea needed order.[26] Despite the State Department's earlier advice on the need for radical change in Korea, Hodge feared threats to his command's tenuous control. In the wealthy, conservative Korean collaborators who spoke English and sought to avoid the punishment many richly deserved, Hodge found the solution to his fears. He believed that it was time to build a protégé government drawn from conservative elements. The general felt it was necessary to return the exile government from Chungking and Syngman Rhee from the United States in order to form an interim government for all Korea. According to Hodge's informants, the Korean people would respect such a regime. A vigorous publicity campaign following the return of the exiles would, he hoped, ease anti-Americanism.[27]

Hodge sent his recommendation through military channels to the State Department and met with opposition. In addition to a long-standing dislike of Rhee, department officials realized that allowing the return of the exiles from China and the United States to form a government almost assuredly strongly anti-Russian would anger the Soviets and probably end any chance of unifying the peninsula. Far Eastern experts remembered the need for economic change; instead of a conservative, hardline regime, they had hoped that some moderate alternative would emerge. The department refused to issue visas to Rhee and Kim Koo for return to Korea.[28]

The instincts of State Department officials were correct, and those of Hodge quite wrong, but the general's desire for stability somehow communicated itself to the exile groups. There followed then a return to Korea of just the sort of politicians the United States government probably did not need. In the confusion of the American command in Korea and with the many other concerns of the Department of State in Washington, initiative passed to the exiles, and they soon were making their way back to Korea. With the help of friends in the War Department, the clever Rhee virtually outwitted the State Department. He was on his way to Korea before the officials knew what had occurred. With his friend Colonel Preston Goodfellow, from the Office of Strategic Services, Rhee first had met with American officials to seek their permission for his return. The meeting was rigged. To represent the State Department, army officers had invited an aging lady from the Passport Division who was ignorant of the complexities of the situation. Unaware of the intrigue, she found Rhee "a kindly, nice-looking old man" and granted him the precious visa. The army officers then rushed Rhee to a waiting military aircraft and flew him to Korea.[29] Kim Koo had a harder time, but he too managed to get back. While Rhee returned in early October 1945, Kim had to wait until mid-November. As soon as news of Japan's surrender had reached Chungking, he sought permission from the United States embassy to return. The question of sending back the Chungking exiles had become a subject of contention between the U.S. Army and the State Department. Happily they arrived at a compromise: the State Department voiced no objection to the use of military aircraft— if available—to transport the Chungking Koreans, so long as the exiles renounced any pretension that they were a returning government-in-exile. Given other military priorities, it took Kim until November to return to his homeland.[30]

Syngman Rhee's reappearance in Korea soon altered the pattern of American-Korean relations. He had waited all his life for this moment. He sensed the need for leadership and the weakness of the military government. The experiences of several weeks in Korea had made Hodge and Benninghoff anxious for such a respected Korean as Dr. Rhee to return and help them reestablish order in the American zone. In reports to their superiors, the two Americans had expressed regularly an insensitivity toward and fear of radical groups in Korea, with a corresponding appreciation for conservative elements. "The most encouraging single factor," Benninghoff wrote, "is the presence in Seoul of several hundred conservatives . . . although many of them have served with the Japanese." The diplomat felt that "well-trained agitators are attempting to bring about chaos in our area so as to cause Koreans to repudiate the United States in favor of Soviet 'freedom' and control." Both men blithely dismissed the problem of collaboration and considered those Koreans demanding retribution as "agitators." Both men failed to see that the once pro-Japanese conservatives, as good Confucians, merely were "moving with the flow" and voicing a desire for Western-style institutions while the radicals had opposed a Japanese-devised economic and social system that damned the peasantry to a subsistence existence. The two Americans turned to Rhee as someone both Korean and American who could help them in their near-impossible task.[31]

Rhee gathered his supporters and moved to dominate the political process. He seized the occasion of an outdoor rally on October 20, 1945, where Hodge introduced him to a Korean crowd. The rally had different meaning for the Americans and Koreans, possibly symbolic of the gap in perceptions between two vastly different peoples, cultures, and countries. Although Rhee had returned several days earlier, Hodge wanted to use the celebration to ease tension. Rhee's return, Hodge thought, would help make Koreans appreciate the Americans. Unfortunately, Hodge's action during the rally did not have that impact. "I want to introduce to you a great man who has given his entire life to the freedom of Korea . . . a man driven from his home by oppressors who has done great work for his country . . . without personal ambition." As Rhee, flanked by American officials, apprached the podium, the situation appeared clear. America was presenting to the Korean people its choice of a leader. Hodge did not recognize the situation for what it was; he simply wanted to use the Korean in an advisory capacity, believing Rhee's advice might bring stability.[32] Moderate Koreans who felt the need for social change thus once again came to believe that America had aligned itself with wealthy conservatives. Korean communists believed that the American military government had revealed its true colors—its antidemocratic beliefs—with its support of Rhee. It was a delicate time and no one was willing to be patient. In future months, Hodge increasingly turned to Rhee and believed he had found a friend in the aging Korean.[33]

The fragmentation of Korean society and the indecision of the military government led to, in the words of Gregory Henderson, "the gates of chaos":

> When liberation came, the tides were at the gates. In the generation of Japan's control, the population had doubled; urbanization, industrialization, education, and communication had multiplied. Alien colonialism had whetted political appetites through repression and economic ones through desire to emulate the colonial power. War brought the further stirrings of mass mobilization. Behind all this stood an ambitious but fluid society without strong intermediary institutions or class identities. Men needed strong leadership; an aroused and impatient peoples sought a way through a sea of economic and political troubles to new shores. Korea's own institutions had no guidance to give. Instead, direction faltered, and the forces of chaos arose.

Perhaps the judgment is too harsh; but America's only real chance to control the situation in Korea had passed and the next five years would witness a belated, sometimes faulty, reaction to an ever-deepening crisis. The military government had lost control of internal events; soon it would concede the initiative over the entire Korean question to the Soviets.[34]

III

As soon as Soviet forces had reached the 38th parallel, they had begun to divide the peninsula. After looting the border city of Kaeson, the troops withdrew. to the north. Setting up barricades, they halted traffic along Korea's few good north-south roads. The Red Army command refused to send trains south and seized those that came north. Telephone lines were cut, mail service ceased, a barrier descended that indiscriminately cut provinces in half, separated farms from village centers, and divided families. Perhaps because they needed some of the industrial production from the American zone, the Soviets did allow electric power from Yalu River hydroelectric plants to flow to the south, but this was about all the cooperation they permitted.[35]

With the border secure, the Russians established control of the north. Careful at first not to show their hand, they allowed a respected Christian nationalist, Cho Man-sik, to emerge from hiding and lead the zone, and they nominally passed political power to local committees. Churches reopened and nationalistic celebrations carefully directed against the Japanese were much in evidence. But appearances were deceiving. Soviet officers governed the zone under the surface of a Korean administrative structure. The Russians sought to create a strong indigenous regime, fashioned after the Soviet system and susceptible to their control. They recognized churches but confiscated church property and ended government subsidies. They encouraged "nondemocratic" elements—those lacking Soviet approval—to go south. Positions of prominence went to well-known native nationalists; positions of power went to men loyal to the USSR. As Red Army political units augmented the combat troops, control tightened.[36]

In time, the Russians brought in their own protégé, Kim Il-sung, to head the puppet regime. Soviet authorities suspected that they could not command loyalty from native communists who were suspicious of outside control and who were as much Korean nationalists as they were communists. They worried about the allegiance of Korean communists who had fought with Mao Tse-tung's guerrillas around Yenan. They instinctively rejected such Christian nationalists as Cho Man-sik. The Soviets wanted a pliant, obedient elite, and to head the elite they chose Kim, formerly a Red Army major. Kim claimed to be a legendary guerrilla fighter from south Manchuria, and hence his name; actually he was educated in Chinese schools in Manchuria, quite possibly had never lived in the peninsula for any length of time, and may have fought with Soviet troops at Stalingrad. He had tenuous ties with Korea and seemed loyal to his Russian mentors. He had returned to Korea in the back of a Russian military transport when Soviet forces occupied the peninsula in August

1945. Other Koreans from Siberia had come with him to spread Soviet control under a nationalist banner.[37]

The Soviet commander, Colonel General I.M. Chistiakov, had pledged that Koreans would "become the creators of their own happiness"; nevertheless, he "arranged" for Kim's introduction to the Korean people. Since the Russians had not yet achieved control, they forced Cho, a native nationalist with much popular support, to present Kim as the people's savior. Presumably many Koreans in the north recognized the implication. By mid-autumn, the Soviets had begun to create a friendly socialist regime. Control of police, education, and the mails passed to Kim's faction. With Soviet help, the Siberian Koreans began to consolidate their power. Soviet soldiers broke up meetings of Cho's supporters under the pretext of searching for Japanese collaborators; border troops denied permission to Koreans who had served with the Chinese communists to cross the Yalu; and the barrier at the 38th parallel cut off opponents from the south.[38] It seemed that the Soviet Union would not compromise on its objectives in northern Korea.

In this manner, Soviet policy divided a largely homogeneous society. For more than a thousand years, the peninsula had possessed a common racial and cultural heritage. Economically, north and south were complementary. Each region relied upon the other. Southern Korea had a labor-intensive rice culture, a few extractive industries, and, since the late 1920s, an industrial sector tied to Japan. Because rice was grown for export to Japan, the south depended upon the north for cheap food grains to feed its increasing numbers of tenant farmers. For its light industry, the south required electricity and coal from the north. The north likewise depended upon the south. Its system of small-farm agriculture which produced mostly wheat and barley did not need as much labor or fertilizer as the south's rice farming. It had sent excess farm workers southward to work in industry or corporate farming. It did require the few minerals the south mined, southern textiles, and other light industrial products.[39]

Soviet policy in the north had important ramifications. American officials during the war had speculated that Soviet leaders might view Korea as the Poland of East Asia. Given Korea's geographic position as a "dagger pointed at Japan" and an invasion route into Northeast Asia, Soviet interest in the peninsula was natural and traditional. The accords with Chiang's regime had given the Soviets an important economic position in Manchuria in the form of railroad joint-stock companies. Control over northern Korea would help solidify their position in Manchuria and lead one day, perhaps, to some sort of political control over that minerally rich, agriculturally productive, industrially developed part of wartorn China. The presence of U.S. troops in southern Korea (in conjunction with fifty thousand marines in north China helping to disarm and repatriate Japanese soldiers), closer to the sensitive maritime port of Vladivostok than was European Russia, may have worried Soviet strategists. Most Koreans feared and disliked Russia. Could the Soviets afford to let the Koreans create their own government? Lastly, Stalin may have meant to use Korea to signal his displeasure over events in Japan. MacArthur followed U.S. policy and his own anticommunist attitude and effectively denied Russians any voice in the occupation of Japan. Did that imply turning Japan into an American surrogate? There were many reasons to account for the uncompromising Soviet actions in northern Korea, and negotiations over the peninsula would be nearly impossible.

The division of the country by the Russians in 1945 caused economic havoc in the south. It also meant political trouble, for American policy regarding Korea only had envisioned breaking that nation away from Japanese control, a course that heightened dependence on the northern zone. The concomitant Soviet division of Korea almost destroyed the south's fragile economy. The south could not pay for fertilizer or coal from the north; without fertilizer, its agriculture could not feed its refugee-swollen population (millions had fled south or returned from Japan), and the flow of electricity across the parallel was inadequate and undependable.[40] The economy in the south deteriorated, prices began to rise in an ever-increasing spiral, and Hodge and the American command found themselves in an increasingly uncomfortable position. American economic policy which first allowed an open market and then fixed prices had accelerated the decline. Hodge had angered most Koreans when the military government maintained the vast complex of Japanese holdings in agriculture, industry, transportation with the same Japanese staff and only a new name: The New Korea Company. Hodge was in a difficult position. He had to satisfy Korean desires for a share of the wealth which Japanese interests had created, but he also had to keep occupation expenses as low as possible to avoid a potential charge of spending too much money to help foreign peoples. Hence, he sought to use profits from the New Korea Company to hold down support from the United States. He could not satisfy an impatient people, and the American-run holding company could not help save the economy from the disastrous effect of the division of the peninsula. Workers rioted for food and employment. Along with Rhee's call for an end to the occupation, north and south, the economic situation made Hodge fear a breakdown of order. Political factions armed their followers, and the resultant private armies easily outnumbered the Americans. The Koreans hated the boundary at the 38th parallel, and Hodge told his staff that they "were walking on the edge of a volcano."[41]

The American commander tried to discuss matters with his Soviet counterpart. Chistiakov would not, perhaps could not answer. It is a reasonable surmise that Soviet leaders at this time were using Korea to indicate their displeasure with American policy in Japan; leaders in the Kremlin continued to seek a means to obtain a Soviet role in the latter occupation. By mid-December 1945, Hodge's G-2 reported that "the Russian attitude discouraging liaison or even contact between our respective forces has recently been intensified." The report stated that the "Russians treat the 38th parallel as a barrier between occupation forces" rather than as a convenient line drawn in the haste surrounding the end of the Pacific war. As Hodge wrote Washington, "The official attitude exhibited in Pyongyang is one of suspicion and cold correctness."[42] It made little sense for the Soviets to arouse American ire unless there was a larger purpose; perhaps it was Japan, Manchuria, or the marines in north China.

Beset by difficulties, what could Hodge do? He decided to ignore the Russians, move ahead with his plan to use Koreans in government, and thereby force his Soviet counterpart, Chistiakov, to cooperate. Once again the American commander wrote the State Department to explain his plan. He wanted to create a "governing commission" headed by Rhee and staffed by members of the provisional government. It would work alongside the military government and demonstrate America's commitment to Korean independence. Along with increased American economic aid, the governing commission would dampen rising tensions in the southern zone. Serving as a model for Korea's future government, the commission, Hodge hoped, would force the Russians to cooperate with the Americans or risk antagonizing public opinion in the northern zone. He had turned once again to his principal supporters in Korea, the conservatives behind Rhee.[43]

In the State Department, this proposal met with little sympathy. To Vincent, Korea seemed a "back-burner" issue, something that could be added to a general agreement with the Soviets. Under no circumstances, he thought, given the limited resources which the U.S. government could devote to Korea and other such areas, should Korea become the main area of contention between the two emerging superpowers. In his mind the need for a Japanese peace treaty and the problem of the developing conflict in China far outweighed the importance of Korea. Writing to Benninghoff on behalf of the department, he condemned Hodge's plan to employ hand-picked Koreans in some form of government. He remarked that the State Department was "well aware of the difficulties and complexities of the political situation which confronts General Hodge," but the military government should not favor any group of Koreans for "such support might encourage the Soviet commander to sponsor a similar group in his zone and thus postpone establishment of a unified Korea."[44] Unaware that the Soviets were already rearranging the north to their taste, Vincent wanted a fluid situation that would permit a variety of compromises with the Soviets.

Vincent's letter caused several weeks of tension over Korean affairs between the State Department and the military in Washington. The War Department saw Korea as one place among several where outnumbered American troops held the line against Soviet Russia, and as a place where thousands of troops precious to a continually shrinking military establishment were wasting away awaiting an elusive Soviet-American agreement. In Hodge's defense, Assistant Secretary of War McCloy wrote Assistant Secretary of State Dean Acheson that the letter "seems to me to avoid in large part the pressing realities facing us in Korea." McCloy urged Acheson to allow Hodge to employ the returning exiles or any other friendly group of Koreans. "General Hodge has an almost impossible task. . . . What shall we do if the Soviets continue to refuse to cooperate?" McCloy remarked that the Russians were using Red Army troops and Koreans from Siberia to take over the northern zone and implied that the Americans must produce their own friendly Koreans.[45]

Vincent appeared to triumph in this initial disagreement with the military over Korea. He told Acheson: "I do not think that there is any serious difference of opinion between the State and War Departments in regard to the instructions which should be sent to General Hodge."[46] He secured the approval of Secretary Byrnes. Over Byrnes's signature he sent a letter to Hodge's new political adviser, William R. Langdon, which set out his position. It was "safer, in the interest of Korean unity and early independence, to negotiate with the USSR before attempting to introduce a new idea such as the Governing Commission with which the USSR has made no commitments." The letter concluded that "support of a 'pg' [provisional government] or even a 'gc' [governing commission] may carry implications such a body has . . . jurisdiction over all of Korea and might prejudice negotiations with the Soviet Union."[47] Still chasing the illusion of postwar cooperation with the Soviet Union, the State Department wanted Hodge to resist the pressure in Korea for a little longer.

The American occupation of southern Korea had encountered many difficulties. Hodge's well-meaning blunders alienated most Koreans. There was the continuing presence of a foreign occupation and the delay in independence. Rhee sought power and verbally attacked both the Russians in the north and the Americans in the south. The Russians were uncooperative; the Soviet military commander cut the country in half. In Washington, State Department officials seemingly ignored mounting problems. Korea seemed a minor matter in a world beset by crises. Hodge's request for increasing Korean participation in government met rejection; the State Department expected the general to survive and the situation in Korea to remain constant while it worked to achieve a general East Asian settlement with the Soviet Union. American diplomats had not yet accepted the impossibility of Soviet cooperation in such strategic areas as the Korean peninsula, nor had they recognized that Korea might become a strategic trap if the United States remained too long.

In four short months, the pattern was set and would remain relatively unchanged through the latter 1940s. It was a problem of perception, or more accurately, misperception. Officials in Washington, military authorities in Korea, Koreans, and Soviets at best all spoke *at* each other. To each group involved in Korea, the peninsula had a differing value and symbolism. Washington officialdom sought to overlook Korea, thinking that the problem might solve itself or disappear. Naturally, Hodge and his advisers had immediate concerns for the security of the occupation and stability of the zone. As frustration and tension increased, Koreans in the south would transfer much of their resentment toward the available target of American military government and fall prey to extremist rhetoric of left and right. As the months and years passed, space for maneuvering lessened, violence would increase and confusion continue, without a solution in sight.

Moscow and Its Aftermath

To American officials in the latter months of 1945, an international trusteeship seemed the best solution for the increasing problems faced by Lieutenant General Hodge in Korea. For four confusing months the general had felt almost helpless in dealing with the restive Koreans under his jurisdiction and the uncooperative Russians to the north. His military superiors had offered little assistance. He had looked to the State Department to find a way to ease the tension. He was not privy to the tug-of-war between the War and State Departments over the situation in Korea. Korea represented a large investment of military means at a time when resources of men and material were scarce. In part because an early solution to the Korean entanglement would allow better use of men and resources tied up in the country's occupation, the idea of trusteeship had gained many more adherents within the State Department. Officials believed it would control Soviet expansion, demonstrate America's cooperative attitude toward the Soviet Union, provide a means to move the Koreans toward independence, and bring the occupation to a reasonably quick conclusion.

The Foreign Ministers Conference at Moscow in December 1945 proved to be the high point of Soviet-American postwar cooperation, and it was at Moscow that the Russians and Americans affirmed their commitment to Korean independence and devised a procedure to lead the divided country through a period of tutelage. This was indeed a cooperative arrangement, although different than what Koreans had envisaged. Each side used Korea as a concession to reach agreement on more weighty matters. The Soviets wished a role in the occupation of Japan and perhaps offered to cooperate in Korea as a sign of good faith. The Americans were unwilling to share responsibility in Japan and perhaps knowingly conceded a Korean trusteeship plan that would likely favor the more powerful left factions on the peninsula. Soviet and American negotiators thus agreed to a series of loosely defined steps that would seek to promote interzonal cooperation while preparing Koreans for unification and independence.

However, the aftermath of the Moscow Conference proved extremely disappointing. The American command in southern Korea watched the hoped-for spirit of cooperation turn to confrontation. From the outset, the Koreans were hostile to the concept of trusteeship. The Japanese had used the idea of tutelage to describe their own system of control in Korea. The notion of a Russian-American tutelage was equally unacceptable—at least in the south. Fearing further delay in the achievement of independence (and reunification), the Koreans reacted with massive strikes. The southern zone passed to the edge of rebellion and warfare between rightist and leftist factions. As for the Soviets in northern Korea, at first the negotiation with them went smoothly. The Soviet commander loosened barriers at the 38th parallel and seemed willing to discuss other urgent problems. Then without warning, the Russians refused to compromise on any issue. In Korea, the American representatives on interzonal commissions found that their Soviet counterparts had so defined matters as virtually to prevent any cooperation between the two military commands and to exclude all but pro-Soviet factions from discussing Korea's future. Once again, the American command in Korea would look to its government in Washington for help.

I

From the beginning of American participation in the Second World War, trusteeship had been an attractive idea to solve the possible problems arising in former colonial areas in Asia and Africa. The concept was uniquely American, even if it had appeared at the Paris Peace Conference of 1919 in the form of mandates (President Wilson had sponsored the mandate idea). It combined a compassion for colonial peoples, the idea of tutelage, and a belief in America's mission. President Roosevelt strongly believed in trusteeship for Indochina, for Britain's imperial possessions, and for Korea. In a sense it was New Deal paternalism internationalized. America had a mission to uplift the colonial and backward peoples of the world; it was within the tradition of Manifest Destiny, for America would now actively change the world for the better rather than continue the older Puritan idea of doing by example. The notion obviously had its defects. It was hopelessly ethnocentric, denying the value of native institutions, culture, and politics in many countries with longer histories of organized government than the United States, especially in Korea, and it ignored the increasing tension with the Soviet Union.[1] During the Second World War, however, the government in Washington had made plans for postwar trusteeships. President Roosevelt believed that the European nations by corrupt and exploitative colonial regimes had forfeited their right to empire. Along with the fiction of a strong, democratic, and Western-oriented China, the trusteeship proposals formed the basis of FDR's (and others') thinking about postwar Asia. Behind a shield of American power, the area would be politically neutralized and economically developed.

Until 1944, the American government had hoped to use the regime of Chiang Kai-shek to replace the French and British and stabilize the region, but as the long and immensely costly struggle drew to a close, an international trusteeship seemed suitable only in Korea.[2] Events in China in 1944, where Chiang had defied and angered the president over military and political issues, had exposed the hollowness of the Kuomintang and caused the United States to modify its plans. As Walter LaFeber has noted, Roosevelt gradually agreed with Churchill to help the occupied nations of Europe reestablish their colonial empires after the war. His successor, Truman, continued that policy. But Korea would be different. One State Department official noted that "trusteeship would prevent any nation from monopolizing Korean resources, some of which are of prime importance to the world economy." Trusteeship, of course, was much more than economic. Soviet power appeared to threaten Korea, and American leaders wanted to prevent the Red Army from handing over power immediately to pro-Soviet Koreans; trusteeship, it seemed, would allow the development of Western-style institutions and freedoms, enabling the peninsula to resist Soviet encroachment. It also would help prepare the Korean people for independence. After thirty-five years of Japanese rule, the people, according to State Department experts, needed instruction in self-government.[3]

As difficulty mounted during the first months of occupation, the interest of the State Department in trusteeship increased. Department officials had placed their hope for Soviet-American cooperation on trusteeship. A report by the State-War-Navy Coordinating Committee (SWNCC 101/4) concluded that "internal and external factors connected with [the] liberation of Korea and establishment of Korean independence are so complex that some form of international trusteeship would seem necessary following military government." Officials hoped that trusteeship would assure the Soviet Union that the United States desired peace and cooperation. Secretary of State James F. Byrnes in an address before the New York Herald Tribune Forum on October 31, 1945, appealed to the American public to recognize "the importance to the Soviet Union of having friendly states as neighbors," and assured the Russians that "America will never join any group in those countries in hostile intrigue against the Soviet Union." While the speech undoubtedly concerned the situation in Eastern Europe, trusteeship in Korea was an important and perhaps crucial part of that policy.[4]

To institute a trusteeship and help ease the difficulties of General Hodge, the department instructed Ambassador Averell Harriman in Moscow to begin negotiations with the Russians. A cable of November 3 informed Harriman of deteriorating conditions in Korea. The department requested Soviet agreement on ten points; the first four were necessary, and the remaining six would be evidence of Soviet good faith. The initial points included delivery of at least 240,000 tons of coal per quarter to southern Korea, continued production and delivery of electric power, resumption of railroad traffic across the 38th parallel and uniform fiscal policies. Agreement to these points was essential to the economic well-being of the southern zone. The other six items proposed resumption of telephone, telegraph and mail service; the free movement of Koreans across the 38th parallel; and delivery to the south of such foodstuffs as soybeans, wheat, and barley, and such industrial items as steel, pig iron, and aluminum. The department informed Harriman that "although these Korean matters are urgent, department leaves to your discretion time and manner of presenting them to Soviets in order not to complicate prompt action on proposals you have already presented regarding Allied organs for Japan." But the urgency heightened as Hodge reported a widespread rumor of Soviet removal of hydroelectric plants and other heavy industry in the north.[5]

Harriman did not think there was much chance for a trusteeship in Korea, for he generally believed the Russians incapable of real cooperation. His reply was discouraging, contending that the Russians were unwilling to negotiate on the Korean issue. He argued that recent Moscow newspaper articles supporting Korean independence and ignoring trusteeship were true indicators of Soviet policy. Harriman cabled that "the USSR has made it clear that historically it regarded Korea as a springboard for attack on the USSR." To secure that border, the Soviets would likely favor an "independent friendly" regime in Korea rather than "any system of international tutelage."[6]

With Harriman's assessment of Russian intent came reports from Korea about local opposition to any delay in independence. The new political adviser to Hodge, William Langdon, cabled the Korean reaction to Vincent's reference to trusteeship during a speech of October 20, 1945, before the Foreign Policy Association. All elements of the Korean press—left, right, and center—had stated that trusteeship as conceived by the former Japanese oppressors was an insult to the Korean people. A week later Langdon cabled: "I am unable to fit trusteeship to actual conditions here . . . and believe we should drop it." It was wrong because "the Korean people have high literacy, cultural, and living standards." It was impractical because "it will not be accepted by Korean people and perhaps will have to be maintained by force." He concluded that "our caution over becoming associated with so-called provisional government in Chungking seems unwarranted."[7] Perhaps Langdon was overly pessimistic; but Hodge, Benninghoff, and Langdon were clutching for explanations of the difficult situation about them and perhaps their pleas for help influenced important policymakers to rethink attitudes toward the Soviet Union.

A *New York Times* editorial also attacked the trusteeship proposal, remarking on the deteriorating situation in Korea and the unexplained delay in independence as reported by the newspaper's Seoul reporter, Richard J.H. Johnston. "Our State Department seems to feel that Korea is one of the 'minor problems' which it will get around to 'in due course,' " he wrote. To the *Times* it seemed incredible that the secretary of state could not see any relation between Korea and MacArthur's activities in Japan, where the supreme commander was ignoring the Soviets and conducting the occupation in his own fashion. The *Times* wanted the department to move forward on the Korean issue.[8]

The State Department remained in favor of trusteeship. According to its Far Eastern desk officers, the Korean trusteeship would be "the first of several trusteeship agreements and should be a model for them." It would assist the expected postwar cooperation with the Soviets. It would seem that Far Eastern experts, realistic about the corruption and inefficiency and even the unrepresentative nature of many American-favored regimes in Asia, feared the Soviet Union less and internal revolution more. Perhaps they feared nationalism, and situations did seem less black-and-white than in Europe. If Byrnes had little support for his policy of cooperation and negotiation with the Soviets, it nonetheless would appear that most of his supporters staffed the Far Eastern desk or overseas embassies. John Paton Davies cabled from China in November 1945 that Stalin would pursue a policy of caution in Korea. The department cabled Langdon that trusteeship "may still be necessary to secure elimination of the barrier at the 38th parallel and present zonal agreements."[9]

As the United States delegation was preparing to depart for the Foreign Ministers Conference in Moscow, Langdon once more argued against trusteeship, without result. Agreeing, of course, that cooperation with the Soviets was highly desirable, he remarked that "our Korean policy so far has been predicated solely on Russian cooperation with no planning beyond this premise. A factor seemingly missing from SWNCC papers is the present mood of the Korean people who are impatient of spoon feeding, conscious of independence and eager to exercise it." Langdon made a strong point but could not turn officials away from seeking a general, comprehensive settlement with Soviet leaders. While Langdon may not have understood fully the complex situation in Korea, he did understand that the solution must develop logically from the situation and not be imposed from without. He proposed to "bypass trusteeship and seek guarantees directly in forthcoming discussions."[10] The department still favored a trusteeship in Korea and, in its haste to prepare for the Moscow Conference, forgot to inform Langdon that it was putting his advice aside.

When the delegation arrived in Moscow, it determined to negotiate with the Soviets over several issues, ranging from details of treaties with Germany's wartime allies and international control of atomic energy to the occupation of Japan. Secretary Byrnes felt that the key to cooperation was compromise. Accustomed to American politics and determined to emerge from the conference as the Great Peacemaker, he believed that a show of friendship and willingness to compromise would generate a similar response from the Soviets. He acted as if this were a congressional get-together, ironing out differences between reasonably agreeable adversaries, rather than a negotiation with a suspicious foe. Byrnes was determined to place his imprint on his country's diplomacy, and the Moscow Conference was to be his personal success. He was willing to ignore the British if it would convince Stalin and Molotov of the community of interests between the two superpowers: the United States and the Soviet Union. The American delegation hoped to use a Korean agreement to ease negotiations on more important matters. The continuing presence of American marines in north China (patrolling railway lines with unrepatriated Japanese troops, thus allowing Chiang to concentrate on the forthcoming battle with communist forces for Manchuria) and the American-dominated occupation of Japan had placed the United States in an awkward position with the Russians; a compromise on Korea might reduce Soviet concern over American intentions in the Far East.[11]

As the conference began, it seemed as if the Soviets were unwilling to reach any agreement on Korea. During the first formal session on December 16, Byrnes raised the issue. He wanted the agenda to reflect an agreement on trusteeship. He also sought to introduce into discussion the difficulties that confronted General Hodge due to Soviet policy in the north. He believed that cooperation between the two commands would be a first step toward a unified administration and a trusteeship. Foreign Minister Molotov protested that Byrnes was straying from the conference agenda. Referring to Harriman's list of ten points, presented prior to the conference, Molotov said that the points "had been transmitted to the competent Soviet authorities," and that Harriman's letter which outlined the issues "contained no reference to or mention of a Korean government." He told Byrnes that he could not see how the two matters were linked. Byrnes sought to explain that a minimum of cooperation between the zones was necessary to establish the trusteeship. Harriman's proposals, he said, were conditions. Molotov replied that such technical matters were beyond his competence to discuss without the presence of specialists or advisers, and their presence surely would violate the spirit of the conference. For Molotov, the important issues were unified administration, trusteeship, and an independent government. Byrnes reaffirmed his desire to discuss all parts of the Korean issue, since they were parts of the same problem. He added that the American delegation was preparing a paper for the following session, and it was agreed to adjourn.[12]

Byrnes was discovering that Korea was neither easy to discuss in isolation nor with reference to other issues, but he refused to give up. On the next day he presented a memorandum on Korea and agreed with Molotov to postpone a decision until the Soviets and the British had time to study it. The memorandum mentioned the necessity for an agreement on some form of trusteeship. As for the division of the country, it argued that without a working relationship between the two occupation zones, it would be impossible to have a unified administration and, therefore, a trusteeship.[13]

The discussion about Korea lapsed for three days and then resumed. During the interim, the Russians apparently had been pleased with the conference negotiations on the occupation of Japan and with American insistence on the temporary nature of the marines' presence in north China. Molotov seemed more conciliatory. He agreed with Byrnes that the first move should be to ease difficulties between the zones. Through cooperation, the two commands would lead the Korean people to independence. Molotov said he wished to present a Soviet proposal to Bevin and Byrnes. The three men agreed to continue the discussion on Korea at a later meeting.[14]

The ensuing Soviet proposal should have been a warning to the Americans. Molotov seemed to accept the need to work out quickly the "urgent" problems in Korea, while diplomats solved "long-term" matters more slowly. The Soviets suggested a joint commission composed of American and Soviet occupation officials to discuss issues arising from the division of the country. The commission would consult the Korean "democratic parties and social organizations." It would result in a "provisional Korean democratic government." But the adjective *democratic* was to prove the sticking point; for the next year, the Americans and Soviets would argue over its definition.[15] Perhaps the experience of negotiating with the Soviets over postwar regimes in Eastern Europe should have suggested future troubles over Korea. While the Soviet Union seemingly agreed to cooperate with the United States and thus ostensibly proved the wisdom of Byrnes's view of Soviet-American relations, in reality Soviet leaders played on the secretary of state's desire for an agreement to ensure that eventually Korea would be communist-dominated. It may have been either Soviet cleverness or Byrnes's naiveté, but the failure to qualify the term "democratic" doomed the negotiations. The Soviet Union had made clear what it meant by the word; it would not accept Syngman Rhee, Kim Koo, Cho Man-sik, Korean communists from Yenan, or possibly even native communists from the south. What kind of compromise Korean government would emerge from this process? Certainly it would be to Soviet liking;

yet the Soviets had done little to deserve it. While the USSR had been primarily responsible for the defeat of Nazi Germany; it had made no significant contribution to the defeat of Japan. American military power in the Pacific and the use of atomic bombs had caused Japan's leaders to seek an end to war. Russia had little to fear from a weakened China or a defeated Japan. It seems rather that Soviet leaders wanted to take advantage of a perceived power vacuum in the strategic Korean peninsula and that Byrnes failed to recognize their purpose.

When the delegations released a communiqué on December 27, the Korean section indeed seemed to represent evidence of notable Soviet-American cooperation after the victories of 1945. It repeated the Soviet phrase of "developing the country on democratic principles." It said that the coming Joint Commission would present its recommendations to the nations which would organize the trusteeship (the United States, Great Britain, the Republic of China, and the Soviet Union), although America and Russia would make the final decision. The commission would promote interzonal relations, working out details of the forthcoming trusteeship. To settle urgent problems that affected the zones, the diplomats agreed to assemble a joint Soviet-American conference in Korea within two weeks.[16]

There were varied reactions to the conference and the agreement on Korea. The chargé in Moscow, George Kennan, believed that Byrnes's behavior illustrated the danger of domestic politicians being transplanted to the international arena. Along with other members of the State Department and Foreign Service, he felt that the secretary had wanted an agreement for its political effect at home. He was sure that the Russians would extract a heavy price for this "superficial success." Republican senators, led by Arthur Vandenberg, found Byrnes too ready for compromise; they feared Soviet objectives. President Truman also was displeased, feeling that the secretary had made his own foreign policy. The two men met on January 5, 1946, and although accounts of that meeting differ, Truman clearly was frustrated with Soviet diplomacy and probably with Byrnes's self-assurance. Truman later claimed that he read Byrnes a stinging letter of rebuttal of the secretary's policies and remarked: "I'm tired of babying the Soviets." Truman was moving away from compromise.[17]

Press reaction around the world favored the spirit of cooperation demonstrated in the principle of trusteeship. The Soviet government obviously liked the idea. A Moscow newspaper editorialized that "this would be the first practical experiment in joint trusteeship on the part of the principal Allied powers and, if successful, it may be applied later to the solution of a number of similar questions concerning the future of one or another mandatory or colonial territories." An article in *Izvestia* expressed confidence that trusteeship would coordinate Soviet and American policies and bring both a swift economic recovery in Korea and a return to political stability. The *New York Times* expressed satisfaction, believing that Korean leaders now would have to demonstrate their political maturity. The *London Times* concurred that the Moscow agreement on Korea heralded a desirable cooperation among the great powers; a five-year trusteeship seemed reasonable after the long period of Japanese oppression.[18]

In December 1945, it did appear that the spirit of cooperation had reached the unhappy peninsula. The conference apparently had initiated an era of conciliatory diplomacy, of which Korea would be a prominent beneficiary. Only two unknown factors remained: Korean reaction to the delay in independence necessitated by the period of tutelage and Soviet behavior during the coming talks in Korea. Most American diplomats assumed that agreement with the Soviets would minimize the possible impact of the two factors.

II

As soon as news of the Moscow agreement reached Korea, an angry cry arose. Hatred of continued foreign rule temporarily united all three major political factions in the south. The Korean translation of the word "trusteeship"—there was no exact equivalent—suggested a continuation of Japan's system of rule. Press reaction was immediate and hostile; writers in the south made clear their opposition to any trusteeship. Leftist, rightist, and moderate papers agreed that here was a "Second Munich," "mandatory rule," "an insult to Korea," "international slavery," "a violation of international treaties." In the United States, *The Voice of Korea* editorialized that the announcement placing Korea under a four-power trusteeship "clouds every Korean mind." In northern Korea, only the strict Soviet control of news prevented a similar outburst.[19]

The Korean people came dangerously close to rebellion. There were massive demonstrations, with the participation of Korean employees of the military government, thus crippling the day-to-day functioning of the bureaucracy. Crowds gathered in Seoul, threatening the military police who sought to protect vital installations. The *New York Times* reported that "public disorder has been spreading and is still growing." The capital's streets were declared off limits to all American troops. To military government officials, it seemed that only a miracle prevented the display of violence and resentment from becoming an armed revolt.[20]

The Moscow agreement surprised General Hodge as much as it surprised the Koreans, for while rumors about the Foreign Ministers Conference circulated throughout the peninsula, he had remained in the dark as to what was occurring. The State Department did not feel that news of the agreement was sufficiently important to be rushed to Hodge. The United Press and Associated Press reported the text of the Moscow agreement a full day before he received it. A delay in transmission from Tokyo to Seoul along with a probable assumption of its low priority had resulted in this time lag.[21] When Hodge finally learned of the conference terms, he did what he could to put a good face on the situation. To the Koreans he urged patience, for he feared a violent outbreak over a delay in independence. He sought to calm Korean tempers by admitting a personal dislike of trusteeship. He met with conservative and moderate leaders to see what could be done. To his military superiors he privately complained of the shabby treatment he and his command had received from the State Department. Hodge noted testily and correctly, one must say, that "this entire unpleasant incident could have been averted if I had been informed of the results of the

Moscow Conference. To do my job I must be kept up to date on all diplomatic developments." He and other local American officials urged modification of the Moscow agreement. They wanted the government to "soften," "drop," or "kill" the term trusteeship owing to its inflammatory connection with Japanese overlordship.[22]

Whatever the confusions within the American occupation command over trusteeship, it is interesting that the result of the American proposal at Moscow proved rather to the advantage of the United States, although this development took place in an odd way. In the first weeks after the Moscow Conference, Hodge allowed a report to circulate in the south that the Soviet Union was responsible for the proposed five-year trusteeship. Officials in Washington had given the public impression that trusteeship was not all that necessary; Hodge believed it meant that the American delegation at Moscow reluctantly had accepted the Soviet argument for some form of international tutelage. Military government officials informed key Korean leaders that Byrnes had sought to resist the Soviets.[23] When the Korean communist party in the south suddenly reversed itself and supported trusteeship, it seemed as if Hodge had been correct. At first, Pak Hun-yung and the communists had joined with other Korean factions to condemn the Moscow agreement. Communist newspapers in the south editorialized against it. In mid-January 1946, the Soviets apparently made clear the party line, and the obedient communists in the south abandoned their opposition; presumably those in the north had no freedom to make mistakes. Korean communists began to attack the supporters of the work strike as saboteurs and singled out Rhee for much scorn. The result was predictable. The Korean people never forgave the communists. Communist leaders found it increasingly difficult to overcome the antitrusteeship feelings among party members. The communist leadership had stood apart from the masses and apparently shown their subservience to a foreign power, a grievous error in a country gripped by nationalist fervor.[24]

Perhaps realizing their tactical error, the Soviets then made a series of charges against the American command in Korea.

They released an account of the Moscow discussion on Korea that cast the American negotiators in a bad light. The Soviet news agency TASS charged that the American military government had sabotaged the Moscow agreement by inspiring "reactionary" protests; "apparently the Korean newspapers are the victims of false and unscrupulous information." The agency noted "a decision in which it is known the government of the United States participated." When Hodge said the release was "without basis in fact," Stalin warned Harriman that since the American government had not corrected its representative in Seoul, the Soviet Union would issue a denial. The Soviets described the Moscow Conference in terms that made Russia appear as the defender of the peninsula against the imperialist, expansionist United States. Cleverly worded statements implied that American officials had stood for a ten-year trusteeship. It was only with great difficulty that the Soviet delegation, the Russians declared, had managed to secure American approval for a trusteeship of five years.[25]

After the Soviets had given their version of the conference, the rightist-led general strike regained the intensity of the previous weeks, and threatened again to turn into rebellion. Many Koreans accepted the Soviet version and began to doubt American intentions.[26] It was a confusing situation for southern Koreans, surrounded by propaganda from the Soviet-dominated left and the Rhee-led right. Many people turned to the Americans because for many years Koreans had held the United States in high esteem. Hodge's puzzlement over the trusteeship issue dismayed those worried men and women who had looked to him for encouragement. The Soviet account of the Moscow Conference offered scant comfort, and many Koreans reluctantly accepted it.

By this time, Hodge had turned to the State Department for a full account of the Moscow Conference and the resulting agreement. He remarked about "not knowing the behind-the-scenes story." He chided the department for paying "little attention either to information painstakingly sent in from those actually on the ground as to the psychology of the Korean people or to the repeated urgent recommendations of the commander and the State Department political advisers." He made clear that "as the significance of the statement . . . sinks in, the Korean people are feeling that the United States has again sold them down the river, this time to the Russians instead of the Japanese."[27] He offered himself as a political sacrifice. "I will gladly accept relief in the role of a sacrificial goat for my muddle here if need be to save face for the United States."[28]

Military officials were crestfallen over Hodge's predicament. The Joint Chiefs of Staff noted stiffly that "in retrospect, it appears there is justification for General Hodge's concern." The chiefs wanted him to be kept informed. Secretary of War Robert A. Patterson, who in November had replaced Stimson, appealed to Byrnes.[29] The State Department defended trusteeship. "Every opportunity is being used to keep General Hodge informed," Byrnes wrote Patterson. The general, he said, knew of the department's support of trusteeship. The department might dispense with it if a capable group of Koreans assumed the offices of government. The department, he said, continued to believe that trusteeship would help the Korean people.[30] Diplomats wanted to hold the military in abeyance as they sought an elusive agreement with the Soviets. Military officials, in a time of low manpower levels and worldwide responsibilities, viewed Hodge's command as one which could be put to better use elsewhere. The impasse would continue.

Meanwhile, the rightists in Seoul were increasing their influence. Rhee and Kim Koo were building a party around which Koreans could rally to express their displeasure with trusteeship. Conservative leaders called for an Emergency National Congress to meet in Seoul on February 1, 1946. Only rightists attended, and on February 6, they announced a National Society for the Rapid Realization of Korean Independence, with Rhee as chairman and Kim as vice-chairman. Adroitly supporting the military government while remaining vigorously antitrusteeship and anti-State Department, the two Koreans virtually became a shadow government alongside the occupation regime of the Americans.[31]

The communist party survived its awkward support of trusteeship and now found itself with two foes: the American military government and Rhee's conservatives. Although the party numbered only from three to ten thousand (its precise membership appears to have been highly uncertain), it exerted a disproportionate influence because it received support from many segments of the population disgruntled over the policies of military government. There had been no significant postwar redistribution of land; Americans continued to hold former Japanese agricultural wealth to help pay for the occupation. Nor had there been punishment of wartime collaborators because American authorities believed that the forthcoming Korean government would better handle their fate. Communist newspapers charged that Rhee, by calling the Emergency National Congress, had sabotaged the Moscow agreement and therefore was "undemocratic."[32]

As the gap between political left and right widened, the State Department sent new advice to Hodge. Korean communists had demonstrated their subservience to Moscow, and department officials expected Hodge to control communist subversion and violence. The department wanted him to move away from such conservatives as Rhee and Kim who would resist reform. It wanted Hodge to discover local leaders with a "firm progessive program which will stress the four freedoms and basic land and fiscal reform," because such a group might appeal to the majority of Koreans who were turning reluctantly to the communists.[33] Given Hodge's near-Manichaean outlook, the conservative tendencies of his advisers and subordinates, and the deteriorating situation in the south, the department's advice, in retrospect, was sent to the wrong people at the wrong time.

Hodge hesitated to support Rhee, but by the spring of 1946, he found himself nearly forced to do it. An outspoken anticommunist, Rhee seemed more responsible than his fellow conservative Kim. Although Rhee's followers used strong-arm tactics, he constantly stated his devotion to democratic principles. Langdon cabled Byrnes that Hodge felt a desperate need for Rhee's prestige even though he would dislike the presence of Rhee in a future government. The military police did move to break up some rightist organizations. On April 21, Hodge dissolved the Young Men's Association; four weeks later Major General Arthur Lerch declared illegal a rightist attempt to reinstate the provisional government; and Hodge rebuked Rhee publicly when the Korean leader claimed backing from the U.S. government in Washington.[34] But Hodge's belief that all critics of his command were leftists and that all leftists were communists and probably Russian-dominated limited his choices, and he was moving in Rhee's direction.

Deteriorating relations between American troops and the Korean population reduced Hodge's freedom of action. Soldiers had found a moral, family-centered society that resented the presence of foreigners. It was a sensitive situation, and the troops did not make much of an effort to behave themselves. Women who favored the troops found themselves cut off from family and friends. Girls working for the military government feared the ostracization that might follow conversation with Americans. The chocolate bar and nylon stockings failed the servicemen. But there were alternatives. The military government had continued Japan's extensive system of brothels, many of which were for officers only. When army chaplains made known their disapproval of apparently army-sanctioned prostitution in which army doctors carried out a widespread program of penicillin injections and regular examinations to control the treatment of venereal disease, the disease rate among the troops reached astronomical proportions. The chaplains' actions caused the army to close the regulated brothels; the rate of venereal disease increased among Korean prostitutes who presumably transmitted it to American soldiers. Frustrated at remaining overseas in a hostile environment, American soldiers began acting outside the law. By the spring of 1946, the *New York Times* regularly reported military trials in Korea for rape and assault of civilians. The situation became so serious that Hodge in mid-March appealed to the troops. "I am deeply concerned," he said, "over a recent increase in the number of incidents reflecting against the good name of US forces in Korea and against the prestige of the American nation."[35]

III

Would negotiations with the Russians hold an answer to the troubles in the south? The Moscow agreement had provided for Soviet-American cooperation. To solve economic problems arising from the division of the peninsula, military representatives were arranging a joint Soviet-American conference. At a more leisurely pace they would organize a Joint Commission to move Korea toward a unified administration and independence.

The joint conference opened amidst a certain fanfare on January 16, 1946. Representatives of the two military commands met in the former imperial throne room in Seoul where the Japanese emperor had entertained when he visited Korea. It was an incongruous sight, as in imperial splendor and secrecy, officials of the world's two great democracies, one capitalist and one socialist, assembled to discuss interzonal matters. The Russians came prepared for oriental pomp and circumstance for the meeting at the Duk Soo Palace. Colonel General Terenti Shtikov led a delegation of 102 persons top-heavy with Soviet brass, including (as advisers) Minister Extraordinary Semeon Konstantinovich Tsarapin, Major General Nicholai Georgevich Lebediff, and Communist party watchdog Gerasim Marinovich Balasanov. Newspaper accounts described the chief Soviet delegate as flanked by a sea of officialdom. In contrast to the overwhelming Soviet party, the Americans came only to negotiate and not to impress their counterparts. American delegates were few and low-ranking technical experts. Major General A.V. Arnold brought Langdon; State Department representative and former embassy secretary in Moscow, Charles W. Thayer; Colonel Robert H. Booth; and SCAP representative, Colonel Frank H. Britton. Arnold wanted to forsake rhetoric and work together to solve the situation in Korea; the Soviets wanted to demonstrate their military strength with a large, mostly useless delegation. Outside the former palace, anxious Koreans awaited news of the meeting.

Buoyed by the spirit of cooperation at the Moscow Conference, American negotiators began the meetings with their Soviet counterparts with considerable hope. Because of their under-

standing of the agreement on Korea, they believed that the talks
would provide for economic unification in such areas as transportation and communication and serve as a prelude to political
unification. General Arnold and his "modest" staff of army colo-
nels and State Department economic experts hoped that a healthy
economy resulting from these talks would solve many of the
problems the Americans had encountered in Korea.[36]

Colonel General Shtikov and the Soviet delegation had a
more limited expectation, for they regarded the conference as
an opportunity to barter goods between two adjoining but separate zones of military responsibility. According to them, the
Moscow agreement allowed negotiation to extend to a few specific matters for "exchange and coordination." In retrospect, it
is clear that they had no intention of dismantling the barrier they
had built at the 38th parallel. Shtikov waited for the Americans
to present their demands for barter, to which he already had his
reply: the Soviets desired rice from the south.[37]

The conference lasted only five weeks and collapsed over the
Soviet demand for vast quantities of rice from the American
zone. The Russians in the north expected to barter on a one-for-
one basis. To all American requests for adequate supplies of
electric power, coal, and resumption of communication and
transportation, Shtikov wanted rice. Apparently he had learned
that the Japanese had exported rice from the south. He assumed
that rice still was plentiful. General Arnold sought to explain
that his zone had exported rice to Japan (and sometimes the
north) only because the Japanese had imported coarse cereals
from Manchuria and northern Korea. Without grain from Manchuria and without supplies of fertilizer, the south had difficulty
feeding its population swollen by hundreds of thousands of refugees fleeing north Korea and returning from Japan. Hodge
informed General Marshall, who then was in China, that the
Russians "apparently believe we are lying." By January 25, 1946,
the Soviet delegation was threatening to cut off the remaining
electric power to the south unless the Americans made good on
Soviet demands. The conference ended ten days later when Shtikov presented a virtual ultimatum: the Soviets would discon-
tinue the talks until the Americans guaranteed delivery of rice.

American conferees could not make clear to their Soviet counterparts that there was no surplus of rice, that the south had serious problems feeding its own people. Since niether side would or could give in, the meetings adjourned.[38]

When the joint conference ended in failure, Hodge made clear his increasingly pessimistic view of Soviet-American relations and the future of Korea. To his staff he remarked that "there is no question but what the Soviets want to have Korea become a Soviet state." At times he would elaborate with talk of Soviet plots to overthrow the American military government through Korean puppets. He noted intelligence reports of Soviet troop maneuvers along the 38th parallel. In reports to his superiors, Hodge sounded a negative note. He saw few chances of success for the coming Joint Commission. Failure would bring increasing difficulties for the occupation. In early February, he met with Ambassador Harriman who stopped over in Seoul on a trip back to the United States, and while they undoubtedly talked about Soviet-American relations, there is no record or recollection of that discussion.[39] Hodge's despairing comments seem to have reached Washington at a critical moment, for Kennan in Moscow about this time was cabling his "long telegram." Having keenly observed Soviet behavior, he sought in a cable of February 26 to reverse Byrnes's policy of cooperation. He offered his views to explain the "logic" of Soviet diplomacy. His opinion urging an adversary relationship with the Soviets coincided with Hodge's request for toughness in Korea.[40]

How important for Korea were Kennan's views on the "sources of Soviet conduct"? Perhaps by early 1946 the moment had come for a change, whatever the momentary moves of American representatives abroad. The previous months in Korea had made clear the problem of drift in policy against the backdrop of a continually worsening internal situation. In Washington, no one figure was exerting control. President Truman had not yet taken over foreign affairs; the domestic responsibilities of the presidency limited the time he had to devote to diplomacy. Secretary Byrnes, hoping to cooperate with his Soviet counterpart and emerge the Great Peacemaker, was dealing in dreams. As the situation in Korea worsened, Hodge and Benninghoff (and his successors) looked about for an explanation. As in other tense places along the Soviet border, they failed to see that their problem was twofold (and, for American policymakers, threefold). In a difficult strategic position they faced a determined Soviet adversary across the parallel; and in the south, they had to control twenty million Koreans who impatiently awaited the opportunity to settle their future (and the government in Washington had to ponder Korea's future political and economic relations with Japan, China, and the Soviet Union and to what extent were American interests affected). The distinction between Soviet communism and the ideologies of awakened nationalism blurred as they saw all opponents of American military government grouped under a leftist banner. Hence, Hodge consistently supported rightwing elements that gave only lip service to the occupation authorities and Western democratic ideals.

Wartime State Department analysts had concluded that Korea needed reform under a left-moderate coalition but neither Hodge nor his political advisers were sufficiently open-minded for the difficult task they faced. They had to mollify Korean pride; wean the noncommunist left to America; and satisfy Korean conservatives that although reforms would lessen their power, influence, and wealth in southern Korea, they would retain a valuable place in society. All the while, occupation officials had to work with inadequate guidance from a distant officialdom in Washington and deal with Soviet obstruction in the north. It required a master politician, if such a person ever existed; Hodge and Benninghoff had lived their lives in a world of good and bad, we and they. They concentrated on the menace to the north. The inequities of wealth, land distribution, and the fate of former Korean collaborators receded into the background before the all-encompassing Soviet threat. Their perception of Kennan's analysis (whatever Kennan meant or did not mean, what would count was the way his ideals were perceived throughout the various layers of government) reinforced their belief in placing the imprint of the superpower confrontation over the reality of southern Korea. They subordinated the myriad problems they could little understand to the Soviet threat in the north.

If Hodge and his political advisers were simplistic in outlook, Kennan and the warm reception received by his "long telegram" enhanced the legitimacy of that thinking. In an important memorandum of January 25, 1946, preceding his telegram, Kennan had urged the State Department to forsake cooperation with the Soviet Union in Korea and support Rhee and Kim Koo: "These men—impractical and poorly organized though they may be— nevertheless represent a pro-American opposition to existing Soviet-sponsored 'democratic' parties and social organizations and the concept of Soviet domination of future provisional government." Kennan thus managed to overlook such anti-Soviet Korean nationalists as Lyuh Woon-hyung and Pak Hun-yung and support expatriates who did not understand the changes in Korean life brought about by Japan's occupation and who found much of their support from among groups that had collaborated with the Japanese. He ignored the rising tide of nationalism that posed a far greater threat to American security than Soviet expansion. The great unanswered question was what side America would take in the final dismantling of former colonial empires, and Kennan's various missives to Washington would suggest that he favored the side that most identified itself as an anticommunist, pro-Western party. Kennan and Harriman in Moscow represented an articulate pair who could put their thoughts on paper with clarity and force. As the men in Korea struggled in an alien environment, Kennan's answer to their plight—befriend the most vigorous anticommunists regardless of internal circumstances—was welcome support.

Perhaps Kennan's nearness to the center of Soviet power and obsession with its communist leaders tended to limit his vision. Behind every crisis along the Soviet border, he saw Stalin's machinations. Perhaps Kennan meant well, but the perception held by most American officials had little relevance to the problems in such places as Korea. In well-written cables to the department, copies of which usually went to nearby stations, Kennan expounded his view. The "long telegram" was merely another in a series of entreaties. As Kennan's worldview gained acceptance in the department (or as a misunderstanding of his view gained acceptance, since Kennan later would claim that he never de-

sired that for which containment came to stand), the few remaining chances for postwar cooperation with the Soviets faded.
The Russians did little to encourage friendship, and American
diplomats would look for the worst in Soviet actions. Tired leaders in Washington who faced never-ending crises at home and
abroad found Kennan's view comforting. Rather than devote
precious time to many individual problems, officials seized the
opportunity to adopt a broad ideology that blamed the Soviets
for world disorder and simply assumed Russian intransigence
on all issues. This view combined well with an emerging military-
industrial complex seeking larger defense expenditures and with
that faction of the political spectrum which viewed the government in Russia as atheistic, anti-Western, and antidemocratic in
a duality of good and evil in which compromise was impossible.
Within the Soviet government, a similar response apparently
evolved. Korea, Iran, and Poland all blended into a grand hostility, soon to be described as the cold war. In the case of Korea,
Soviet actions brought on the hostility. Soviet leaders must assume the larger burden, but American leaders must bear some
blame as well. By adopting the ideology of containment and by
imposing the superpower confrontation in all areas where Soviet
and American interests, power, or forces might meet, American
officials blinded themselves to a multipolar world, to local problems, and to regional complexities. American policy would act
and react upon the misperception. In Korea, the U.S. government redefined the situation and considered intelligence only as
it fit a preconceived notion of the emerging bipolar struggle.
There would be no shadings of gray until it was too late. The
damage was wrought by well-meaning, but sadly close-minded
men.[41]

As Kennan's view made its way from desk to desk in the
State Department and around embassies abroad, SWNCC 176/18
was offering Hodge guidance for organization of the Joint Soviet-
American Commission. The commission's discussions, read the
document, should bring about among Koreans "a definite majority of strong, competent leaders who are not extremists of
either left or right." The leaders might represent the "will of the
people." After several pages of repeating the hope for cooper-

ation with the Soviets, SWNCC 176/18 accepted the need for independent action in Korea. "If it is not possible for the Joint Commission to reach agreement on the above methods of selection or on the composition of this group of leaders," the American commander should choose individuals from the south.[42] Was Hodge (or his State Department advisers) capable of selecting someone such as Lyuh or Pak who resolutely opposed the American occupation but also were determined to resist Soviet control? Or would he naturally choose Rhee, who seemingly cooperated with him, even though Rhee had support from among the worst elements in Korean society and a perspective hopelessly out of tune with the situation within the peninsula.

It seemed from SWNCC 176/18 that the department and American representatives in Korea had come closer together in their understanding of Soviet diplomacy, but Hodge still did not feel that his instructions dealt with the real problem. The issue was not creation of an interim government, he said, rather it was removing the Soviet news blackout in the north. He asked for the Four Freedoms as a basis for negotiation. He believed that Soviet insistence on rice during the recent joint conference was evidence of the difficulties Russia faced in the northern zone. "The more we open up the country and convince people of our real aims, the greater will be the chances of achieving truly democratic rather than Soviet-directed communistic Korean Government." He concluded that the State Department had based SWNCC 176/18 on theory and not fact.[43]

When the Joint Commission opened its sessions on March 20, 1946, Hodge's pessimism seemed borne out. The Soviets displayed their intention with Shtikov's address, which noted that Korea should be "a true democratic and independent country, friendly to the Soviet Union, so that in the future it will not become a base for an attack on the Soviet Union." This statement precluded compromise, for it meant that Korea had fallen into the same category as the nations of Eastern Europe. Only loyal communists would ensure Soviet security. Fearing the anticommunism of Rhee and Kim Koo, who appeared the only noncommunist opposition favored by the American command, the Soviets now wanted Korea under their domination.[44] Soviet actions in the north had demonstrated the USSR's decision to create a socialist state indirectly controlled by Russians. Shtikov's opening address to the Joint Commission was evidence of Soviet policy to incorporate the south into a puppet regime. Soviet cooperation extended only as far as American negotiators would retreat.

Within a week, the commission reached an impasse over interpretation of the word "democratic." The Moscow agreement had authorized the two military commands to consult democratic elements in Korea. After a suitable period of international tutelage, Korea's future leaders would emerge. Based on instructions from the State-War-Navy Coordinating Committee, American negotiators held a flexible notion of "democratic": "Any Korean party or organization or individual regarded as democratic by either the US or Soviet members should be accepted by both sides." They only excluded former collaborators. The Americans would allow Soviet consultation with leftists in the south and expected that the Soviets would permit Cho Man-sik and other noncommunist leaders in the north to participate. But the Soviet view developed logically from Shtikov's opening statement. The Russians wanted to exclude any group or individual opposed to the Moscow agreement. Of course, every political group in the south except the communists had protested the agreement because it delayed independence. In arranging discussion of Korea's future, the Soviets sought to exclude the noncommunists in the south, and with Kim Il-sung's control of the north, they thus could dominate the consultative process. Russian negotiators described such conservatives as Rhee and Kim Koo as reactionaries and antidemocratic.[45]

The chief American delegate, General Arnold, attempted to modify the Soviet position. Benninghoff had advised Arnold to issue unilateral communiqués after each of the sessions so as to inform the Korean people of any progress. Publicity also would modify Soviet intransigence, or so he hoped. If it failed to change Soviet behavior, the Americans felt that evidence of good faith would help make the Koreans appreciate the American side.[46] In mid-April, it seemed that Arnold's policy had triumphed, for the Soviets offered a compromise on consultation. Shtikov proposed that the commission require an oath of support for the

Moscow agreement *and* trusteeship from all parties wishing to participate in the forthcoming government. The Soviet formula offered Koreans the chance to repudiate their "reactionary" leaders; in fact, the Russians feared Rhee's prestige among the masses or, more realistically, his control of the peasantry through rightwing groups. For a few days there was hope for progress.[47] Then Shtikov reverted to his earlier position and refused to consult with those leaders who had opposed trusteeship. Shtikov, to be sure, had acted on orders, and once again Korea was a victim of the cold war. The final chance for compromise in Korea disappeared when the commission, on May 8, 1946, adjourned *sine die*. Shtikov told Arnold that he had received orders to return to Pyongyang. He then reiterated the Soviet position on consultation. The Soviet Union demanded that a future Korean government be friendly. Reactionaries such as Rhee "would be instrumental in organizing hostile actions." He refused to modify the barrier at the 38th parallel. Arnold moved to adjourn.[48]

The United States government quickly drew conclusions from the failure of the Joint Commission. Some officials still clung to the illusion of postwar cooperation, but for many American diplomats, the events in Korea reinforced lessons of previous negotiations with the Russians. Assistant Secretary John Hilldring represented those State Department officials who continued to seek agreement with the Soviet Union. Hilldring tried to persuade the State-War-Navy Coordinating Committee of his views on the importance of Korea, as he felt that "US insistence upon respect for the principle of freedom of speech clashed with Soviet determination to prevent certain avowedly anti-Soviet Korean leaders from participating in a provisional government." He remarked that "while the United States should hold firm to its basic objectives with regard to Korea, it should be recognized that an amicable agreement with the Soviet Union over Korea is to be desired not only as a means of achieving our objectives there but also as a factor facilitating a Far Eastern and general understanding with the Soviet Union."[49] Even so, Russia's rejection of peaceful overtures embittered most American diplomats. The embassy at Moscow made clear its position on the Korean problem: "To the USSR, Korea is in east what Poland is in west.

USSR has no more intention of permitting Korea to gain real autonomy than to allow Poland freely to determine its own destiny." Officials concluded that time favored the Russians, and that a Korean agreement was impossible except on Soviet terms. A briefing paper for Secretary Byrnes accepted the remoteness of Soviet-American cooperation on the future of the peninsula and proposed that the military government should act unilaterally in the south to cope with the many problems it faced. It was at this time that the special counsel to the president, Clark Clifford, was forming his view of Soviet-American relations. A paper of May 15, written largely by Clifford's assistant, George Elsey, noted that "in our dealings with the Soviets we must conduct a global policy and not expect to advance our interests by treating each question on its apparent merits as it arises." Soviet policy is "carefully planned and integrated with moves on other fronts. . . . The United States must so organize itself that it can act with dispatch, decisiveness, and consistency in dealing with problems of foreign relations."[50] Spurred by Soviet intransigence, the U.S. government was revising its view of the world. It would come to perceive all problems along the Soviet periphery as emanating from specific decisions by the Soviet leadership. It would give the Soviet Union credit for an internal unanimity and decisiveness it could not possess, and it would ignore problems and solutions that did not fit this preconceived mode.

For nearly a year the United States government had continued to tie the solution of economic, social, and political matters in the southern zone to a general Soviet-American agreement, and in the meantime the situation had deteriorated. The economy had nearly collapsed; society moved closer to violence and anarchy; and as the chance of Soviet cooperation lessened, the political lines hardened into an extreme right, led by Rhee and Kim Koo, and a communist-dominated left.

As in many other troubled areas along the Soviet periphery, the United States found itself confronting an unyielding foe, and it subordinated the local reality to the superpower confrontation. Byrnes had made an ill-starred effort to arrange a compromise. Government officials now turned to what Kennan and Harriman had been saying in order to understand particular problems. In coming months, the United States would announce a series of makeshift plans to help rebuild the economy, institute reforms, and allow Koreans to choose leaders to work with the military government. The U.S. government began elevating troubled Soviet-American relations to prime status; it allowed the local situation to worsen beyond repair; and it demonstrated a blindness to a leftwing nationalism that, in varying degrees, characterized the nationalism in most colonial or former colonial areas in Asia. The government subordinated the reality of Korea to the cold war confrontation and thus began the emergence of an unwanted symbol, created by American policy.

The Turning Point

THE years 1946 and 1947 were a discouraging time in the history of the American occupation of south Korea, for it marked a period when the American military government vainly sought a way to end the increasing difficulties. When the Joint Commission adjourned on May 8, 1946, General Hodge and his advisers tried a new policy; they undertook to bring together a coalition of moderate leftists and rightists under Lyuh Woonhyung and Kimm Kiu-sic. As soon as the coalition should acquire credibility, Hodge would authorize the election of an interim legislative assembly. Unfortunately, the time for a coalition had passed. Rhee had organized the police, landlords, and armed "youth associations" to control the peasants. Pak Hun-yung and the communists had organized groups of assassins and gained the support of many urban workers. The moderate political groups were powerless, given their unwillingness to use force and/or inability to organize paramilitary units. Rhee's friends had already demonstrated their strength. Communist-led violence threatened American control in September and October; and before the year had ended, Hodge was forced to admit to his superiors that the initiative in the south had passed to the extremists of the left and right.

When officials in Washington realized that Hodge virtually had lost control in southern Korea, they proposed a complex plan for economic assistance of $500 million over three years. The Soviet barrier at the 38th parallel and the forced separation of Korea from its traditional trading partner, Japan, had made great trouble for the south Korean economy, and State Department experts wanted to strengthen the depressed agricultural sector, develop industrial exports to pay for imports of raw materials and energy, and thereby find employment for the hundreds of thousands of refugees that were overburdening the American zone.

Then events brought another proposed course. Affairs in Europe caused President Truman to drop the economic plan for south Korea in March 1947 when the British approached the Americans with news that they would have to abandon Greece and Turkey to the communists. The president and his advisers believed that the situation in Greece and Turkey directly threatened the security of Western Europe and was more important than Korea. Nor would the economy-minded Eightieth Congress have approved two large aid programs. The American government therefore sought to reconvene the Joint Comission. Although Soviet leaders quickly agreed to recommence the talks in Seoul, their action did not signify a new attitude of cooperation. Soviet negotiators insisted that only such Korean parties as the communists and socialists were democratic and that the commission should not consult with conservatives and moderates. The American delegates believed that any Korean party not tainted by collaboration with the Japanese was acceptable. Within a few months, the commission deadlocked over the same issues as it had the year before.

I

At the outset, in May 1946, Lieutenant General Hodge attempted a new initiative in Korea based on coalition politics and zone-wide elections. As the State Department's Hilldring wrote the Operations Division of the War Department, "Hodge should start using Koreans in local level government, set up shadow national government of Koreans, start some reforms and go it alone but not completely in case any chance for negotiations with the Soviets." Military authorities were at odds with Syngman Rhee and the conservatives who wanted a separate, noncompromised south Korea. Far Eastern experts in Washington sensed that because of his xenophobia about communism and his extreme rightwing views, "Rhee has outlived his period of usefulness and should be gently eased out of the Korean political picture."[1]

Hodge and his advisers had decided by early 1946 that they could not trust the communists in the south. In the first days of occupation, the American command had assigned the native communist party one of the larger and more modern office buildings in the capital, and now it had uncovered a counterfeiting operation. In the basement of the building, printing presses had poured forth newspapers and pamphlets attacking the American occupation, and when during the spring an estimated nine to eleven million counterfeit yen flooded the south, government security officers learned from a Korean informant that the yen were printed by the basement presses. The counterfeit yen threatened to undermine the fragile economy of the south and convinced Hodge that local communists took orders from the Soviet command in north Korea.[2] In fact, it is possible that the counterfeiting operation was a sign of the desperation of native communists, who felt themselves cheated out of their just reward by a Russian-picked exile regime in the north and an American-supported one in the south.

Leaving the communists out of the proposed coalition, Hodge hoped to unite the moderate right and left behind Dr. Kimm Kiu-sic and Lyuh Woon-hyung. Kimm was a beloved conservative, afflicted by poor health, whose hold on such rightist elements as the traditionally conservative peasant farmers and tenants varied markedly with his physical condition. Unlike Rhee and Kim Koo, Kimm received almost no support from the wealthy, and he wanted former collaborators (who supported Rhee) punished. Lyuh had been the leader of the People's Committees that had greeted the American liberators in September 1945, and a strong contender with Pak for leftwing nationalist support. He was in a difficult position. Hodge and Benninghoff had considered him a communist dupe and would not deal with him during the initial phase of the occupation; the communists believed that he had sold out to the capitalists and pro-American collaborators. From these weaknesses and hopes came the Coalition Committee with Kimm as chairman and Lyuh as vice-chairman. Through the summer of 1946, occupation authorities assisted the committee in gaining respect, but as violence by the extremists increased, the committee appeared ill-equipped to fight for power in the deteriorating situation.[3]

Economic reform would help the Coalition Committee, and during the spring, the military government considered plans to redistribute land and wealth to provide the peasantry with a stake in the new regime. Hodge was under pressure for reform because Kim Il-sung's dictatorship in the north seemingly had redistributed land (the regime later would force peasants to return land to the state) and nationalized industry (all opponents had fled south to further complicate Hodge's reform problems). The Americans planned to create "The New Korea Company," a temporary holding company that would sell land to farm tenants at low prices with payment stretched over many years. Money collected would help the new Korean government support agriculture.[4] In mid-summer 1946, the Americans unveiled the remainder of their new initiative: elections for an interim legislative assembly which would help satisfy Korean desires for independence and provide practice in democratic process. If the Coalition Committee dominated the October elections, the Americans hoped that such a regime would please the Russians and move Korea toward unification and independence.

However, Syngman Rhee saw the coming elections as representing a golden opportunity to gain power. Among his supporters he counted business and landowning interests threatened by economic reform, most village headmen, the military government's Korean employees, and the police (and others) who had been tainted by collaboration with the Japanese and still awaited punishment. Wealthy conservatives would finance his election campaign. Village headmen would make sure that illiterate peasants, regardless of their wishes, voted for Rhee. Government workers would supervise the campaign and voting. The police and other collaborators represented Rhee's most powerful supporters for they were the most worried about their status; the radical left and the Coalition Committee had agreed to punish them if either of their groups won the elections. The former collaborators would provide the force to terrorize the populace. Having spent the years of Japanese rule safely in the United

States and consumed with his hatred of Russia and the desire to rebuild a traditional Korean society, Rhee seemed unaware or unconcerned over the inequities of wealth and the issue of collaboration in postwar Korea. Throughout the summer, he remained above politics while the police waged a virtual war against his enemies.[5]

The communists, as one might have expected, denounced the proposed elections. Pak and the native communists were in a difficult position. Throughout the years of Japanese oppression, they had represented the only resistance movement and had concentrated in the south where the impoverished peasantry seemed susceptible to communist ideology. The end of the war had dealt them a hard blow, for an expatriate regime ruled in the north, while in the south the Americans supported the conservatives. The proposed elections might lead to a permanent division of the peninsula, and there was little likelihood, with the forces supporting Rhee, that voting would be a free expression of the popular will.[6]

In late summer, Hodge turned openly on the communists, fearing attempts to sabotage the elections. Responding to increasing leftwing violence (while ignoring the violence of Rhee's supporters), Hodge suspended three communist-oriented newspapers, saying that their editors had violated ordinances prohibiting the inciting of revolt. He ordered the arrest of party leaders for "the safety of the occupation troops and for attempted sabotage of military government administration." He also allowed the brutal police a freer hand in dealing with "subversives." Pak and his chief lieutenants evaded arrest by escaping north of the 38th parallel.[7]

The communists who remained in the south did what they could to stir up trouble. A series of strikes and related violence nearly overwhelmed the military government. Communist-controlled railroad workers in Seoul walked off the job on September 14, demanding wage increases and improved working conditions. Within two weeks the strike had spread through the southern zone to the entire mechanism of transportation. Communist saboteurs sought to wreck the transportation system; assassins targeted key rightist politicians. As the level of violence rose, the workers moved from economic to political issues and their demands mirrored the communist party platform. The economy ground nearly to a halt.[8]

Hodge managed to reestablish order, but the cost was enormous. He let loose police on striking workers and called in rightwing "youth associations" to control the countryside. One observer likened Korea to an "armed camp on the eve of insurrection." Another noted that the police carried out the suppression of communists with "unusual alacrity." The violence almost destroyed the authority of the American command. Conservatives had tasted power and would not relinquish it easily. Workers who had participated in the strike perceived a close relationship between the supposedly neutral Americans and Korean conservatives (and former collaborators). And the violence destroyed the fragile Coalition Committee. Extremists had armed followers; the Coalition Committee did not embrace violence. Extremists intensified hatred of military government; Kimm and Lyuh were dedicated to gradual and peaceful change. As Korean society began to break down into armed camps, the Coalition Committee could not make its voice heard above the din. Several weeks after the strike, Hodge wrote Vincent that "there is an open and growing aversion to American Military Government and every move made by Americans is being subjected to strong criticism and propaganda as another move to prolong AMG or colonize Korea for American imperialism," including, perhaps, the Coalition Committee.[9]

The elections for an interim legislative assembly turned out far differently than the Americans had hoped, for Syngman Rhee won a great victory, his supporters capturing thirty-eight of forty-five assembly seats. The remainder were divided between moderates and leftists. The victory had been assisted by fraud. In the villages, headmen voted for all peasants; in certain districts only taxpayers and landholders (i.e., the wealthy) voted. Observers rightly charged that the election was undemocratic and superficial. The Americans had set the voting date in mid-October, at a time when leftists and moderates were unprepared and the police remained in uncontested control following the riots. Leftists boycotted the elections, for they feared that Rhee would use a victory as a referendum on the issue of independence for southern Korea.[10]

Hodge admitted irregularities in the electoral process and appointed forty-five assemblymen in addition to the forty-five elected members. Although he and his advisers were pleased that leftists had done so poorly, they had hoped that the Coalition Committee would do better. To strengthen the committee, Hodge appointed seventeen unaligned rightists, many of whom had been followers of Kimm Kiu-sic; fifteen centrists who represented urban, Western-oriented and educated Koreans; and twelve leftists who had followed Lyuh. One appointed member declined his seat.[11]

Victory in the election encouraged Rhee to become a strident critic of the American presence in Korea, and as leftists had anticipated, he demanded immediate independence for the southern zone. He flew to the United States to plead for an independent government before the United Nations. Langdon wrote the State Department that Rhee had decided to fight and wreck U.S. policy for Korea. Meeting with American officials in Washington, he proposed a six-point formula that would have handed control of the south to his followers. After he returned to Korea, the Americans learned that he had hoped to release an inflammatory message while in the Unites States, causing his people to riot against the occupation; he then would have volunteered to control these "patriots" if the Americans would accept his six-point plan. Upon return, Rhee began viewing Hodge as an enemy, along with the communists, and authorized his followers in the military government to sabotage whatever the general desired to do.[12] Rhee's allies then turned the interim legislative assembly into a forum to embarrass the American command. Hodge's appointments to the assembly only confirmed that body's overwhelming conservative majority. Although the assembly was a consultative group serving at the pleasure of General Hodge, it rapidly assumed quasi-governmental powers. It claimed to represent the people in the south. It passed resolutions condemning trusteeships, indigenous communists, and even General Hodge. (These actions drove many moderates into communist ranks because they were the only effective opposition to the conservatives and collaborators and the only group with power that desired reunification of the peninsula.) The assembly went so far that Hodge had to make a public statement criticizing its pronouncements, a sign of weakness and the American dependency on Rhee to help maintain order. Hodge should have confronted Rhee and his followers, but the military government had too few men to control the resulting chaos. The initiative had passed to Syngman Rhee.[13]

It is difficult to know what Rhee might have done in his effort to undermine American authority in Korea had it not been for the announcement of the Truman Doctrine in March 1947. Rhee probably would have found one reason or another to move against the Americans. After all, he was an intense nationalist and wanted control in Korea; the Americans stood in his way as they sought a middle group of Korean politicians who were neither communists nor reactionaries. In any event, when Truman announced a worldwide opposition to communism (though he specifically mentioned only Greece and Turkey), Rhee seized upon Truman's address as a long-awaited justification of his virulent anticommunism. His supporters renewed their attack on trusteeship, while rightist armed units took to the streets. They believed that Truman would chastize General Hodge and favor the conservatives in Korea.[14]

II

An economy-minded Congress in 1947 forced the War Department to reconsider the army's occupation of Korea. Appropriations for fiscal year 1947 had allowed $50 million for Korean relief, and occupation planners had calculated that two or three times that amount was necessary. They recommended that the United States should "get out of Korea" if funds remained inadequate. Army leaders wanted Secretary of War Robert Patterson to end the occupation. Budget cuts had reduced troops to a minimum, and Korea seemed not worth the presence of forty thousand American soldiers.[15]

Patterson sought to relieve the War Department of Korean responsibilities and approached the State Department with two alternatives. The department would have to assume responsibility for Korea, secure funds from Congress, and bring about a civil administration in the south. Failing this, the United States should terminate its involvement in Korea as soon as possible. He forwarded the recommendations of Hodge and MacArthur; the generals wanted submission of the Korean problem to the United Nations, formation of a commission of disinterested nations to survey and recommend, further meetings of the Big Four "clarifying" chapter three of the Moscow agreement, or "highest level" meetings between representatives of the United States and Soviet Union.[16]

The State Department, however, would not allow the army to pull out of southern Korea. Vincent advised Secretary of State George Marshall that the occupation must continue. To solve problems in Korea and move that country toward independence, the United States needed, he believed, to reach an accord with the Soviet Union. If the Russians would interpret any American request for high-level meetings as weakness and impatience, a continued show of American determination would eventually lead to negotiations. Vincent noted that Korea had become a symbol of the cold war, and that if the army left Korea, the Japanese might (would?) question America's strength of purpose and seek an accommodation with the Soviets. A continued American presence might help Chiang Kai-shek in his struggle with the communists in Manchuria. Vincent did believe the occupation structure needed reform and agreed to replace the military with Korean civilians in the everyday working of government.[17]

Realizing the need for initiative on the Korean situation, the department created a special interdepartmental committee on Korea, and the five-member group met during January and February 1947. Department officers wrote to the new political adviser in Korea, Joseph E. Jacobs; to Langdon (who returned to his permanent assignment as consul in Seoul); and to economic expert Arthur Bunce that senior officials finally were paying attention to the confusing situation in the peninsula. Within a few weeks, the committee circulated a report that stated the object of American actions was "psychologically, to demonstrate to the communists and Koreans, that [the U.S.] meant to stay in business in Korea and, practically, to create a viable economy in South Korea capable of withstanding subversion." It recommended a three-year grant-in-aid program supervised by the department. The committee rejected the continuance of present policies because they were ineffective and the American position too untenable given Soviet unwillingness to negotiate an end to the division of the peninsula. It noted that early recognition of an independent government in south Korea, as Rhee demanded, would be a superficial response. The committee believed that referring the problem to the United Nations would be a premature move and expressed few hopes for cooperation with the USSR. It urged adoption of an aggressive, positive program for south Korea.[18]

The committee's report marked a turning point in Korean-American and possibly the whole range of Soviet-American relations. Until 1947, Korea had mattered little to high-level American officials; at best it was viewed as a ready concession to assist compromise on more important issues if the Soviets wished to cooperate. Thus the period until early 1947 witnessed a continual deterioration of conditions in the peninsula as Korea remained, in Vincent's words, "a back-burner issue." While the Soviet Union caused a great many of the problems faced by the occupation, American officials failed to develop contingency plans in the event of Soviet intransigence. Valuable time passed; perhaps the moment for the United States to extricate itself without a loss of prestige had passed as well. Moderate politics had been discredited; violent leftists and rightists competed for political control. Few American officials understood the reality of Korea, and Korea now found itself raised to a symbol in the cold war. The less strategic an issue (and the less understood) the greater its value as a symbol, precisely because of its unimportance. Korea was becoming a bellwether of American intentions, a sign of American determination and, in time, the symbol would grow so large that it nearly controlled its creator.

The three-year economic program was the key provision of the committee's proposal. A well-financed aid program would place Korea on a "self-sustaining basis." The committee wanted

Congress to appropriate $500 million to $600 million for fiscal years 1948-50; it was a tremendous sum of money. A distant relative of the Marshall Plan, this program would provide assistance for rehabilitation of the south Korean economy and help find new trading partners since the Soviets prohibited interzonal commerce.[19]

State Department officials approved the report, believing it to be sound: congressional approval would convince the Soviets of American determination and continued Soviet obstinacy would help convince Congress of the need for an aid program. Hilldring and Vincent wrote Marshall in late February 1947 that he should "coordinate timing of an approach to the Russians with Presidential submission to Congress of proposed special legislation for a grant to Korea."[20]

The aid program received the reluctant approval of the War Department. Patterson "agreed not to oppose it" although he believed the United States "should get out of Korea as soon as we could do so 'gracefully.' " Major General Daniel Noce, chief of the Civilian Affairs Division, wrote Hilldring that he was glad both for the forthcoming aid program and for State Department assumption of responsibility of civil affairs in Korea. Hodge and his advisers in Korea cabled thanks for belated attention to the Korean situation.[21] As February drew to a close, the outlook for Korea was good. After months of drift, the situation was receiving the reluctant attention of the government in Washington.

Then the European situation intervened. In late February 1947, the British informed the American government of their problems in the eastern Mediterranean. Britain never had recovered economically from the Second World War and by 1947 found its imperial obligations too great for its resources. On February 21, the Foreign Office privately informed American officials in Washington that it could no longer support the governments of Greece and Turkey. Unless the United States assumed the financial burden, those governments would have to fend for themselves after April 1. While the British may have raised the communist specter merely to have the Americans protect the empire, it truly seemed that the United States had little choice; and in a dramatic speech of March 12, President Truman addressed a joint session of Congress to ask support for a $400 million aid bill. The president said: "I believe that it must be the policy of the United States to support free peoples who are resisting attempted subjugation by armed minorities or by outside pressure." The precise meaning of the Truman Doctrine has been a subject of some controversy, but John Lewis Gaddis has argued convincingly that it did not presage a worldwide commitment to containment;[22] nonetheless, the policy seemingly signified a new level of commitment.

The meaning of the Truman Doctrine for Korea was at first unclear, and Rhee praised the president for his stand against international communism and repeated his own demands for an independent government in the south. American officials in Korea were pleased that their government had awakened to the red menace. The State Department hoped for a Korean aid bill, noting that Korea was one of two places in the world where American soldiers confronted Soviet troops. The Russians complained more about American policy in south Korea than in the American zone in Germany. The *New York Times* reported Russian criticism of the interim legislative assembly: "The legislative body in the US zone is attacked as a creature of US administration and reactionaries." The department hoped that Congress would accept the nation's obligation to the Korean people and the need to resist the Russians.[23]

But the aid program then ran into difficulties with the Eightieth Congress. Under Secretary of State Dean Acheson appeared before the Senate Foreign Relations Committee, and other department representatives made themselves available to Congress. Although such Republican legislators as Senator Arthur H. Vandenberg accepted the need for aid to Greece and Turkey, they resisted an aid program for Korea, seeing a contradiction in the administration's policy for China and Korea. They feared that too much foreign aid would bankrupt the American people. Congressman Hubert S. Ellis of West Virginia remarked in mid-April 1947 that "there is no doubt that a transfusion for Korea and a bloodletting for Uncle Sam to the tune of $600 million is in the making and will be presented to Congress after the disposal of the Greek-Turkish question." Vandenberg sought to cooperate with the State Department and drew a parallel between American responsibilities for Korea and Germany, stating that "there is an inescapable obligation in Korea. . . . Yes, there will have to be a Korean program." Congressional Republicans refused to follow the senator's lead. Pennsylvania Congressman Robert F. Rich said that "we must economize or bust. . . . We will wreck our country unless we can balance our budget" and control foreign aid programs and spending.[24] There was one major difference between aid for Greece and Turkey and assistance to Korea: administration officials could demonstrate the strategic importance of the eastern Mediterranean and the positive benefits of foreign aid for that area, but not show that the aid would be effective in Korea, nor prove that Korea was important strategically to American security.

State Department officials continued their planning for Korea as if Congress would appropriate the money. Speaking before the Economic Club of Detroit on March 10, 1947, Hilldring said that "the problems we have encountered in Korea constitute one of our most formidable challenges in the entire field of foreign relations." He stated that American democracy must rehabilitate that nation. Vincent wrote Hilldring in late March that, if necessary, the U.S. should "go it alone" in Korea to discharge its responsibilities. The department also moved to assume control of civilian administration in Korea from the War Department. It wanted General MacArthur's political responsibilities terminated and a political adviser of ambassadorial rank appointed. Within two to three months, American civilians should replace military personnel in the occupation. When that change had taken place, the American command in Korea should have the interim legislative assembly pass a general election law. A report on March 31, 1947, by the special interdepartmental committee on Korea summarized this viewpoint:

> Korea's principal political importance to the US is perhaps the effect of developments there on the whole cause of Soviet-US relations. It is important that there be no gaps or weakening in our policy of firmness in containing the USSR because weakness in one area is invariably interpreted by the Soviets as indicative of an overall softening. A backing down or running away from the USSR in Korea could easily result in a

stiffening of the Soviet attitude on Germany or some other area of much greater intrinsic importance to us. On the other hand, a firm "holding of the line" in Korea can materially strengthen our position in our other dealings with the USSR.[25]

It is a remarkable report, indicating the serious problems of perception that already afflicted American foreign policymaking. While admitting differences within the government (notably between State and War), it assumed that there was but one voice in Moscow and that Korea, an area of minor importance, could affect the future of Germany, an area of prime importance. Regardless of what Kennan meant by "containment" in February 1946, a year later it had come to mean "a firm 'holding of the line.' " Although, as Gaddis argues, the means were lacking to back up the verbal commitment, Korea had begun to emerge as a symbol of American determination to hold the line against the Soviet Union in East Asia.

The State Department believed that the aid bill for Korea would solve a great many problems. Vincent informed Acheson that the department could agree to an "early date" for withdrawal (within three years) if the War Department would support the Korean aid bill before Congress. A staff meeting on Korea concluded that the department's program for Korea would lead to early withdrawal. Besides helping to save the deteriorating situation in Korea, it also would further commit Congress to the containment view of U.S.-Soviet relations that was gaining increasing support among State Department officials.

By early summer 1947, it began to appear that Congress would not pass a Korean aid bill. The department had sought funds for a one-year program. Within a few weeks, the department accepted that there was no way to obtain even this limited support from Congress. Vandenberg would not permit the Foreign Relations Committee to take up Korean aid legislation because he felt that the Senate would only approve a limited number of rehabilitation programs and that pushing Korea would jeopardize more important funding proposals. Although he suggested taking it up before the Armed Services Committee, the department had little hope for more favorable treatment elsewhere given the senator's reading of his colleagues' feelings about authorizing vast new spending programs. Vandenberg made it clear that he did not want any more relief bills for such marginal areas as Korea, for he "feared the political consequences of a defeat on this issue—vis-a-vis other rehabilitation programs."[26] The Korean aid bill passed into history when Hilldring on July 8 recommended to Secretary Marshall that "there be no further efforts this session to obtain Congressional action on the Korean aid program." Hilldring recommended making the program a part of the general appropriation for economic reconstruction at a later date.[27]

III

How could Hodge raise the prestige of the occupation, now so far jeopardized, in danger of complete, utter collapse? Hope reappeared when Secretary Marshall, in Moscow in March 1947, sought to persuade Foreign Minister Molotov to reconvene the Joint Commission in Korea. When officials in Washington sought Hodge and MacArthur for consultation, the generals recommended reassembling the commission. Hodge told the president the Soviet agents were building up a five-hundred-thousand-man north Korean army to overwhelm the south. He believed that war was certain unless the United States and Soviet Union acted immediately to reunite the zones. MacArthur agreed, urging that "measures be taken immediately to break the US-Russian deadlock in Korea by diplomatic means." The interdepartmental committee on Korea seconded the recommendation, and Truman approved. The president instructed Marshall to approach the Soviets toward the end of his stay in Moscow for the Foreign Ministers Conference. In early April, Vincent had cabled Marshall that matters in Korea hinted that the Soviets "may be willing to reconvene the Soviet-American Joint Commission for discussions on establishment of a provisional Korean Government and a unified administration for Korea" (although he failed to explain "matters"). Marshall on April 8 gave Molotov a letter proposing to reopen talks and blaming the Soviets for the delay. He wanted progress reviewed after a few months. Seeking to obtain public pressure for renewed cooperation in Korea, he released the letter to the press.[28]

After a bitter denunciation of American policy in Korea, Molotov agreed to reopen the talks on Korea. At first he accused the Americans of causing the delay, claiming that the United States "excluded such large democratic parties and social organizations as the all-Korean peasant union, Korean-National revolutionary party, all-Korean youth union, etc." He charged that the Americans fostered antidemocratic elements in Korea, that is, Syngman Rhee and his conservative supporters. He proposed that the Joint Commission convene on May 20 and that the two governments review progress in July or August. Molotov's readiness to reopen the commission may well have come from a fear of congressional passage of the Korean aid bill (attesting to the strength of the commitment implied in the Truman Doctrine), for in mid-April, Congress had not yet rejected such legislation.[29]

News of the great-power agreement quickly reached Korea, exciting political passions. Rhee and his allies, fearing a Russian victory at the talks, charged that Hodge was procommunist and "intended to sell us into communism through the operations of the Joint Commission." American officials feared that Rhee would sabotage the proceedings. Moderates hoped that this act of great-power cooperation might produce an acceptable compromise of left and right politics (and revive the hopes of the Coalition Committee). Communists were exuberant, for an agreement surely would be a prelude to an all-communist Korea.[30]

Once again the two delegations met at the Duk Soo Palace, and an easy informality warmed the first few sessions of the reconvened Joint Commission. Colonel General Shtikov and his four fellow delegates only brought sixty-five staff members to assist them. Shtikov refrained from "fulminations against reactionaries or other name-calling characteristic of last year's address." The chief Soviet delegate emphasized the need for speedy agreement. Major General Albert E. Brown, who had succeeded General Arnold, and his staff expressed a cautious optimism.[31]

For a month, proceedings went smoothly and American delegates, weary of Soviet machinations in the long, tortuous negotiations over Korean unification, were encouraged by the progress of early sessions. The two delegations easily agreed to form various subcomissions to interview Korean parties and social organizations, study the economy, and look into the problem of zonal reintegration. Shtikov and Brown seemingly overcame the problem that had deadlocked the commission the previous May; they issued a communiqué setting forth who was eligible for consultation. The Joint Commission would consult with Korean parties and/or social organizations on the structure of a future, unified Korean government which would declare their support for the Moscow agreement of December 1945 by "signing the declaration in Communiqué No. 5." The Americans wanted to promote a spirit of compromise and agreed to the Soviet position on consultation even though it limited Korean freedom of speech to criticize the Moscow accords. Still the Soviets acted reasonably, perhaps until Congress recessed for its summer vacation without passage of Korean aid, before they revealed their true attitude toward the talks.[32] The failure of Congress to authorize a Korean aid program may have caused the Soviets to rethink their worry over America's commitment to contain communism.

The bubble of optimism burst on June 27 when a Soviet delegate announced in subcommittee that his side would insist on excluding parties now or formerly opposing trusteeship from further consultations. Soviet members explained that this action affected eight parties with a membership totalling about three million (the core of Rhee's strength). The Russians wanted only leftists to take part in the consultations. The Soviet delegation claimed that leftist membership in more than four hundred organizations totaled 62 million in south Korea. Hodge thought that total amusing, for the American zone had a population of only 30 million.[33]

American officials soon realized that no compromise was possible on the issue of consultation. General Brown told Shtikov that he would stand firm on the matter of conservative organizations, for Rhee and his allies had respected the commission's guidelines. Over Marshall's signature, John M. Allison of the Northeast Asian Affairs Division wrote the political adviser in Seoul, Jacobs, that the "department believes there can be no, repeat, no compromise on this issue." He repeated that as long as Korean parties would cooperate with the commission, the commission should consult with them regardless of past views on trusteeship or the Moscow decision. From the embassy at Moscow, Ambassador W. Bedell Smith sent Marshall the embassy's views: "The unwillingness of Soviet delegation on JC to compromise on its definition of democratic organization is symptomatic of the whole Soviet attitude on Korean questions. We fail to see where agreement can be reached save at sacrifice our principles." Hodge informed Washington that compromise was impossible and said, "If the JC fails, I expect to see terrorism by both factions begin on a scale that may approach an oriental-style civil war." The general found both sides preparing for hostilities.[34]

As weeks passed, the commission deadlocked in recrimination. Russian delegates charged that the Americans had violated the spirit of the Moscow decision by desiring consultation with such antidemocratic elements as Rhee, Kim, and their allies. They claimed that the Americans welcomed a permanent division of the peninsula. The Soviets used the sessions in Seoul as a propaganda forum from which to attack Rhee. Perhaps the Russians no longer feared an American plan to rehabilitate the south, perhaps they were using their on-again, off-again attitude toward cooperation in Korea to indicate displeasure with the course of relations elsewhere (especially Germany or Japan), or maybe they wanted to take advantage of the confusion they perceived in American policy. Regardless, they revealed their intentions for Korea. The Americans also expressed bitterness, for they felt that all parties in the north and south were eligible for consultation. They charged that the Russians wanted to eliminate all noncommunist parties from contention. It was an ironic situation, for American delegates had to defend Rhee's right to "freedom of expression" while they had to defend themselves from Rhee's attacks on their purpose and integrity.

As chances for compromise faded, the American command in Korea decided to make public the commission's deadlocked status and inform south Koreans that the USSR was responsible for the lack of progress toward unification. Hodge remembered that the volatile south Koreans had turned to violence at previous delays in independence. He wanted to demonstrate that the United States had acted in good faith while Soviet negotiators had procrastinated, and he hoped to achieve a great propaganda victory for the much-maligned military government. But interviews with the Korean press and political groups did not gain the desired purpose. Rhee praised the American delegation for resisting the Soviets and claimed the proceedings proved the need for a separate government in the south. Communist and leftist parties attacked the Americans, fearing that the breakdown of the commission would lead to a communist regime in the north and a reactionary one in the south threatening their very existence. Most Koreans were impatient and blamed both sides in their anger and dismay.[36]

The American delegation made one last attempt to resolve the problem of consultation with Korean parties. Under instructions from Secretary Marshall, they presented a series of proposals to their Soviet counterparts in late summer. Brown suggested to Shtikov that Soviet and American commands conduct separate meetings in their respective zones with those Korean parties and social organizations that had filled out written questionnaires the previous month. Shtikov insisted that the Americans adopt his interpretation of the situation and disqualify conservative organizations in the south from a Korean government. He feared that Rhee's popularity whether real or forced might rival that of Kim Il-sung, the Soviet choice for an all-Korean regime. On August 1, American delegates, on behalf of the Soviets, offered to consult with those Korean parties that owed allegiance to Rhee and Kim Koo. The Soviets again demanded that the Americans "fulfill" the Moscow agreement and consult only those parties that the Soviets had approved. The Soviets also rejected the final American proposal. Jacobs asked the Soviet delegation to agree to set aside oral consultations with Korean parties and continue plans for a provisional government based on the written questionnaires received during late June. However, the Russians rejected every American attempt at compromise.[37]

When the Soviets rejected the final American proposals, the

U.S. delegation vainly sought a joint report on the commission's progress. The embassy in Moscow asked Molotov to instruct Shtikov to prepare a report by August 21. Molotov stated, though it is difficult to believe, that he had no power over the Soviet delegation. For the next few weeks Brown repeatedly asked Shtikov to join him and sign a report for their respective governments. By the end of August, Jacobs would report to Marshall the delegations could not even agree that they had disagreed.[38]

The situation in and about Korea had reached a turning point. Hodge's days of neglect were over; the period of chaos and confusion was passing. The government in Washington belatedly was paying attention to the crisis as it sought a way to fulfill its obligations to Korea. In the months since liberation, the situation had steadily deteriorated. Korean society had been polarized between north and south, between violent left and violent right. The Coalition Committee arrived too late; the Joint Commission appeared doomed from the beginning. It is clear that of all the groups involved, only the United States sincerely sought compromise. This was of little consolation as a year of hopes for peaceful unification ended with a stark confrontation across the negotiating tables at the Duk Soo Palace.

A new period was setting in, with significance beyond Korea. The Truman administration was beginning an exercise in symbol creation; it was ignoring the reality of Korea and creating a symbol that was little understood by allies or adversaries and one which would take on a life of its own. As the months and years passed, Korea would increase in importance as a symbol of American determination to resist Soviet aggression. As the adversarial view of Soviet-American relations gained credence, Korea became an ideal location to prove American strength of purpose. Unfortunately, congressional rejection of the $500 million aid program caused the administration to retreat momentarily into renewed attempts at cooperation. Then, having been rebuffed for the last time, the administration would in the future accept greater risks in demonstrating its commitment to Korea.

Enlisting the United Nations

THE period of cooperation largely had passed; it was a time of confrontation, and the government in Washington would seek to involve the United Nations in a series of actions designed to further the containment of the Soviet Union. Part of the broad American initiative to enlist the world organization in the cold war, the "Korean Question" would give evidence of a new United States attitude toward allies, neutrals, and opponents as American leaders saw themselves leading a reluctant world into battle with Soviet-dominated communism. The result of this new policy for Korea (and the United Nations) would be as surprising as it was significant.

Whatever the original hopes of American planners who conceived of an august international body devoted to peace, government officials had decided by 1947 that the United Nations must resign its neutrality and take sides in the increasingly hostile relations between the Soviet Union and the United States. It would help further containment by bringing to bear whatever influence the United Nations possessed against the USSR and its client states. Along with dramatic assistance programs for such areas as Greece and Turkey, the new United States policy toward the UN would show American determination to resist Soviet expansion. Involving the United Nations in the affairs of the peninsula would mark an important step in that policy.

Although the United States government achieved its goals in the UN General Assembly, the cost would outweigh the gain. By forging the United Nations into an American tool in the superpower confrontation (the Soviets most likely tried to follow a similar course), the United States probably destroyed that body's influence for peace since its effectiveness depended upon great-power cooperation. It may well have furthered the well-developed Soviet sense of paranoia and forced Kremlin leaders into a military expansion they might have wanted to avoid. It certainly affected Canadian politics (and Canadian-American relations) and demonstrated American insensitivity toward allies. Policy-makers in Washington assumed that American interests mirrored those of its allies. In leading the free world into battle with atheistic Russian communism, it was assumed that the free world must willingly fall into line and submit to American direction.

I

When the United States took the issue of Korea to the United Nations General Assembly in the autumn of 1947, it was difficult to believe that the American government was willing to force a decision on Korean affairs. In the two years since the end of the Second World War, people had come to think that the uneasy confusions of the past would continue, that trouble might arise in Europe or the Middle East, perhaps even in Latin America or Asia, but that Korean problems would only simmer and not boil. Korea had been in a state of confusion since the 1880s, and the people of the peninsula had survived. They had been un-happy to be sure; Syngman Rhee as a young man had appeared at the Paris Peace Conference and sought the intercession of Colonel Edward M. House. Word of Korean discontent reached President Woodrow Wilson, who decided that he could do noth-ing about it. The end of the Second World War marked only another episode in the travail of Korea. What would be the role of the United Nations?

Admittedly, the UN was a court of last resort. When the Truman administration's special interdepartmental committee on Korea prepared its report in February 1947 (which resulted in the ill-fated attempt at a Korean aid bill), it had rejected the idea of taking the Korean question to the four powers which had negotiated the Moscow agreement or to the United Nations. Such admission of failure "would have a most damaging effect on U.S. prestige"; the Soviet Union would charge that the United

States had violated an international agreement by abandoning the talks in the Joint Commission. The committee noted carefully that such a course was "hardly likely to result in hastening a solution to the problem." It suggested that if it were "conclusively demonstrable that the Soviet Union is deliberately preventing a solution of the Korean problem," then "it might eventually become desirable to refer it to the United Nations."[1]

The State Department at this time was placing its hopes on the Korean aid bill and the reconvened Joint Commission. Officials in Seoul felt that referring the matter to the United Nations was "either a confession of failure or a move to embarrass Russia." The assistant chief of the Division of Northeast Asian Affairs, John Allison, prepared "an outline of program for Korea," in which he considered approaching the Security Council but rejected acting independently of the Soviet Union, believing the United States had no case for moving beyond the Moscow agreement.[2]

When it became apparent that the aid bill would not pass and that the Joint Commission had reached a stalemate, Allison presented a detailed plan, a series of steps that, if the Soviets refused to cooperate, would place the Korean question before the United Nations. A letter from Secretary Marshall to Foreign Minister Molotov would suggest that, if the Joint Commission continued without progress until mid-August, the "two delegations be requested to report to their governments and that the governments then consider what further steps can usefully be taken to bring about a unified, independent Korea." Should Molotov refuse to cooperate, "consideration might also be given to the possibility of presenting the Korean question to the United Nations." Allison was certain that Russian obstinacy would give the United States such "freedom of action that it might take any steps deemed necessary." He noted three problems: the politics of Rhee and his group, elections in south Korea, and the nature of the subsequent provisional or interim government.[3]

A few days later, the administration approved a version of Allison's proposal as SWNCC 176/30, and over Marshall's signature, Vincent wrote the political adviser, Jacobs, in Seoul that the department was "giving urgent study to a course of action for Korea in case of breakdown or indefinite prolongation of the present stalemate in the Joint Commission." Allison brought up his proposal at a meeting of the Ad Hoc Committee on Korea on August 4, and the committee sent the State-War-Navy Coordinating Committee its recommendations pointing out the increasing ideological importance of Korea as well as its strategic liability. Immediate withdrawal from the peninsula, desired by the War Department to ease the strain on its limited resources, would lead "inevitably" to communist domination: "This would seriously damage United States prestige in the Far East and throughout the world and discourage those small nations that now rely upon the United States." The committee noted that extremists in the south might well force a hasty withdrawal of U.S. troops if internal disorder continued. It concluded that the U.S. government must set a timetable that would force the Korean question to a resolution. A proposed letter to Molotov on August 7 would request the Joint Commission progress report by August 17. Since the commission would report no progress toward elections, the committee wanted the secretary of state to call for a meeting of the Four Powers in Washington in late August, and, if this meeting achieved little, the government in mid-September would announce its intention of bringing the Korean question to the United Nations. The committee recommended that the department establish a group to prepare the case for submission to the United Nations. Hilldring received Marshall's approval on August 6, and that of the president a few days later.[4]

The approval of SWNCC 176/30 marked an important step. Circumstances, perceptions (and misperceptions), and actions combined to elevate Korea in the cold war struggle. Considerable naiveté had marked American dealings over Korea through 1946, but it became increasingly obvious that the Soviet Union would not negotiate in good faith. Kennan's "long telegram" and the reception it received caused many to view the Soviets as aggressive and expansionist, orchestrating a global movement. The containment thesis argued that a retreat anywhere along the line of confrontation would signal Soviet leaders to test American strength elsewhere. It also implied that the United

States must contest areas of little significance in order to convince friends and adversaries that it would contest the priority areas. Korea became a symbol of American prestige because administration officials publicly so stated. They felt that nations throughout the world were regarding the Soviet-American confrontation in Korea as a test case. By making Korea a symbol of American commitment regardless of adverse conditions, the government in Washington became trapped in its own imagery.

Secretary Marshall wrote Molotov requesting that the Joint Commission report "the status of its deliberations." He reviewed the history of the Joint Commission, the problems it had encountered, and the obligations of the great powers to the Korean people. He remarked that the United States could no longer allow delay and proposed that by August 21, 1947, "the Joint Commission report the status of its deliberations so that each government may immediately consider what further steps may usefully be taken to achieve the aims of the Moscow Agreement." He desired a prompt reply.[5]

As Marshall sent what proved to be the first of several letters to the Soviet foreign minister, State Department officials were preparing the case for submission to the United Nations, a complicated task. If Korea were a final step in the "liquidation of the Second World War," then it was outside the jurisdiction of the UN; if it were a problem of peace after the war then the international organization could consider the issue. Even that distinction was fuzzy, for department legal experts decided that Article 107 of the UN Charter did not, in the case of great-power disagreement, preclude consideration of the matter by the General Assembly. A few months before, Allison had rejected bringing the Korean question to the Security Council, for the Soviet representative certainly would exercise his veto. Dean Rusk, who would coordinate American strategy on Korea at the UN, felt that the U.S. delegation must present the question to the General Assembly. At first, the department based its case on Article 10 of the Charter, but legal experts decided that it was too weak and resorted instead to Article 14, which stated that "the General Assembly may recommend measures for the peaceful adjustment of any situation, regardless of origin, which it deems likely to impair the general welfare or friendly relations among nations." Department officials felt they could prove that the Korean situation threatened peace and stability in Northeast Asia. They hoped to use this situation for larger gain; the Assembly could be "a suitable instrument for mobilizing political and psychological pressures on the Soviet Union." One officer even noted that taking the Korean issue to the United Nations would complete the encirclement of the Soviet Union begun with Palestine and Greece.[6]

While the department worked on the Korean presentation, Acting Secretary of State Robert A. Lovett informed Molotov that the United States had a new proposal for Korea. Lovett recounted the course of Joint Commission negotiations. He noted that the commission had difficulty agreeing to a report, that it was stalemated. It had failed to bring independence to Korea. "The United States Government cannot in good conscience be a party to such delay in fulfillment of its commitment to Korean independence." He wanted the Four Powers to meet in Washington on September 8, 1947, to consider seven American proposals: including early zonal elections for legislatures, choosing a provisional government in Seoul, the presence of UN observers, withdrawal of occupation forces, ratifying provisional zonal constitutions, and, finally, national elections under UN supervision. He wanted an early reply.[7]

Although the Chinese and British governments agreed to reconvene the Four Power Conference, the Soviet government finally answered that it saw "no possibility of accepting the proposals advanced in Mr. Lovett's letter." The Chinese were happy to continue the fiction that their nation was a great power as the fateful battles with communist forces raged in Manchuria. The British Foreign Office reluctantly assented to the American proposals, but noted orally that it was "sanguine over the outcome of the proposed Washington Conference," although the department's proposals were a "logical step in the development of the Korean problem" and would, at least, "clarify the Korean problem to the world."[8] Molotov replied on August 5 that the United States was responsible for the problems of the Joint Commission. He reiterated that the Moscow agreement had entrusted the

Joint Commission to assist in formation of a "provisional Korean democratic government." When the commission completed its work, it would forward recommendations to the Four Powers. Molotov wanted nothing to interfere with that process. He claimed that any imagined problems were "primarily the result of the position adopted by the American delegation on the consultation of the commission with Korean democratic parties and social organizations." Molotov expected the Americans to exclude Rhee and the powerful conservative faction from consultation, as if the United States would willingly consign the peninsula to communist rule. Perhaps he feared that the new American initiative signalled the beginning of an aggressive, anti-Soviet policy. He complained that the Americans had acted unilaterally by informing the Chinese and British of its disappointment with the Joint Commission, and he refused to consider seriously Lovett's proposals.[9]

As the American government readied itself for the next step on Korea, it considered the ideological importance of the peninsula. The political adviser in Korea cabled his views about the situation, noting that it was so dismal that the American and Soviet delegations were not even close to an agreement. Jacobs maintained that the American military command was "in the unenviable position of being shot at by both leftists and rightists." Although withdrawal seemed the only prudent course, he warned that abandoning an obligation to Korea would endanger American prestige in other areas of importance. The assistant chief of the Division of East European Affairs, Francis B. Stevens, wrote that while Korea "is without strategic value to us, there are important ideological imponderables." To withdraw would invite painful comparisons with more sensitive areas, or so Stevens and many department officers now felt. "If we allow Korea to go by default within the Soviet orbit," Stevens wrote, "the world will feel that we have lost another round in our match with the Soviet Union and our prestige will suffer accordingly." The department had come to the regretful decision that the Korean situation, or as it perceived the Korean situation within the superpower confrontation, was critical. Although the Joint Chiefs of Staff had informed the department that Korea had no strategic value to the United States (though it might have an effect on Japanese political developments), State Department officials realized that the military's desire for withdrawal had to be balanced with the area's increasing political importance. The years of neglect were beginning to reap a bitter harvest: early recognition of either Lyuh or Pak would have given Korea a left-leaning but nationalist regime possibly able to resist Soviet encroachment. Now there were unenviable choices: withdraw and suffer a loss of prestige, be forced to withdraw, or conclude an alliance with Rhee and accept a continuing commitment to a regime whose philosophy would not be compatible with American ideals.[10]

At last, and according to plan, Lovett on September 16, 1947, wrote Molotov that the U.S. government would refer the problem of Korean independence to the United Nations. He told the foreign minister that the United States would not acquiesce in continued delays over independence, that no progress could come from the Joint Commission, and that "it is the intention of my government to refer the problem of Korean independence to the forthcoming session of the General Assembly of the United Nations."[11] The next day, the U.S. representative at the United Nations, Senator Warren F. Austin, wrote UN Secretary General Trygve Lie and requested that "the problem of the independence of Korea" be added to the agenda of the forthcoming session of the General Assembly.

II

The United Nations by September 1947 had become a troubled international organization, and it seemed unlikely, despite American hopes, that it could do anything about Korea. In the last months of the Second World War, the idea of a new world organization to succeed the moribund League of Nations had attracted Americans of all varieties of political opinion. There was a feeling that the troubles of the world could find peaceful solution in the parliament of man; that if the battle flags were not completely furled, if war did not end, the United Nations at least would prevent any holocaust. But for Korea, the hopes of 1945 had become the troubled times of 1947. Statesmen had not foreseen the division of the world into two hostile camps. As Acting Secretary Lovett pointed out at a meeting of August 30, 1947, "The world is definitely split in two." Perhaps that was not true, but American officials believed it. Bipolarization, or the perception of it, as well as the decision to use the UN as an instrument of American policy, would affect the power and prestige of the world body.[12]

When the second annual session of the General Assembly opened in September 1947, the State Department sought to use the meeting as a forum from which to press the Soviet Union into cooperation on several important matters. The United States had an overwhelming majority of votes in the Assembly; the Soviet Union only controlled its European satellites. By avoiding the Security Council, the U.S. delegation expected to enlist the United Nations on its behalf.

Secretary Marshall addressed the Assembly on September 17, informing it that the United Nations faced difficult decisions during the session. He told the Assembly that decisions reached in the following weeks would affect its influence as an agency for world peace. The *New York Times* reported that "the issue was no less crucial than the existence of the U.N. and the whole dream and plan of international cooperation of which it is the symbol and the instrument." Marshall spoke in a quiet, unemotional voice, forsaking gestures or rhetoric. He stated that the time had come for action, and described proposals to reform procedures in the Security Council, to limit the right to veto, to place greater responsibility in the Assembly, to force action on Greece, to break the stalemate in Korea, and to control atomic energy. As he finished his speech, the "hushed and startled audience understood that the United Nations had reached a crisis."[13] Marshall announced that the situation in Korea required prompt attention: "It appears evident that further attempts to solve the Korean problem by means of bilateral negotiations will serve only to delay the establishment of an independent, united Korea." Stalemate made UN assistance necessary, and he wished for the "impartial judgment" of its members. Although the secretary said that the U.S. delegation had prepared a resolution

on Korea for consideration by the Assembly, he welcomed proposals from other delegations.[14]

The new Soviet foreign minister, Andrei Y. Vishinsky (Molotov had become premier), angrily rejected Marshall's call for
UN assistance in the Korean question. As soon as Marshall finished his speech, Vishinsky approached the podium. "Mr. Marshall," he said, "submitted a proposal which is a direct violation
of the Moscow Agreement on Korea." He charged that the
Americans sought to cover obstructionist tactics in the Joint
Commission with the authority of the General Assembly. Observers remarked about the vehemence of Vishinsky's rebuttal
that "left many of his listeners stunned and heartsick." Delegates
later expressed "shock and dismay" as the Soviet representative
accused the United States of creating a war psychosis against the
Soviet Union and demanded that the United Nations "forbid
war propaganda within their borders." He claimed that Marshall's proposals were a continuation of the Truman Doctrine
and Marshall Plan wherein "the U.S. Government attempts to
impose its will on other independent states." Vishinsky understood, and quite possibly feared, Marshall's purpose and he sought
to scare the United Nations away from involvement in the Soviet-
American confrontation or, at least, make it aware of the stakes.[15]

Quickly the other communist envoys fell into line. Soviet UN
Ambassador Andrei Gromyko insisted that taking the Korean
issue to the General Assembly was illegal. Oscar Lange of Poland
explained that "the United Nations had jurisdiction over problems of peace after the war, and had nothing to do with liquidation of the Second World War including Korea, a former
possession of the Japanese Empire." One by one, delegates from
Byelorussia, the Ukraine, and Yugoslavia approached the podium to denounce the American proposal. Each repeated, as if
from memory, the accusation that the United States followed
reactionary policies in south Korea and that its Korean plan was
illegal.[16]

But the General Assembly agreed on September 23 to consider the "Question of the Independence of Korea" for the
agenda. A few days later, the First (Political) Committee of the
Assembly voted overwhelmingly to include Korea on the agenda;

there were six nay votes (the three Soviet delegates and their three European satellites) and seven abstentions (the Arab nations seemingly had not forgiven the United States for support of the Jews during consideration of the Palestine question the previous spring). Although the United States had world opinion on its side (at least as far as considering the Korean question), there was a price to pay, for the Assembly vote had increased Soviet hostility, making a satisfactory settlement of the Korean issue even more difficult.[17]

As the General Assembly began discussion of the Korean question, the Soviet representative at the Joint Commission talks in Seoul made a headline-seeking announcement to ease the deadlock. Reiterating his government's belief that the great powers had to resolve the stalemate in Korea without UN involvement, General Terenti Shtikov proposed simultaneous withdrawal of all occupation troops in Korea beginning in January 1948. He explained that as soon as the troops withdrew, the Korean people could organize a government without outside interference. It was a clever scheme: the Russians offered the United Nations a means to avoid entanglement in the superpower confrontation. The General Assembly could hand the problem back to the Americans and Russians. While the proposal seemed reasonable and may have had its origins in Kremlin officials' fear of encirclement, it would make certain Russian domination of the peninsula. When the troops had withdrawn, Soviet-trained (and armed?) north Koreans and communists in the south would combine their forces to overwhelm resistance below the 38th parallel and create a communist, pro-Soviet regime.[18]

For the next few weeks, the U.S. delegation worked behind the scenes at the United Nations, garnering support for its Korean resolution. After meeting with Marshall and Lovett, George Kennan outlined the strategy: "We will not turn down the Soviet proposal . . . but will pass it on to the U.N. together with our recommendations," thus making it appear the Soviet proposal fit well into the larger, American scheme. He wanted the U.S. delegation to describe the Soviet proposal in Seoul as an intermediate step in the American resolution, suggesting the two powers were in agreement, which clearly they were not. The low-key approach worked well, as John Foster Dulles, a member of the U.S. delegation, told the British that such problems as Korea and Austria were unexpected and "might have to be referred to the United Nations for settlement in view of the inability of the Great Powers to agree." The British lent support, and the Chinese followed, fearing the consequences of a hasty American withdrawal. The United States convinced other delegates that UN consideration of the Korean question was reasonable, successfully arguing that it would demonstrate the organization's purposefulness. Dulles summed up the American position: "We felt that the interests of thirty million Koreans took precedence over a technical claim that the U.S. and the U.S.S.R. should be confined to working under an unworkable agreement."[19]

While the U.S. delegation slowly moved its resolution through the Assembly, Syngman Rhee and his supporters in south Korea naturally sought to make matters difficult for the Americans. When news reached Korea that the United States was turning to the United Nations, Rhee began campaigning for an official Korean representative at the discussion. He wanted the interim legislative assembly in the American zone (which his supporters controlled) to choose a delegation that he would dominate. When Jacobs turned him down, he persevered, writing world leaders to demand representation during discussion of the Korean question, as Arabs and Jews had been present during the discussion of Palestine. His conservative supporters informed American authorities that the people might riot if denied representation at the United Nations. Jacobs wrote Marshall that Rhee was "determined to force the United States to hold an election in the south before a decision is reached at the U.N. or to compel the U.S. to take action against him so that he can appear in the light of a martyr."[20]

Late in October, the First Committee of the General Assembly considered Soviet and American resolutions on the Korean question. The Soviet delegation submitted two resolutions, the first repeating the call for simultaneous withdrawal of troops in early 1948, leaving to the Korean people the establishment of a national government for the entire peninsula. The Soviets also wanted to invite to the UN the elected representatives of the Korean people from the north and south. The Soviets considered the only democratic election to be the one in north Korea in November 1946, and they sought to arrange a Korean delegation in their favor; but the Americans met the challenge. Dulles suggested to his fellow delegates that the immediate withdrawal of troops might imply a shirking of responsibility by the two powers. He called for withdrawal "at the earliest practicable date."[21] The second Soviet resolution was more difficult to meet.

The course of debate favored the Americans. The British delegate, Sir Alexander Cadogan, pointed out the flaw in the attempt by communist diplomats to delay solution of the Korean issue. "It is hardly possible," he said, "to have the true representatives of the Korean people come to New York and participate in the debates [where] one of the primary and unsettled differences between the U.S. and the U.S.S.R. had been the question of who were the true representatives of the Korean people." Dulles questioned the "free character" of the November 1946 elections in the Soviet zone. Rather than submit a second set of resolutions to the First Committee, forcing the United Nations to choose between the Soviets and Americans, the U.S. delegation offered amendments to the Soviet resolutions, changing them to call for troop withdrawal; zonal elections by March 31, 1948, under the observation of a special UN commission created by the General Assembly; proportional representation in a national assembly based on population (two-thirds of all Koreans lived in the south); the commission to travel and observe throughout Korea. Gromyko was opposed. If, he said, the United Nations adopted the American amendments "without the participation of representatives of the Korean people in that body's discussion, the U.S.S.R. would not be able to take part in the work of that commission." The First Committee nevertheless adopted the U.S. amendments (the Soviet bloc abstained in the voting): the UN would "establish a United Nations Temporary Commission on Korea (UNTCOK) to be present in Korea, with right to travel, observe, and consult throughout Korea."[22]

A bitter discussion began as the General Assembly opened consideration of the American plan for the Korean question. Gromyko spoke first. "This resolution," he charged, "has been imposed by the United States ... based on the designs of the United States." He claimed that the American plan to postpone troop withdrawal until nationwide elections was designed to foil the aspirations of the Korean people and "ensure the election to representative institutions of persons upon whom the American military authorities have long been relying in Korea, that is to say, arrant reactionaries." The Byelorussian delegate, K. V. Kiselev, noted that "the United States reactionaries see in Korea an important strategic base and the real cause for failure to reach an agreement on Korea was the U.S. attempt to impose its own will on other countries." Gromyko turned bitter: "These proposals are designed to convert Korea into an American colony." He concluded that "politically, South Korea is being turned into a center of reaction in eastern Asia. Territorially, Korea is apparently regarded as a kind of United States base." As discussion moved to other issues, it was clear that the Soviets would not cooperate with the commission.[23]

The next day, the Soviet bloc continued its attack on the American proposals. Bebler of Yugoslavia pointed out that "Greece has her Tsaldarias—Korea, her Rhee; both in Greece and South Korea there are numerous prisons filled with democrats; in Greece and South Korea quislings are in power." He noted a political reality: "The commission which you dispatch will have a majority that will be a reflection of the majority in the assembly. It will therefore find exactly what it is desired to find." Kiselev added that "unbelievable terror is raging throughout South Korea. ... The present situation in South Korea surpasses the darkest days of unbridled reaction during the Japanese occupation."[24]

The six-member Soviet bloc could do little to control the American-dominated General Assembly, and as Soviet bloc delegations turned the rostrum over to other member nations, the sentiment of the Assembly became clear. Dulles had made a telling point: "Although conditions are painted as being such a hell on earth in South Korea, it was the U.S. delegation which took the initiative in urging that the U.N. should send a commission to Korea to see for itself what is going on, and it was the U.S.S.R. delegation which took the position that it would have nothing to do with such a commission." As successive delegates took the rostrum, the strength of Dulles's argument became apparent. Delegates from Europe, Latin America, and Asia all felt that the American proposal was reasonable and committed the Assembly to no irrevocable position. After a few days, the General Assembly voted in favor of the American resolution as, once again, the Soviet bloc voted against it and Arab nations abstained.[25]

The final move in the creation of UNTCOK came when the U.S. delegation suggested member nations to be represented on the commission. It seemed that the Americans had acted in good faith, for the commission apparently represented a cross-section of the Assembly: East, West, and neutral. After a perfunctory debate, the Assembly approved selection of members from France, Canada, Australia, India, El Salvador, Syria, China, the Philippines, and the Ukraine. The Ukrainian delegate stated that regardless of the Assembly's vote, the Ukrainian SSR refused its place on the UN commission.[26]

The Soviet Union refused any connection with the commission. For the past year, Soviet leaders had sought to establish loyal regimes along their nation's long border to serve as buffers in future wars. They felt that American ideals of self-determination, freedom, and personal choice were irrelevant for Eastern Europe and Korea, given their security needs. Did the United States use rhetoric to hide its true intentions? The UN Korean commission represented a threat to the Soviet plan to create a socialist republic in northern Korea. While Secretary Marshall wanted to reunite the Korean people and withdraw foreign armies form the peninsula, Soviet diplomats wondered whether the United States might replace Japan as a threat to the Soviet Far East. Suspicious of the West, angered at defeat in the General Assembly, worried over security, Soviet officials rejected calls for cooperation and announced they would deny the commission entrance into north Korea.

III

Having secured approval for UNTCOK, the Americans anticipated little trouble securing acquiescence of the nations they had nominated for the commission. During the Christmas holidays, Secretary Marshall instructed embassies in France, El Salvador, the Philippines, Australia, India, Syria, and Canada to explain to the respective foreign ministries the purpose of the commission, the costs and expense allowances, and the need for prompt action. While they were visiting south Korea, the State Department intended to house commission members in army-run lodgings, transport them in army vehicles, and feed them at the officers' mess hall. The anticipated cost was low.[27]

Most commission nominees accepted the burden of this task. The French agreed grudgingly. The Salvadorean and Philippine governments apparently welcomed the opportunity to place the United States in their respective debts. To the Australians, the obligation to make the United Nations work outweighed the possibility of failure. The Indian government saw itself the leader of neutral, non-Western nations, and enjoyed the chance to lead the commission, although it had deep misgivings about the Soviet-American confrontation. The Syrians continued to resent American support for the creation of a Jewish state in Palestine and possibly viewed membership on the commission as a means to embarrass the United States.

Canadian approval seemed imminent, for the Canadian government recently had shown great interest in the United Nations. The minister for external affairs, Louis St. Laurent, and his chief deputy, Lester Pearson, had come to believe that the UN's ability to deal with serious political and security questions required a "less humble role by Canada." During St. Laurent's tenure, "Canada's foreign policy changed from a rather indifferent, at times even skeptical, attitude towards the U.N. to a positive determination to make the world organization work and to commit Canadians to it as the cornerstone of their relations with other countries." He had supported Marshall's plan to move major issues to the General Assembly from the Security Council. Although the U.S. delegation nominated Canada without first clearing the matter with the Canadian delegation, St. Laurent, Pearson, and the minister of justice, J. L. Ilsley, saw the commission as of temporary and routine significance. Ilsley and Pearson had questioned the wisdom of appointing a commission on Korea given Soviet opposition; neither wanted Canada to be a member, but Ilsley had yielded to American pressure. The Canadian delegation believed it was important to maintain the solidarity of Western nations.[28]

However, Prime Minister William Lyon Mackenzie King made the minor issue of the commission into a subject of major importance, illustrating one aspect of the fallout from America's creation of a Korean symbol. He had returned to Canada to learn of a decision "taken without my knowledge." Basically, the prime minister was an isolationist, "hostile towards any Canadian involvement in the affairs of the Far East." He even disliked Canada's involvement in the United Nations and had opposed acceptance of the seat in the Security Council vacated by Australia after a two-year term. He wanted the Canadian government to limit its influence and energies to such traditional Canadian concerns as the British Commonwealth. Behind it all lay an increasing fear of the inevitability of war. Upon his return from Europe in December 1947, he believed actions taken (or soon to be taken) by Britain and America in Germany might well cause a Russian response that would lead directly to war. He felt that the Korean situation approximated the German one and that the UN commission would heighten superpower confrontation. He neither wished to stretch his nation's concern, influence, or power too thin nor let the Americans make Canada the "point man" in a future crisis.[29]

The ensuing difficulties in the Canadian cabinet over the nation's involvement in the Korean commission were a reflection of the rivalry between the two principal figures of Canadian politics: Foreign Minister St. Laurent and Prime Minister Mackenzie King. St. Laurent was one of Canada's leading lawyers, the major figure in French-Canadian circles. He had joined Prime Minister King's cabinet in 1941 to help in the conduct of the Second World War. His presence placed French Canada in the government party, and he risked his political future to support national conscription. After the war, he reluctantly continued in government and became secretary of state for external affairs. He steadily expanded his horizons from French Canada to the nation and then to the world. As the cabinet now began consideration of the Korean question, he was the nation's most brilliant exponent of internationalism. Believing in the United Nations and Canada's "mission" in diplomacy, he was prepared to accept a place on the Korean commission. Prime Minister King, unlike St. Laurent, was not a lawyer by profession but an academician-turned-politician. He had received a Ph.D. in political science at Harvard University and then turned to politics. Becoming minister of labor in 1909, he soon reached the top in Canadian politics, and in 1947 he celebrated his twenty-six years as prime minister. His ambition and opinion of himself gradually increased. He once likened himself—with an ingratiating smile—to Abraham Lincoln and William E. Gladstone, and many Canadian observers felt he thought of himself in terms of historic statesmanship and was wearing himself out "no longer merely for office, but for rank in world history." Concerned for his place in history, he was wary of policies that might threaten his reputation. And, as his diaries indicate, he approached his desired retirement from politics with apprehension, for he feared a cataclysmic world crisis and worried which of his colleagues—if any—had the mettle to lead the nation. The Korean commission touched many points of importance to him.

The cabinet meeting in December 1947 revealed that an intellectual gulf separated King and St. Laurent. The latter sought to compare the unimportance of the commission with the "importance of exercising a wholesome influence at the United Nations." He asked for what he believed was routine approval of the appointment of Dr. George S. Patterson, counselor of the Canadian embassy in Nanking, as the commission's Canadian representative. King immediately "blew a gasket," displaying an unwonted annoyance, anger, and irritability. King was not going to have anything to do with Korea (his diaries indicate in somewhat rambling fashion the depth of his anger). He could not "understand how a matter of such dangerous import could have been dealt with in this offhand fashion." President Truman, he said, once had confided a worry about the situation in Korea and Manchuria. Truman nearly expected war. King feared Canada might be caught up in that conflict, for the French and Canadians "would be made spearhead of whatever arose" in the commission. The meeting ended uncertainly with King expressing, he declaimed, anger at American treatment of Canadian sovereignty. Canada followed an independent foreign policy and was not committed to the notions of the American State Department. St. Laurent believed King acted irrationally; King felt St. Laurent and Pearson were too easily influenced by the Americans and by the idea of exercising power.[30]

A week later when the Canadian cabinet resumed discussion of the Korean commission, tension had increased, for St. Laurent was assailing King's isolationism. As a member of the United Nations, he said, Canada was obliged to accept such responsibilities as serving on a Korean commission. He suggested that his personal honor was at issue, for he had promised the Americans that the Canadian government would appoint a representative to UNTCOK. St. Laurent must have felt that the six years of his participation in the cabinet of Prime Minister King, years of support of the European war, a time when he had risked his leadership of French Canada for what he thought were the necessarily higher concerns of not merely Canada and not merely the Western Hemisphere but Europe and the entire world were now being called into question by the man whose cabinet he had entered. St. Laurent's career, as well as that of King, seemed to tremble in the balance, because of the American decision to appoint a commission for Korea.

Caught in the middle of what had become a major argument in Ottawa, St. Laurent's deputy, Pearson, tried to be reasonable. For nearly two decades, Pearson had served his country as a diplomatic envoy and mediator. He told King that if the Soviets refused to admit the Korean commission to their zone, it would have to return to New York. "For the commission to act in the south alone was contrary to the express provisions of its terms of reference." Pearson wanted to make clear that the commission would not find itself in the middle of a Soviet-American confrontation. But King continued in opposition. Except as a vehicle for Russian propaganda, "the United Nations counted for nothing so far as any help in the world was concerned." Canada was not a "latter-day Sir Gallahad" attempting to "save the whole world." As a participant noted later, "the atmosphere in the room became electrically tense."[31]

The Korean issue threatened the stability of the Canadian government, Brooke Claxton, a supporter of St. Laurent, pointed out that the Soviets would interpret Canada's refusal to serve on the commission as "a lack of unity among U.N. members supporting the American resolution." Things went so far that King announced his intent to resign and take his case to the people; he would not continue in the government if forced to appoint a representative to the commission. St. Laurent voiced thoughts of resignation. If King carried the cabinet, Canada's position would be a veritable rebuke of his diplomacy. Other ministers joined in the resignation talk. Fortunately, the atmosphere eased when St. Laurent and King met at Laurier House for dinner one evening and told each other not to resign. Perhaps, as one observer suggested, they sought a solution that "would save King's face and still let Canada accept membership." The Korean question, at least publicly, remained unresolved.[32]

At this point, the American government recognized the crisis in Ottawa, and Truman instructed his ambassador, Ray Atherton, to meet with Canadian leaders. Atherton handed King a note from the president asking a delay until Under Secretary Lovett could "prepare and send you a personal message fully setting forth our views . . . explaining our deep concern regarding the possibility of such withdrawal." When the prime minister finished the note, Atherton expanded on the letter. He stated that his government wished to withdraw troops from Korea and that the commission was an opportunity to do so without charges of retreat. He added that, since Canada was on the Security Council, it would be "quite serious" if Canada failed in its responsibilities. King then lectured the American ambassador. Canada must not "waste her strength ineffectually in other areas of the world." Although Korea was potentially dangerous, King resented "the unhappy, ill-advised haste" with which the United

States had forced the Canadian delegation to come to a decision. He would not, he said, appoint a Canadian representative.[33]

Atherton reported to the State Department that the issue required understanding of Canadian sensibilities. King was making the Korean commission issue "a declaration of independence to show that Canada reached decisions independent of the United States." If the government persisted, it would force a cabinet crisis "during which Canada's relation with the United States might become the issue before the Canadian people." King's intention to limit Canadian intervention to areas of concern to the British Commonwealth resulted from British Foreign Secretary Ernest Bevin's displeasure at Canada's lack of help during settlement of the Palestine issue. Atherton concluded that caution was necessary to avert an international crisis. Sadly, throughout the entire crisis in Canadian-American relations over the Korean commission, Atherton alone among American officials understood the issues involved.[34]

When Lovett wrote King on December 30, 1947, to persuade him to support the American position, it seemed that he had ignored Atherton's advice. He agreed that the Soviet Union would not cooperate with the commission but said it was difficult "to understand the basis for Canada's withdrawal." He argued that Canada had "a direct and urgent interest in the restoration of peace and stability in East Asia." He sought to force the issue: "Those unfriendly both to the United States and Canada [might] find, if Canada does not see her way clear to participate in the work of the commission, grounds for propaganda that Canada's action reflected irritability and difference of view with the policies of the United States." The letter itself was an example of the take-Canada-for-granted attitude that so incensed the prime minister (and many Canadians). It also illustrated the predominant American view that its world perception was the only one and that Canada (and other allies) must accept it.[35]

The day that Lovett's letter arrived, the Canadian cabinet met again to consider the Korean resolution, and King and St. Laurent again assumed uncompromising positions. King believed the commission was "on a fool's errand." As for Lovett's letter, he said he did not think it was part of the duties of any official of the U.S. government to "begin to tell me what should or should not be done by the Canadian Government." The prime minister felt that the State Department was "simply using the United Nations as an aim of that officer to further its own policies."

But once more the clouds lifted. Before the discussion could turn to talk of resignation, Pearson offered to go to Washington to discuss the matter with the American government. King insisted that Pearson make clear the Canadian government's concern with American interference in its policymaking. The cabinet agreed that Pearson must receive American guarantees that if the commission did not meet U.S. expectations, it would not lead to superpower conflict in the Far East. If Pearson failed, King would stand firm and the remaining cabinet members would resign.[36]

Pearson had hoped for a friendly review of relations between the two allies, but found Lovett and the State Department angered by perceived Canadian intransigence and President Truman ignorant of Canadian sensitivities. When he sought to state King's fears to Truman, the president replied, "Don't worry, you won't get into any trouble over there, and if you do, we are behind you." That was precisely the point. King felt that the government in Washington wanted to use Canada in its confrontation with the Soviet Union. Pearson was afraid to tell King of Truman's comments and suggested that the president place a direct call to the prime minister. Department officials vetoed the idea; the president "did not know very much about the Korean business and they were afraid Mr. King might overwhelm him on the telephone." They agreed that Truman should write to King. There thus was a dilemma, for Pearson found that where Truman lacked facts, the U.S. State Department lacked understanding. In a meeting with senior members of the department, Pearson sought to explain Canadian thinking, and Lovett replied that the commission could nevertheless achieve success if it decided on elections which would result in the establishment of a democratic Korean government in the south. Lovett passed over the possibility that such action would create a UN-sanctioned division of the peninsula or contribute to heightened tensions between America and Russia, fears of King's. He concluded with a veiled threat: "Should Canada . . . feel constrained to limit its responsibilities . . . its position as a member of the Security Council and its interests in areas other than West Europe would have to be regarded in an entirely new light."[37]

As Pearson returned to Canada, Truman's letter to King arrived, reiterating the American position. After reviewing the Korean question and the UN resolution on Korea, Truman wrote that "we do not expect the work of the Korean Commission to lead to or contribute to a clash with or even intensification of the present tension with the USSR." He concluded: "I hardly need add that the USSR would exploit Canada's absence to the fullest in its propaganda." Truman, his advisers, and department officers who drafted the letter believed that what they felt was good for the United States was good for Canada and that the Canadian government should follow their lead.[38]

It marked the final crisis in the Canadian cabinet on the Korean commission. King succumbed to cabinet pressure and agreed to appoint George Patterson to the commission. St. Laurent pointed out that if a Canadian representative joined the commission, the organization still was powerless without co-operation from the Soviet Union. It would have to return to the General Assembly, report that it could not carry out orders, and disband. Canada would not become embroiled in a superpower confrontation. Although King still was angry at the Americans, he agreed that the commission could do little harm. A compromise ensued. The Canadian delegate would remain on the commission as long as the Soviet Union and the United States cooperated in Korea. Once cooperation ceased, Patterson would leave.[39]

The crisis resolved, Patterson seemed ideally suited to represent Canada on the Korean commission. The Canadian government united in praise of his talents. By his nature Patterson would help preserve the commission's independence. St. Laurent noted that "Patterson had no intention of becoming a tool of American diplomacy . . . and he was strongly opposed to any policy which threatened to prolong the political division of the Korean peninsula." Patterson was an essential part of the compromise between St. Laurent and King.[40] A few days later, the chief of the Division of British Commonwealth Affairs, Edward T. Wailes, reported to Lovett the terms of the compromise: "If on arrival in Korea, the commission finds that the USSR is agreeable to its dealing with Korea as a whole, the Canadian appointee to the commission will carry on as a member. If not . . . the Canadian appointee will request that the commission call upon the interim legislative assembly for instructions."[41]

The United States had used the United Nations to press the Soviet government. The nation's preeminent economic position and full usage of diplomatic pressure made victory in the UN certain. It did not make much difference that the Korean commission had no chance to fulfill its terms of reference because the Soviet Union would refuse to cooperate. The American government had pushed the international organization to play a partisan role. If the UN had had a chance to serve as an impartial forum to hear world problems, the American use of the General Assembly to further its own policy, over the relatively minor Korean question, helped destroy those idealistic hopes.

Adoption of the resolution on Korea probably worsened Soviet-American relations. In retrospect, it does seem reasonable the Soviets might have believed the worst about American policy and feared a new and more powerful aggressor surrounding their borders. They believed that Marshall meant to use the United Nations to encircle the Soviet Union. Speeches by Soviet (bloc) delegates clearly demonstrate that this suspicion was in their minds during discussions on Korea. The vehemence of speeches, the angry denunciations of American diplomacy, the fear that the United States might intend to use southern Korea as a military base all attest to a serious misreading of American intentions. Again, perception and misperception lay at the heart of the superpower confrontation.

There also was damage to Canadian-American relations. For years, American leaders (and the American people) had assumed a commonality of beliefs with their northern neighbors, but it was another sign of American ethnocentrism. They had taken Canadian leaders and policy for granted. American officials raised the issue of relations with the Soviet Union to a moral crusade and expected Canadians willingly and perhaps eagerly to join. American officials certainly had the right to employ various means to obtain Canadian approval for the Korean commission; such is diplomacy. However, it was inexcusable that save for Ambassador Atherton no American official understood Canadian views on the Soviet-American confrontation and the Korean question. It bespoke a moral certitude which the United States had no right to appropriate for its use. Happily the opposing factions in the Canadian cabinet were willing to see common ground despite brief thoughts of resignation. How many other cases were there where insensitive American diplomats offended an ally in their overly zealous drive to close ranks against the Soviet menace? Possibly, this was the true tragedy of the cold war—not damage to Soviet-American relations (which might have been inevitable) but the damage to relations between the United States and its allies.

Korea thus emerges as an unwanted symbol in American foreign policy. The U.S. government decided quite on its own to raise the strife-torn, economically weak, politically chaotic southern zone into an example of American determination. Was it the path of least resistance to cover up the failure to secure a Korean aid bill by overblown rhetoric? The government did not realize at that early juncture that having said Korea was of symbolic importance, it would be difficult to avoid a greater commitment, a deeper involvement. A further catalyst was needed, but the major crisis was brewing just over the horizon.

Trying to Get Out, Forced to Stay In

It was an eventful year for the United Nations and the people of Korea as the UN Temporary Commission on Korea supervised the election that led to the inauguration of Syngman Rhee as the first president of the Republic of Korea (ROK). The commission, gathered in the American zone, observed the first election campaign in Korean history, although not without problems. Soviet officials would not allow commission members to cross into the northern zone; communists in the south boycotted the election, charging their opponents with seeking a separate government; Rhee's conservative supporters allegedly used corruption, fraud, and terror to ensure victory. When the polls closed, Rhee received an overwhelming majority and began a new chapter in Korea's history. The Soviet Union reacted to the elections (and perhaps to events elsewhere) by cutting electric power to the south and handing over control in the north to the people's committees run by Kim Il-sung's communists. Southern communists looked to violence, and rightist-led police units responded in kind. Syngman Rhee achieved his life's goal of the presidency and continued to ignore American advice on democratic ideals and economic stability. The United Nations found itself caught between the superpowers and being a guarantor of sorts to the infant and unrepresentative Republic of Korea in a situation that seemed a prelude to civil war.

For the United States, after years of the nagging problem of Korea, the UN-supervised election was fortuitous. When the United Nations certified Rhee's victory, it marked the final step in the American government's plan to replace its presence in Korea with the moral authority of the world organization. In involving the UN in the confusing affairs of the peninsula, the United States had used strength to mask weakness. But total withdrawal was far from easy as a variety of factors led to increasing entanglement.

Events in and about Korea took place against the backdrop of changing U.S. government policy toward the Soviet Union. A series of State Department Policy Planning Staff papers and documents authored by the newly organized National Security Council accorded the situation in Korea increasing weight. American perceptions of the cold war made it imperative that the United States suffer no loss of prestige in extricating itself from Korea and that a noncommunist government in south Korea continue. This analysis led the government to increase its political/symbolic involvement at the same time as it moved to end its military presence. A few weeks after the UN-supervised elections, the government in Washington decided to recognize the new regime of Syngman Rhee (setting up competing regimes of North and South) and to seek a program of financial assistance not unlike the one Congress rejected in 1947 to rebuild the South Korean economy, further that nation's chance to resist communist subversion, and to integrate the economies of the former American zone and Japan into a complementary whole. Much like brer rabbit and the tar baby, the more the U.S. government struggled with its Korean involvement, the deeper and deeper ties it developed. The symbol, one might say, was beginning to exert a disproportionate influence over its creator.

I

The United Nations Temporary Commission had come to the peninsula in the first months of 1948 to travel, observe, and consult throughout both zones prior to the UN-sponsored election. It had to tutor Korean politicians in democratic practices, make sure that Soviet and American authorities remained neutral, and approve the election as a demonstration of the will of the people. Given the circumstances, it seemed like a near-impossible task. The commission arrived in Seoul amid celebration and cheering throngs. Commission members received a tumultuous reception as they proceeded from the airport to the city. The bitterly cold January weather seemingly had little effect on the crowd, and for three hours thousands of Koreans waited along the twelve-mile route to cheer the commission.[1]

The goodwill so carefully displayed in Seoul did not extend north of the parallel, and from the beginning Soviet authorities refused to deal with the commission. The chairman, K. P. S. Menon of India, wrote the Soviet commander requesting permission to enter the north, but the letter went unanswered. American liaison officials in Pyongyang reported that the impression given them by Major General Shanin, chief of staff of Soviet headquarters in the northern city, was that the Soviet government and particularly Soviet forces in Korea would have no dealings with UNTCOK. Radio Pyongyang and Radio Moscow both condemned the commission as a tool of American imperialists and a product of the "mechanical majority" in the General Assembly. Soviet officials in New York and Moscow reiterated their opposition.[2]

It is difficult to understand the Soviet refusal to work with the commission. At this point, Kim Il-sung presumably was in complete control and had eliminated all opposition in the north; in the south, the commission would have to conclude that the native communists under Pak Hun-yung and, possibly, the moribund Coalition Committee were more representative of the majority of Koreans than Rhee's conservative faction tainted by charges of wartime collaboration. It would appear that, had the Soviets cooperated, the UN commission would have found in their favor, and the USSR would have found itself with at least a leftist and possibly a Russian-dominated communist regime on its eastern flank. It is possible that Soviet leaders saw a linkage in Anglo-American attempts to work together in their zones of occupation in Germany, American actions in Japan, and American manipulation of the United Nations in Korea. This hypothesis will become more clear when the electric power shutoff in Korea coincides with the crisis over Berlin.

Surprisingly, after the initial amenities, Korean politicians in the south soon had few encouraging words for the commission's efforts to unite the zones, north and south. Rhee's supporters felt that a UN-sanctioned reunification would hand power to the communists; Pak and other communist officials regarded the commission as a tool of the U.S. government; and American intelligence agents noted that "the extreme left will openly oppose it [the UN commission] while the extreme right . . . most likely will try to sabotage it in secret." Moderate politicians such as Kim Koo, who had broken with Rhee in opposition to a permanently divided Korea, and Kimm Kiu-sic told commission members that "unless the present situation is improved there will not be any free elections." There was concern over police interference and communist violence. Most members of the commission agreed with moderate Koreans that "setting up a government in South Korea under U.N. auspices would lead to setting up in North Korea by the Soviets of a North Korean government and thus permanently divide Korea into two states." Many of them found it difficult to reconcile the political immaturity of the people with their desire for independence and unification.[3]

American officials sought to convince the commission to proceed with its work in the south, despite difficulties. Secretary of State Marshall cabled Langdon and Hodge to urge the "importance and urgency of proceeding without delay with the observation of an election in south Korea. . . . After all twenty of the thirty million Koreans live in south Korea." Jacobs told the commission that circumstances had divided Korea and UN action in south Korea would not make the present situation any worse. The Americans hoped that the Soviets would feel virtually forced to open up the north or suffer a tremendous propaganda defeat if the UN commission carried out its duties in the south.[4] The government in Washington was counting desperately on the commission to salvage its Korean difficulties.

Commission members were unsure what to do, and, in late January, Menon told the press that the group was "undecided whether to conduct elections only in southern Korea or admit failure to carry out the assignment and quit." Menon, Patterson of Canada, and Robert Jackson of Australia, to whom American officials referred derisively as the "British bloc," believed the United Nations should not perpetuate the division of the peninsula by observing elections in the south. They felt that permanent denial of Korean unification was more important than Soviet disobedience of a UN resolution. The Syrian, Philippine, and Salvadorean delegates believed that the United Nations could not back down before Soviet rejection of a UN resolution, and they wanted to hold the election. The French delegate noted that the situation was serious but offered no solution. (The Ukrainian SSR had refused its appointment.) All of the delegates questioned their authority to act, given the situation and the commission's terms of reference.[5] Hence, members waited in Korea while Menon returned to New York and handed the problem to the Interim Committee of the United Nations. The "little assembly" was an American brainchild proposed by Marshall during the previous session of the General Assembly. American officials envisioned that the IC would handle problems when the General Assembly was not in session and thus keep critical issues from suffering a Soviet veto in the Security Council or from awaiting reconvening of the General Assembly.

As the Interim Committee prepared to hear Menon's report, American newspapers concluded that the Korean question was "a crucial test of UN determination." The *Chicago Daily News* editorialized that the "U.S. and U.N. have been outsmarted. Both have lost face in a region where to lose face is to lose everything. U.S. and U.N. can write Korea off as total loss and charge it up to experience." Most American newspapers expected the "little assembly" to order UNTCOK to observe separate elections in south Korea, and the *New York Times* remarked that "the United Nations cannot accept open defiance of its will without sinking into impotence." The Catholic weekly *America* said that the UN "will have to act promptly and decisively if we are to avoid in the Far East a debacle like that in Hungary and other Eastern European countries." Editorials in the Scripps-Howard newspaper chain commented that "far more than Korea is involved. If Russia can defy the UN with ease in this case, it can do so in any other case."[6] The editorial opinions, in part, testify how far Korea had come as a symbol. Although it was without value strategically, Korea had become a litmus test of American and, according to the newspapers, United Nations determination to

stand up to the Soviet Union. Little by little, pressure was mounting on the government in Washington; how could it ever relax
its vigilance in Korea? Further, since department officers sent
summaries of newspaper opinions to the relevant embassies, it
is possible that the hardening of newspaper editorial opinion
might have affected policy discussions.

On February 19, 1948, the Interim Committee heard the
report of the UN commission, and delegates listened as Menon
recounted the history of UNTCOK, how the commission found
the problem so complicated, so difficult, so important that it had
to ask the Interim Committee for guidance. He described Soviet
obstinacy, the tense political situation, and American pressure
for a UN-supervised election. He told delegates that the UN
commission wondered if it would be detrimental to the best interests of Korea, and if it would be inconsistent with the terms
of the General Assembly resolution to proceed with an election
in south Korea. He outlined three alternatives: (1) the commission could admit failure and disband, although members of the
commission agreed that the United Nations had accepted a responsibility toward the Korean people and could not ignore it;
(2) the commission could observe elections in the south and recognize that government as a government of all Korea, but Menon
argued that such action would lead to permanent division of the
peninsula; or (3) the commission could observe an election in
south Korea for "the purpose of consultation with the elected
representatives of the people." However, the third alternative
was too similar to the second choice. Menon finished his presentation by asking: "What, then, can the commission do?"[7]

Meanwhile, the U.S. delegation to the Interim Committee
had convinced most of the delegations that the Korean commission should observe the elections in southern Korea. Marshall
had written Ambassador Austin that "you are authorized at
meeting of IC on February 19 following presentation by Menon
of KC's report to agree to a brief adjournment in order that the
report may be studied by members of the IC. Such adjournment
should under no circumstances extend later than February 24.
We have not altered view that IC should advise KC to get on
with its job and observe elections in such parts of Korea as are

open to it." Perhaps it is unfortunate that, as the State Department continued to enhance Korea's importance in the test of wills with the Soviet Union, few department officials accepted the ideas advanced by the director of the Policy Planning Staff, George Kennan, in yet another paper. Kennan argued in a long analysis of February 24 in favor of a unified concept of foreign policy based on a realistic analysis of the situation, recognizing both the problems of emerging nationalism in Asia and the way many Asian leaders might view the United States. Disapproving of stopgap measures applied to Korean matters, he wrote: "We have not yet worked out realistic plans." The department nonetheless continued to press its position before the Interim Committee. British delegates agreed that "we could not put ourselves in the position of having Soviet-noncooperation block the carrying out of the mandate of the General Assembly." Belgian and Venezuelan delegates told Philip C. Jessup of the U.S. delegation on February 10 that they would support the American position. Pierre Ordonneau of France said that "a decision not to hold elections in Korea would be a backward step which should be avoided." By the time Menon appeared at the Interim Committee, the Americans had gained approval of all members of the IC except the Soviet bloc. Two points were important. The Soviet Union had opposed a UN resolution, and two-thirds of the Korean people lived in an area accessible to the commission. UN delegations found that having agreed to "A"—authorizing the commission in spite of vehement Soviet opposition—they now had to continue with "B": observing the elections or revealing the impotency of the world organization.[8]

When the committee met on February 26 to advise the leader of the Korean commission, the session proved to be only a formality; and the U.S. delegation secured an overwhelming majority of votes. An international crisis had strengthened the American position, for a few days earlier a coup had occurred in Czechoslovakia and memories of Munich swirled through the corridors of the United Nations. After the vote, the Interim Committee expressed a view that "it is incumbent on UNTCOK to implement the program as outlined in Resolution II of the

General Assembly in such parts of Korea as are accessible to the commission."[9]

The vote of the Interim Committee committed the United Nations to a program supported by one superpower and resisted by the other. It would contribute to the installing of antagonistic regimes in Pyongyang and Seoul publicly committed to liberating the people under control of the other; it helped bring war that much closer. It certainly exacerbated tensions within Korea and increased cold war hostility. The United States, however, now drifted into an adversary relationship with the commission. Although the IC had given approval to the U.S. position and expected the commission to follow orders, the latter remained unsure of its direction. According to the commission's terms of reference, only the General Assembly could order it to observe the election. The committee united in the desire to preserve its independence.

When General Hodge announced plans for an election, to be held on May 9, 1948, the commission reassembled in Seoul and defied the Interim Committee. Patterson of Canada spoke for a majority of the commission: "The view of the Little Assembly ran counter to the views of a majority of the Temporary Commission delegates. Since the Interim Committee had merely offered us its advice, it was extremely regretable that the public had inferred that the commission had already reached a decision to hold the elections." Jackson of Australia noted that "elections will be boycotted by all parties in Korea except the extreme right group" and stated his opposition to such a policy. French and Syrian delegates did not favor elections. Menon wanted to follow IC advice, but he too opposed elections. Members from China, El Salvador, and the Philippines favored separate elections in the south, most likely to curry favor with the U.S. government.[10]

Patterson left Korea on March 10 and precipitated new trouble in Canadian-American relations. He believed the Interim Committee had no power to change the commission's terms of reference and that the situation in Korea was far different from that imagined during UN debates and as described by the United States the previous fall. Unable to convince the commission to request new instructions from the General Assembly, he decided to block its activities by departing. He told the press in Korea that he was returning to consult with his government.[11]

Officials in Washington made known their irritation. Niles Bond of the Division of Northeast Asian Affairs reported that Pearson, in Washington, regretted Canada's opposition but "asserted that his instructions were, while holding firm to his position, to give as little comfort as possible to the Soviet Union and as little discomfort as possible to the United States." Jacobs, Walton W. Butterworth, and Allison called in the Canadian ambassador, Hume Wrong, "to account for Patterson's attitude." Wrong defended his government, and State Department officers, caught up in the containment crusade, expressed a sense of betrayal.[12]

The Canadian government found that its fears about the Korean commission had come true. The Ministry of External Affairs thought of abandoning the commission, telling the Americans that Canada was "no banana republic" and would not come to heel at U.S. orders. Assistant Secretary of State Charles Saltzman explained the Canadian attitude to George Marshall as reflecting the personal viewpoint of Prime Minister King, who believed "the situation in Western Europe is now so critical that Canada must concentrate its efforts in that area and cannot afford to become involved also in the Far East." King suspected that UNTCOK was an American effort to use lesser powers as "front men" in the Soviet-American confrontation, and to some extent it was. He believed the commission was doomed, because of Soviet opposition and the difficult situation in south Korea. Despite King's strong feelings against continued participation on the commission, the Canadian cabinet postponed a decision until Patterson returned and reported.[13] After hearing his discouraging account, the cabinet reluctantly instructed him to return to Korea. St. Laurent and Pearson had gained strength, for King made clear his intention to leave office in the near future. The Canadian government believed it had to support the Interim Committee. The Soviet Union had shown contempt for a UN resolution and Canada, St. Laurent felt, had to reaffirm its commitment to the world organization despite misgivings about the situation in Korea. He told Patterson to remain on the commission but avoid any initiative.[14]

When Patterson returned to Korea, the situation had not improved. The Soviets continued to avoid the commission; communists in south Korea declared that they would boycott the election and threatened to disrupt it. Moderate Korean leaders despaired, for it seemed that the outcome of the UN-supervised election would entrench a leftist dictatorship in Pyongyang and a rightist one in Seoul. Only Rhee and his allies looked forward to the May elections.

In early April, Kim Koo and Kimm Kiu-sic proposed an All-Korean Conference, hoping to prevent a division of the peninsula, realizing that the Soviets would declare a people's republic in the north if the UN approved the election in the south. They clung to a naive faith that the Korean people's desire for unification and independence would somehow overcome the problems that separated them.[15] Much to everyone's surprise, the north Korean communist party welcomed the Kims' call for a national conference and offered to hold it in Pyongyang. The controlled press in the north made a propaganda victory certain; no rightist politician would attend the conference. Delegates from north Korea were party members, and they had an opportunity to embarrass both the United States and the United Nations. The conference was set for late April, just prior to the UN-sponsored election.[16]

In the south, talk turned from the coming election to the national conference. Once more the Korean people raised their hopes. Rhee and his allies denounced the conference as communist trickery and charged that Kim Koo and Kimm Kiu-sic were communist dupes. Rhee was certain of victory in the election and wanted no obstacles placed before him. Leftists praised the north Koreans and accepted the invitation. The Korean commission, particularly Jackson, Patterson, Menon, and Djabi of Syria, thought that the people had nothing to lose and a united nation to gain, and therefore awaited conference developments. American officials were wary that the conference would give the commission another excuse to postpone the May election.[17]

As the Korean conference dominated politics in the peninsula, the newly organized National Security Council in Washington approved NSC-8, a paper which defined the American position with respect to Korea against a backdrop of other decisions analyzing Soviet-American relations. According to NSC-8, in April 1948, the U.S. government had three courses open to it: to abandon Korea, admit that it had used the United Nations "as a convenient vehicle for withdrawing from Korea," and suffer a grievous loss of prestige. The council rejected a guarantee of political independence and territorial integrity for south Korea. Military leaders had shown that such a guarantee might commit the United States to an Asian land war where the Soviet Union had the advantage. The council decided to bring about a situation in south Korea where further U.S. withdrawal could take place "with a minimum of bad effects." NSC-8 made a UN-observed and UN-sanctioned election in south Korea, leading to a separate regime, a goal of American policy. The document did not define the middle ground between a precipitous withdrawal and political/military guarantees; there were too many shadings of grey between the stark alternatives. NSC-8 most logically followed NSC-7, a report of late March 1948 which defined the position of the United States with respect to "Soviet-directed world communism." The officials who drew up the document clearly saw a bipolar world of good and evil in which the United States must fight or be destroyed. It implied that a strong war-making capacity was the best defense against Soviet aggression. It recommended increasing the military capacity of the United States and its principal (and more secure) allies and placing civilian sectors in line with military needs in case of war. The planners clearly believed a gain for the Soviet Union meant a defeat for the United States and vice versa. The implications for Korea, despite NSC-8 urging a timely withdrawal without loss of prestige, were strong and obvious. Regardless of the reality of the situation in Korea, the government would subordinate it to the world conflict it perceived.[18]

In view of NSC-8, American officials feared the propaganda value of the Pyongyang conference. Lovett wrote Jacobs that if too many Koreans "shift allegiance from the elections to the conference it may well result in decision by UNTCOK to disas-

sociate itself from such elections." Jacobs noted that the conference had attracted much attention among the Korean people
and asked permission to issue a statement that elections were a
better way to unification than a propaganda conference. The
department approved.[19]

In late April, Kim Koo and Kimm Kiu-sic journeyed north
for the conference on unification. Although they had few hopes,
they were disappointed by what they saw. North Korean leaders
showed little concern for the people; the Kims saw few signs
that the people had much freedom or choice; and land reform
had led to an unpopular collectivization. North Korean leaders
used the conference as a propaganda forum, destroying the slim
hopes of the Kims and their remaining influence. When the
conference ended, the Kims returned to the south, disillu-
sioned.[20] With this failure, however, no more obstacles remained
before the elections on May 10. Hodge had changed the date
from May 9 for fear that an eclipse of the sun predicted for that
date might overly influence the Koreans. Given the nature of
East Asian folk beliefs, it was possible that the people might
interpret the eclipse as a sign of heavenly disapproval of the
elections, the Americans, and the candidates they favored.

II

A great majority of Koreans in the south went to the polls
on May 10, 1948, and elected mostly conservative candidates to
a Korean National Assembly. Eighty-five percent of eligible voters made a seemingly indisputable expression of their will. When
ballots had been counted, Rhee's followers won a commanding
position in the new assembly. American officials were happy with
the elections. Hodge felt that the Korean people "had responded
to the challenge of a democratic voting campaign." Secretary
Marshall congratulated them: "The fact that some ninety percent of the registered voters cast their ballots, despite the lawless
efforts of a communist-dominated minority to prevent or sabotage the election, is a clear revelation that the Korean people are
determined to form their own government by democratic
means."[21]

But the UN Temporary Commission on Korea was reluctant to declare that a "reasonably free atmosphere" had existed in south Korea during the election. Some observers commented that conservative parties broke up meetings of moderate and leftist parties. Others reported that the police acted in behalf of rightwing candidates. The structure of Korean society raised real doubts about whether the rural voter (and most Koreans lived in rural areas) was able to exercise his franchise with any degree of freedom.[22] When Rhee met with the commission, he noted that "there is too much freedom, which permitted communist activities such as strikes, riots, assaults." Moderate politicians had disagreed, and the commission was inclined to believe them. Kimm Kiu-sic maintained that in southern and northern Korea there was "no genuine freedom of expression, freedom of press and information, freedom of assembly and association, freedom of movement, protection against arbitrary arrest and detention, or protection against threats of violence and violence." The chief justice of (south) Korea pointed out that there was no *habeus corpus* in the south and moderate politicians wanted the commission to investigate the thousands of illegally detained political prisoners they claimed were in jail.[23]

Admittedly, there was a problem with observing the election. The commission's thirty non-Korean personnel found themselves working with an area of about forty thousand square miles and a population of 20 million. Because of limited personnel and inadequate transportation facilities, observers inspected several random sites. They had to depend on Korean civil servants and on the police who supported Rhee. There were charges of fraud and terror. Peasant farmers voted because their village headmen told them to vote for conservative candidates. Rhee and his supporters equated voting with patriotism; communist sympathizers, according to him, boycotted a free election. American officials also wanted a large turnout. The voters had little choice, for most moderates and all leftists did not participate. The large turnout merely served to display Rhee's control of police and "youth associations."[24]

The deeply divided commission eventually approved the election. The "British minority" wanted to downplay the election, and Jackson submitted a resolution that "the assembly elected by ballot on 10 May 1948 though acceptable as an elected body for consultative purposes, is not qualified by its mandate alone to establish a National Government of Korea." Jackson, Patterson, and Menon did not think that Koreans voted in a "free atmosphere," but they knew that the commission would not approve such a strong denunciation. They hoped nonetheless to commit UNTCOK to rejection of Rhee's claim that the election had brought about a new government for all of Korea. When the commission voted, a majority supported an innocuous Philippine resolution that left the matter up to the General Assembly.[25]

Having at last surmounted one major obstacle, the United States faced another when electric power transmission, from north to south Korea, ceased on May 14, 1948. Soviet and north Korean authorities had threatened for months to cut off power supplies to the American zone. They apparently acted in retaliation to the American-supported elections. During the previous October, Soviet authorities had informed American officials that payment for electric power was unsatisfactory and that they were turning the matter over to the People's Committee of North Korea. They wanted payment in scarce goods at favorable prices—the Americans had offered to pay part of the amount in dollars—and wanted the Americans to negotiate with a de facto Korean government in the north. Langdon had reported the attitude of north Korean representatives as truculent. The matter languished for months, but then as the elections approached, the problem of payment for electric power became serious. Hodge received a letter in mid-March from Kim Il-sung demanding payment "of approximately $4,620,000 for power furnished south Korea from August 1945 to 31 January 1948." Kim threatened to cut power transmission by midnight, April 15. Hodge cabled Marshall that Soviet authorities had notified him that "any communication from Kim is official and bona fide and that hereafter such economic matters would be handled by the People's Committee of North Korea." The Soviet command informed American liaison officers in Pyongyang that because payment had not been met Soviet forces in north Korea would no longer act as mediator between the Americans and Kim's regime in the electric power dispute. "I am informing you that any further negotiations on this matter must be conducted directly with the People's Committee of North Korea which is in charge of electrical power stations in North Korea."[26]

American officials could not explain Soviet tactics. Langdon saw "an attempt to expedite payment through a veiled threat . . . that north Korea will shut off power more readily than Soviet forces will." Arthur Bunce believed that the Soviets were not satisfied with the goods Americans had offered in payment for electric power. Hodge told local correspondents that it was a typical example of Soviet obstinacy and refused to communicate with the Russian-sponsored north Korean government.[27] U.S. officials viewed the problem as local in origin, local in solution.

Soviet leaders may well have had in mind a more important matter than several million dollars worth of goods in payment for electric power. There may have been a strong connection (and certainly an intriguing coincidence) in the timing of the emerging crises in Korea and Germany, i.e., the blockade of electric power (Korea) and the blockade of surface access routes (Berlin). Most obviously, the Soviets may have wished to demonstrate their anger at the UN-sponsored elections in the south and at American attempts to go it alone in southern Korea. Soviet leaders perhaps used the electric power shutoff to protest the changing course of the unilateral American occupation in Japan, to state their worries about British and American attempts to create a German state around which to rebuild Western Europe, and to express their paranoia about an American-reconstructed Germany and Japan. The power cutoff in Korea seemed an ideal solution. It was not an area of vital American concern, so it would not provoke an overreaction. Nevertheless, the signal would not be missed. South Korea received eighty percent of its power and coal from the north; without it, the shaky economy most likely would collapse, riots and strikes might follow, and southern communists could take control. In addition, turning the administration over to north Korean organizations was another step forward from the September 1947 call for withdrawal of foreign troops. The Soviets would show the Korean people that, regardless of any election in the south, Kim Il-sung controlled their destiny. If American officials negotiated with the People's Committee of North Korea, that would imply recognition of Kim's puppet regime and undo U.S. efforts at the United Nations. If the Americans found matters so difficult that they withdrew, it would be a great propaganda victory for the Soviets. Soviet leaders were using the electric power dispute in Korea as a test of wills. The question was (and is): for what purpose?

No officials then and few scholars since have noted the connection between blocking electric power transmission in Korea and blocking surface transportation routes in Germany. Perhaps it was coincidental that the Korean crisis occurred in the midst of the confrontation over Berlin; there are several interesting hypotheses. Most scholarly accounts agree that the Soviets instituted the mini-blockade of rail traffic to the Western zones in Berlin in response to Anglo-American actions that moved beyond currency reforms to unification of their occupation zones and reconstruction of the still-shattered economy, exacerbating Soviet fears of a resurgent German nation possibly at the front of a hostile Western alliance. The mini-blockade occured in late March to early April 1948 (Daniel F. Harrington places its beginnings even earlier); in mid-June the total blockade began. Why was there a break of several months between the tentative attempts at blockade and the onset of the more complete one that led to the Berlin airlift? The Russians (or their north Korean allies) cut electric power across the 38th parallel on May 14, 1948, in the midst of the two phases of the Berlin crisis. Later, as the Western allies demonstrated their ability to maintain West Berlin (Harrington argues that the winter of 1948-49 proved their capability to supply Berlin), the Soviets used Korea to hint at an end to tensions in Europe. The Polish press commented in September 1948 that "the United States should withdraw its occupation forces from southern Korea and thus furnish a precedent for solution of the German problem." Soviet authorities in Austria noted: "Is it not clear why Austria three years after the end of war is still occupied? Northern Korea proves that if Russians had their way Austria too would be freed from occupation troops. Southern Korea on the other hand proves that Americans only are interested in prolonged occupation to exploit countries as colonies and strategic outposts." Belatedly, in January 1949, Perry Laukoff of the Division of Central European Affairs noted "increasing Soviet propaganda on parallels between Korea and Germany."[28]

There was a connection between events in Korea and Germany, at least as perceived by the Soviets. Robert Jervis in *Perception and Misperception in International Politics* argues that officials of one power tend to view adversaries as operating from a master plan, emphasizing the confused diplomacy of the perceiver and the organization and force of the perceived. Alex George's article, "Nothing Happens in Russia by Accident," in *International Studies Quarterly*, points out that Kremlin leaders are particularly prone to this sort of perception, for as far as Moscow is concerned nothing happens by chance or coincidence. Adam Ulam's biography of Stalin affirms this point. Such a worldview would have great significance for the crises in Korea and Berlin. Howard Schonberger, for instance, has argued that the changing course of American occupation policy in Japan, beginning in 1948 as the U.S. government began viewing Japan as the anchor of the American position in East Asia and began rebuilding the economy to make Japan an ally against Soviet expansion, came not from external sources, that is, Russian action or threats, but from internal pressures and politics having little to do with the superpower confrontation. The timing is important. Kremlin leaders, with their fear of encirclement, their vision of a world full of enemies working from a master plan, saw a connection between diverse situations in eastern Asia (Korea and Japan) and Western Europe and thus may have undertaken reasonably coordinated action in Korea and Berlin to protest such a worldwide American plot. Perhaps they undertook the two blockades to test American intentions.[29]

Did American officials have a master plan directed against the Soviet Union? There is no published evidence suggesting that the government in Washington coordinated policy in Western Europe and northeastern Asia to fit the precepts of such a strategy. There were no official and probably few unofficial contacts between officials designing policy for Korea (and Japan) and for Germany. Yet, while there was no great conspiracy, policymakers in Washington did talk about a unified foreign policy. Kennan urged "a unified concept of foreign policy" in February 1948. In fact, NSC-7 delineated a *Soviet* master plan and urged creation of an American strategy to counter "Soviet-directed world communism." Ambassador Smith in Moscow wrote the department in late June 1948 that while the Soviets adapted their tactics to various areas based upon local circumstances, their strategy remained unchanged. Smith's acceptance of the concept of a Soviet master plan implies that he desired an American one. NSC 14/1, from early July 1948, stated that the United States had an obligation "to supply countries vital to our national security."

It raised an important question: at what point does arming for defense appear aggressive? As Smith wrote the secretary of state in August 1948, the Soviets at least publicly believed in an American master plan. Smith reported Soviet propaganda stating that the United States lead an "offensive for war," organizing hostile blocs and using its occupation duties as "an instrument of aggression." Further: "The United States in Germany and Japan seeks [the] revival of reactionary ruling groups, suppresses democratic tendencies, prevents democratization and demilitarization. . . . [This] military offensive embraces [the] conversion of Germany and Japan into place d'armes against the Soviet Union."[30]

III

In Korea, when Kim Koo and Kim Kiu-sic traveled to Pyongyang before the election, they talked about the power problem, and Kim Il-sung implied that if the south Koreans could stop the election he would continue to supply power. The Korean moderates returned to Seoul, and Radio Pyongyang that day destroyed their political influence in the south by broadcasting that it would have to suspend the power supply "if the American command persists in showing unwillingness to make fair settlements of outstanding power bill."[31] The Russians must have been dictating Kim's actions, for it made more sense for him to postpone the election and work with southern communists for a unified Korea.

Power ceased at noon Friday, May 14, 1948. Soviet and north Korean officials acted because, they claimed, "American military authorities were in default having paid only 15.6 percent of the bill by April 1." General Korotkov informed Hodge that he had turned control over to north Korean officials.[32] The cutoff caused immediate difficulty in the American zone. South Korea had only a few, badly deteriorated, Japanese-built electric plants, and there were two offshore floating power barges that required scarce and expensive fuel oil. American experts calculated that the south could produce sixty percent of its need, but only at great expense. It would slow economic growth, require increased U.S. aid, and possibly further social instability.[33]

As they moved to increase electric power output in the south, American officials prepared to approach the Soviet government. Marshall wrote Molotov on June 24 (the day the blockade began in Germany) to resolve the situation, telling the foreign minister that Hodge had sought to settle the account in dollars because of delays in delivery of specified material. Hodge had acted in good faith. Marshall claimed that the Soviets had acted unreasonably to cut power when forty percent of the goods (for payment) waited in Seoul for the Russians to take possession. He told Molotov to stop parading the fiction of an independent north Korea controlling electric power output. He wanted transmission restarted.[34] But the Soviets brushed off Marshall's attempt to negotiate, Vishinsky replying that American authorities in Korea had not delivered payment on time and must negotiate with the People's Committee.[35] As long as Marshall failed to understand that the power cutoff was serving an as yet ill-defined larger purpose, he could have little success approaching leaders in Moscow.

Hodge began an exchange with General Merkulov, writing the Soviet commander on May 17 and releasing the letter several days later. "In view of my repeated efforts to arrange for equitable payment, this action is all the more unjustifiable and leads to the conclusion that your publicized statements concerning nonpayment for electric power are only a subterfuge to hide the motive behind the act." He claimed that the Soviets wanted to punish south Korea for voting in the elections. He informed the Russians that more than sixty carloads of goods—valued at $2 million—waited in Seoul. Before he would send payment north, Hodge wanted transmission of electric power resumed.[36] Merkulov answered that Hodge should direct his letter to north Korean authorities. Hodge replied in mid-June that "so long as Soviet forces remain in occupation of North Korea, the Soviet command cannot divest itself of responsibility to supply electric power." Merkulov wrote on June 25 that "the North Korean People's Committee informed me that immediately the American government pays for electric power supplied to South Korea . . . it will resume supplying electric power to South Korea." He again told Hodge to deal with the People's Committee and that its representatives would come to Seoul to take delivery of the goods.[37] The Americans, however, would not negotiate with north Korea. Kim Il-sung and Syngman Rhee would not deal with each other. The power supply remained off.

Another problem arose that would also affect Korean issues through the remainder of the year. After UNTCOK had approved the May 10 election, American diplomats considered recognition of the Republic of Korea in late spring. Butterworth asked the department's legal adviser, Ernest A. Gross, for his opinion, remarking that he felt advantages outweighed disadvantages even if the United States acted before the UN General Assembly met in December. Recognition would strengthen the republic and American prestige was tied to the fate of the country regardless of its stance on early recognition. Gross suggested, and the department concurred, that prior recognition was a serious move. He recommended de facto recognition by appointing a special representative of the president with ambassadorial rank.[38]

The State Department began to seek de facto recognition of the republic by nations represented on the UN commission before inauguration day 1949. Over Marshall's signature, Allison wrote embassies in London, Canberra, Damascus, Manila, New Delhi, Nanking, Paris, and Ottawa that "the department is contemplating issuance of statement that the U.S. Government regards new government as 'the national government of Korea envisaged by the General Assembly resolution.' " The letter made clear that the department expected its representatives to argue that nonrecognition would mean UN weakness and a victory for the Soviets over the United Nations.[39] The result proved disappointing. The British were very dubious because Rhee's regime would exercise control over half of the territory where it claimed sovereignty, recognition would bypass the General Assembly, and it would give the USSR justification for proclaiming a puppet government in the north. Australian officials informed the American embassy they would wait until the General Assembly considered recognition. A Syrian foreign ministry official commented that Syria probably would support the United States. The Philippine government, a close supporter, raised no objection. Menon refused to consider the new Korean government as "a national government of Korea envisaged by the General Assembly resolution," and he controlled the Indian vote. The Chinese were eager to gain allies in the Far East as the civil war worsened and quickly assented. The French and Salvadoreans wanted to wait until the General Assembly met in Paris. The Canadian government was divided.[40]

The U.S. delegation to the United Nations disapproved of early recognition. Jessup, Noyes, and Hyde advised Marshall that "the United States is in weakest position in the General Assembly if it took any steps without UNTCOK or other UN approval." They recommended that the department wait until UNTCOK had made its report and raised the Korean question.[41] Department officials decided nonetheless to grant "qualified recognition," Jacobs writing Marshall that "we are doing no more than the USSR has already done in north Korea—i.e., transferred government functions to local authorities." He received word on August 6 that Marshall approved his suggestion. Six days later the State Department announced that the United States welcomed the new nation into the family of nations and appointed John J. Muccio of Rhode Island as a special representative with ambassadorial rank.[42]

Syngman Rhee was inaugurated on August 15, 1948, as the first president of the Republic of Korea. He had invited Generals

MacArthur and Hodge to celebrate his inaugural and the third anniversary of liberation from the Japanese. When he addressed the crowd at the stadium in Seoul, he basked in the glory, threatening his enemies and raising the specter of a patriotic war against the north: "Our joy is clouded with sorrow as we look to the north. . . . No nation however powerful should be allowed to occupy the territory of its weak neighbors." MacArthur addressed the crowd with less than diplomatic words: "Yet in this hour, as the forces of righteousness advance, the triumph is dulled by one of the greatest tragedies of contemporary history—an artificial barrier has divided your land. This barrier must and will be torn down. Nothing shall prevent the ultimate unity of your people as free men of a free nation."[43] The State Department released a statement that "it is the view of the U.S. Government that the Korean government so established is entitled to be regarded as the government of Korea envisaged by the General Assembly resolution of November 14, 1947." China and the Philippines quickly extended recognition, but few other governments took that step. They would not act in advance of the General Assembly.[44]

Establishment of the government in South Korea presented an opportunity for the abolition of the U.S. Army Military Government in Korea (USAMGIK), and General Hodge returned to Washington to await a new assignment. For over a year government officials had sought to replace the man they belatedly realized was unqualified for such a political task. They waited until Rhee's inauguration, thus relieving Hodge "after a job well done." Despite criticism directed at his many mistakes in Korea (most of which resulted from inadequate guidance and assistance from officials in Washington who now wished to replace him), the praise was strong and convincing. President Truman congratulated Hodge: "The achievement of constitutional government in southern Korea completes the difficult task that was assigned to you. Your mission has been accomplished with outstanding success." MacArthur praised Hodge. Rhee had kind words, despite the animosity between the two men during the prior two years.[45]

The inaugural signalled the beginning of more problems for the United States government at a time when it wished to decrease its Korean commitment. The constant threat of a North Korean attack or a communist-inspired popular uprising in the south forced the U.S. Army to postpone withdrawal. And Rhee began to be extremely difficult. Perhaps understanding the value of the symbol that Korea represented, he sought to involve the American government in his byzantine maneuverings. Since American prestige was tied to the success of the new republic, a large aid program was necessary. American diplomats were committed to securing General Assembly approval of the new government as the government of all Korea.

A new National Security Council document, NSC-20, suggested that the continuing superpower confrontation would place new importance on the American involvement in Korea. In July 1948, Secretary of Defense James Forrestal had asked the NSC "for an appraisal of the degree and character of military preparedness required by the world situation." Kennan, director of the Policy Planning Staff, asked for a few days grace, noted a series of qualifiers, and promised a document that would become NSC 20/2. The department delivered NSC 20/2 on August 25, 1948; the document argued for a large increase in resources for national defense. "It is necessary that this government maintain armed strength . . . as a source of encouragement to nations endeavoring to resist Soviet political aggression. . . . It is necessary for this country to maintain the outward evidences of firm armed strength and resolution as a means of stiffening the attitude of those people who would like to resist Soviet political pressure." A strong defense, vigilant and flexible, would discourage Soviet miscalculation. NSC 20/2 implied a renewed commitment to Korea. Since Korea was one of the few places in the world where American and Soviet forces faced one another, the relative insignificance of Korea in *realpolitik* terms was magnified by its symbolic value as a sign of American determination to resist Soviet pressure. The problem was that the United States was committed to psychological/symbolic battlegrounds with serious disadvantages: a politically repressive regime to legitimize, a shaky economy to maintain and rebuild, a strong insurgency movement to combat, a strategically indefensible half-peninsula to hold. The document also used cold war language to describe a problem largely caused by emergent nationalism in the Third

World. By creating a symbol that did not fit reality, by using language and perceptions that mattered little in Korea, the United States would begin creating the trap from which there would be no escape.[46]

State Department officials by mid-1948 (in light of NSC 20/2) felt that American troops had to remain in Korea despite the army's need for them elsewhere. NSC-8 had authorized early withdrawal, and the army wanted no delay. Secretary of the Army Kenneth C. Royall wrote Marshall on June 23 that the army would complete withdrawal by December 31, 1948, as envisaged in NSC-8. But Far Eastern experts in the State Department worried over how other foreign ministries, particularly the Soviets, would interpret a hasty withdrawal. They insisted the army recognize that its withdrawal plans were inconsistent with NSC-8 as well as American goals in the UN, and that NSC 20/2 implied greater allocation of resources to the military, thus making the Korean commitment less expensive. Several days later they modified this stand when Lovett sought to compromise with the army. He had no objection to the withdrawal as long as army leaders were flexible. If the demands of the moment called for delay, then Lovett wanted the army to adjust.[47]

The department wanted to suspend the withdrawal of troops because it realized that most nations would delay recognition until the General Assembly met in December. Allison and Bond requested that senior officials look into the issue so that withdrawal was "not inconsistent with the overall policy which we are following in other parts of the world." A hasty military withdrawal, before either the General Assembly or the Republic of Korea had made known their feelings, would damage American prestige in China, Europe, and the Pacific. Rusk and Butterworth agreed that "there should be no public announcement of troop withdrawal until after the General Assembly has completed consideration of the Korean problem." They convinced Marshall the army should take no immediate action.[48]

When the Washington press learned of withdrawal plans, it expressed displeasure. Joseph and Stewart Alsop said that "more honest State and Defense Department policymakers frankly admit the ultimate effect of the decision to withdraw will be to throw all of Korea into the expanding Soviet empire. . . . American abandonment of Korea will have an immediate, disastrous psychological and political effect on all forces of resistance to communist expansion throughout Asia." The *Denver Post* agreed with the Alsops: "If we withdraw in Korea it may be the first of a series of little Munichs wherein the U.S. throws aside its promises and its moral strategy to pursue a short-sighted, short-range program of military and economic retrenchment." "What is to be gained," questioned the *Philadelphia Inquirer*, "if we pull the props away from Rhee and his new administration?" In the crusade against communism, newspapers felt it sacrilegious to give up territory to the Soviets and were unable to see (as many government officials were unable to see) that situations such as Korea were not simply matters of Soviet expansionism. Again, department desk officers sent news summaries to interested embassies. What was the effect of this "we-they" distortion of reality? By 1948, the government had taken its first tentative steps to making Korea a symbol of American determination. The press was helping tie the administration to Rhee's regime; soon domestic political pressures would do the same.[49]

To make matters more difficult, the Soviet Union on September 19 announced it would withdraw its troops from North Korea by January 1, 1949. Here was a shrewd gesture, risking little, for Soviet forces would fall back a few hundred miles to their own territory. A call for mutual withdrawal would embarrass the U.S. government. The Russians suggested that the powers also withdraw troops from Germany, noting a link between the two divided lands, with communist newspapers stating that "Soviet evacuation of northern Korea is proof conclusive that the Soviets genuinely are concerned about freedom not only of Korea but also Germany and Austria."[50] The Soviet announcement hardened feeling within the State Department that the troops should remain in Korea. Department spokesmen noted that withdrawal was part of the larger issue of Korean independence. They told the press that the United States would wait until the General Assembly considered the Korean question. In early October 1948, Lovett gained Marshall's approval to suspend withdrawal until January 1949. As incidents of violence along the 38th parallel increased, the department felt the troops should remain until the UN sent observers to replace them.[51]

In addition to the question of withdrawal, the U.S. government had problems with Syngman Rhee. Difficulties had appeared during the decades when he was in American exile and felt himself the personification of the Korean people. Jacobs wrote Marshall that the problem had magnified by mid-1948: "First indications of coming difficulties with Syngman Rhee have appeared. He is definitely suffering from a messiah complex . . . as if he had been appointed by the Korean people to lead them into the promised land of independence. Some of his own friends say that in the mornings he is usually rational, but by afternoon he is completely 'off the beam.' " A few weeks later, Jacobs added to his warnings: "He assumes more and more messiah pose and speaks in the third person of what he will do." Jacobs was certain that Rhee would antagonize both the UN commission and moderate Koreans, but offered no ideas on how to deal with Rhee.[52]

When Rhee became president, the situation worsened. In public speeches he said that "Koreans must fight Russians" and would not explain his meaning. He welcomed a North Korean surrender and warned them that "the people" would rescue their land from the Soviet aggressor to the north. He seemed incapable of running a government. His administration suffered mounting deficits despite nearly $100 million a year in American relief. Korean officials were corrupt and incompetent, for Rhee preferred loyalty over efficiency and knew little about managing a bureaucracy.[53] Within a few months, the special representative in Korea, Muccio, would report to the State Department that Rhee could not bring stability to Korea. By mid-October, Rhee's popularity had "never been so low." Muccio noted: "I have never seen Rhee show his age as much as he did on this trip. . . . He disclosed a tendency to surrender to 'fixed ideas' in thinking." A month later it was worse: "Rhee often evidences inability to cope with major problems and direct government[,] . . . possibly this incompetency verges toward incipient senility." Muccio warned of corruption, internal rivalries, and irresponsibility in government. Rhee meanwhile spoke of "recovering 'lost territories' " and "using force of arms if possible."⁵⁴ There was little the United States could do since it could not replace Rhee. There was no other major figure except for Pak, the communist, and a few members of the now-defunct Coalition Committee. The government in Washington could only hope for the best.

Rhee had difficult relations with the United Nations commission, even though it had instructions to "advise" the new government. At one meeting he remarked that commission members "come as our guests, at our invitation." When he asked the commission to consult with him, it turned out to be a formality. He was unwilling to discuss alleged repression of rights in the south. He told the commission to limit its efforts to "implementing the General Assembly's program of UN-supervised elections in North Korea." Rhee's attitude made it harder to convince the General Assembly to accept his regime as the government of all Korea.⁵⁵

The State Department realized that propping up Rhee's government required a well-financed aid program. In March 1947, the department had prepared a three-year relief and rehabilitation program for Korea. Events in Greece and Turkey and congressional reluctance to fund a great many aid programs had caused the department to put the plan aside. Now, no doubt encouraged by the implications of NSC 20/2, it updated the old program to present to Congress. The department had worked out an economic assistance program when Rhee assumed the presidency of the Republic of Korea. The army would continue to administer relief aid until it completed troop withdrawal (then figured to be by January 15, 1949); when it had left Korea, the Economic Cooperation Administration (ECA), an agency created to dispense aid authorized under the Marshall Plan, would take over control of the program. Because the aid program would take three years, ECA officials agreed that "ECA was the logical agency to assume the responsibility for the economic aid and rehabilitation program." President Truman ordered the army to turn over responsibility to ECA not later than March 15, 1949.⁵⁶

The department had chosen its course of action by early September 1948. The United States could not drop the aid program, for such action would be inconsistent with NSC-8. State Department officials rejected a relief program simply to keep

Korea from immediate collapse, for they saw no end to it. A stopgap year-to-year program for relief and rehabilitation would not help rebuild the Korean economy. Department officials agreed on a three-year program that would provide "greater internal stability through increased production and employment." To overcome congressional reluctance to fund long-term aid programs, the department decided to tell the Congress that it was a one-year program "to avoid the implication of a commitment to Korea."[57] However, despite the urgency of securing aid legislation, the department concluded that a comprehensive relief and rehabilitation program would have to wait for the next fiscal year (FY). It was too late to include the program in FY 1949, and the ECA wanted more time before it presented the program for FY 1950. Putting the idea aside temporarily, the department authorized the army occupation to continue relief assistance for another year.[58]

The department meanwhile had begun campaigning for recognition of the Republic of Korea at the General Assembly session in December. Department experts wanted the assembly to approve the regime as the government of all Korea and authorize a new commission to observe mounting violence along the 38th parallel and to continue UN involvement in the peninsula. In September, the director of the Office of UN Affairs, Dean Rusk, instructed the delegation in Paris on policy for Korea: "The Republic of Korea is the government of Korea envisaged by the General Assembly resolution." He told the delegation not to oppose a Soviet move to declare a government in North Korea but to remind the delegates that "UNTCOK had not observed elections in the northern zone."[59] When the delegates assembled in Paris in December 1948, the Americans believed they had a good chance to secure United Nations recognition for Rhee's government. While the British Foreign Office would oppose calling the ROK "a national government of all Korea," the British delegate, Sir Alexander Cadogan, sided with the Americans. The Australians felt that the American plan "seemed reasonable." French delegates favored a strong stand against the Soviet Union, and most of the Latin American delegations were behind the American proposal. The United States benefited from continued Soviet refusal to honor a UN resolution.[60]

The discussion on Korea at the General Assembly began on December 6, 1948, and communist delegates sought to invite North Korean leaders to speak out about repression in the south. They claimed that because ninety-nine percent of the North Korean population had voted in elections as opposed to seventy-two percent in the south, North Korea was truly representative and free. It was a ridiculous argument and Dulles exposed its fallacies. He compared terror and force in North Korea with freedom of expression and the UN-supervised elections in the south. He urged the delegates to avoid such delaying tactics. Dulles argued that the United Nations should "fulfill its task of assuring independence and unity for Korea" by "stamping the government of the ROK with the seal of legitimacy."[61] Debate continued for several days, repeating arguments raised in September and October 1947. It seemed that the fourteen months in between had done little to change minds, for when it came to a vote the Assembly sided with the U.S. delegation. On December 12, it declared "that there has been established a lawful government (the government of the ROK) . . . and that this is the only such government in Korea." The U.S. delegation also gained another victory as the Assembly created a permanent UN Commission on Korea (UNCOK I) with six members. Canada and France withdrew while the other six nations from the temporary commission continued as members on the new one. The new commission was to assist the development of democracy in South Korea and observe conditions along the 38th parallel.[62]

American diplomats had thus gained a partial success, for they had made the United Nations a defender of Korean independence, yet the cost of the slight success was great. To communist bloc nations, Arab states, Canada, and some members of the British Commonwealth, the United States had forced its view on a reluctant majority at the United Nations. The Korean question may have heightened Soviet fears of American purpose. It caused unnecessary problems with Canada and exposed some of the worst aspects of the cold war crusade, including permanent division of the peninsula into antagonistic halves.

It was an ironic situation, for the more American leaders sought to extricate their nation from Korea, the more circumstances forced them to deepen the commitment. It seemed that a communist tide threatened the world in 1948, and American policymakers typically felt that a "gain" for the Soviet Union was a "loss" for the United States and a diminution of its prestige. In Korea, many nations expected the United States to make a stand as did many American newspapers. The State Department sensed that the country would suffer a loss if it withdrew from the peninsula without leaving behind a stable Korea. How could the United States withdraw? Instead it continued to follow the path of least resistance: to remain in Korea, to seek a new aid program, to elevate Korea's importance as a symbol of American determination, to overlook many unpleasant aspects of Rhee's regime. American officials would not back down from the (self-created) challenge. Circumstances in coming months would make final the creation of important cold war symbolism around the issue of divided Korea.

Unprepared for War, Tied to Korea

IN the weeks and months after the formal proclamation of the Republic of Korea, American officials worked long and hard on the problems they faced in their efforts to help establish and maintain an economically sound and militarily secure South Korea and thus allow the United States to withdraw from the peninsula without a loss of prestige. They began 1949 again asking Congress to fund a relief and rehabilitation program for the former American zone. As the bill stalled in the House of Representatives, the administration turned its attention to the situation in Korea. Officals feared a breakdown of the fragile peace in the peninsula. They worried that North Korean communists would invade the south; they feared that the UN Korean Commission might attempt to disband, leaving hostile Korean armies facing each other across the 38th parallel; they wondered if Syngman Rhee understood the deteriorating economic situation in his country, and if, anticipating communist aggression, he might launch an attack northward. Administration officials recognized that peace and economic stability in the south would require American financial assistance and moral support. They sought passage of the stalled Korean aid bill under difficult and trying circumstances following the "fall" of Nationalist China. When Congress finally approved the Far Eastern Economic Assistance Act of 1950, it was February and the outbreak of war in Korea was only a few months away.

More important than the fate of the Korean aid bill or American attempts to assist the infant Republic of Korea was the emergence of Korea as an unwanted symbol of American determination to defend the noncommunist world against communist aggression. It had been a slow process from 1945 to 1949 as more and more segments of American politics discovered that Korea represented American values and deserved support. Paralleling this process was a steady increase in the resources available for Korea (via NSC 20, NSC 48, and NSC 68). Culminating in the critical months of January and February 1950, the final year and a half before the outbreak of war would witness the symbol manipulating and somewhat controlling its creator. Korea had risen from an expendable "back-burner" issue during Byrnes's secretaryship to an increasingly vital point in an increasingly hostile superpower confrontation. As the perceived Soviet threat came to dominate the views of most American officials, the reality of Korea faded from sight. As image conquered reality, the government in Washington would describe (and possibly believe its description of) Korea as a Western-oriented democracy valiantly striving for social justice and political harmony while facing a communist neighbor bent on attack. It was a useful if largely inaccurate description. The appearance of a strong stand in Korea, allowing the administration a "grace period" between the hoped-for withdrawal from the peninsula and the fall of the south, might quiet critics of the administration's China policy. A strong stand might help convince Japanese leaders to cast their lot with the United States. Determination in Korea might allow the administration to attempt an understanding with the communist rulers of mainland China and possibly keep the world's most populous nation from falling under the control of the Kremlin. A show of American support for South Korea would encourage allies and discourage adversaries. Korea mattered little for its own sake; rather, the perceived requirements of the cold war made it important. The problem, however, was that the more potent a symbol Korea became, the more difficult it would be to reduce or eliminate U.S. ties or deal realistically with the fate of the corrupt, undemocratic, and tyrannical regime that had come to power in the former American zone and which hid behind the respectable mantle of the United States.

I

During January 1949, the State Department outlined Korea's importance for American policy. Mao's impending victory in China would leave the Republic of Korea as the "only remaining foothold of democracy" in Northeast Asia. If the red tide overran this "continuing challenge to communist ideology," it would encourage Japanese communists and discourage "those Japanese who are now striving to build into the fiber of Japan democratic principles and practices." The cold war confrontation so dominated American thinking that department officials could describe without qualms Rhee's Korea (where the as yet unpunished wartime collaborators constituted the core of his support and helped administer the country) as a "foothold of democracy." It caused American policymakers to believe that Rhee's half-hearted promises of social justice implied future action. Before the onset of the cold war ideology, few people in government in Washington wanted anything to do with Rhee or had any faith in his commitment to reform; now in 1949 he emerged an upholder of the American way of life.[1]

The department convinced the National Security Council to reconsider NSC 8, its paper on Korea. The council had decided in 1948 to cut the American commitment as quickly as possible "with a minimum of bad effects." The NSC 20 series had somewhat changed considerations. While the document and its revisions did not deal directly with Korea, it apparently favored a strong stand in Korea and a greater commitment of resources to encourage American allies and discourage Soviet expansion. NSC 20/4 warned that the United States must prevent "lessening of U.S. prestige and influence through vacillation or appeasement or lack of skill and imagination in the conduct of its foreign policy or by shirking world responsibilities," presumably including its role in Korea. Under State Department pressure, in a March 1949 meeting, the National Security Council recognized that Korea had become a symbol in the cold war and authorized the department to develop a Marshall Plan program for Korea.[2] Government officials recognized a dilemma: given America's military responsibilities and resources, Korea remained a strategic liability.

As the National Security Council confirmed Korea's increasing importance, department officials refurbished a two-year-old relief and rehabilitation program. In 1947, the plan would have allowed the U.S. government to retire from the peninsula gracefully; now it would demonstrate a national commitment to defend governments threatened by communist aggression. Although the State Department would defend the assistance program before the Congress, it planned for the Economic Cooperation Administration to administer the aid. The ECA had carried forth State Department objectives in running the Marshall Plan, now it received the added obligation to do in Korea what it had done in Western Europe. Secretary of State Dean Acheson would appear as the principal witness before congressional committees. The department intended to call upon its most senior officials for appearances before the legislative branch to impress a reluctant Congress with the gravity of the situation in Korea and the importance of large-scale economic assistance.[3]

The State Department intended that the program reassure nervous allies that the United States would stand up to aggression. As the army began the final phase of withdrawal, it would indicate a continuing commitment to the Republic of Korea and other democratic nations. Despite misgivings about the wisdom of Korean assistance, department officials felt that a political/symbolic (but not military) line had to be drawn in Korea. Yet, the aid package illustrated a basic contradiction in Korean policy: as the department made Korea into a first-rank symbol, how could the government in Washington (despite its professed belief to the contrary) avoid military involvement to retain credibility should the situation degenerate into war?

To dramatize the issue's importance, President Truman included a personal message with the proposed legislation he sent to Congress on June 7, 1949. He called for $150 million for fiscal year 1950. "The Korean Republic, by demonstrating the success and tenacity of democracy in resisting communism, will stand as a beacon to the people of northern Asia in resisting the control of communist forces which have overrun them." Truman told Congress that his request was "the minimum aid essential during the coming year."[4] The next day, Under Secretary of State James C. Webb opened hearings before the House Foreign Affairs Committee. Webb sought to impress committee members with Korea's importance after the collapse of Nationalist China: "The legislation . . . is among the most important which the Department of State is supporting at this session." He characterized Korea as the key outpost of democracy in the Far East. He concluded by noting that "the rest of Asia is watching us in Korea."[5]

Witnesses sought to convince the committee of the value of the Korean Assistance Act of 1949, but they faced a difficult task given that the United States was in a general retreat from the Asian mainland. Southern Korea was a strategic liability. There was no provable link between the security of the United States and the continued existence of the Republic of Korea. At a time when the administration was abandoning Chiang Kai-shek, how could it convince skeptics that the place for a stand against communism was in southern Korea and not southern China? And worse, it could not demonstrate that Rhee would prove more successful than his Chinese counterpart.

The director of the department's Policy Planning Staff, George Kennan, bore the brunt of congressional dissatisfaction. Kennan had received attention as the exponent of the containment policy which, to many Americans, relegated the nation to defense against a communist conspiracy. Republican Congressmen wanted to question him. He was in an awkward position, for he could make no extravagant promises or exaggerated claims (and, within the department, he had questioned the value of the symbolic commitment to South Korea). He admitted that "the real danger is the question and probability of armed forces coming down from north Korea." He would not be surprised "if a civil war did develop in the next two or three years." The government had no plans to use American troops in South Korea, but "we cannot say we have a plan for civil war." He conceded that the situation in Korea was bleak but told the committee that "it is a chance worth our betting on . . . if we give them economic aid." Kennan's honest assessment caused some committee members to question the wisdom of making the south a more inviting target for an invasion from the north.[6]

The skeptical attitude of some committee members did not equal the outrage of Republican members of the China lobby. Walter Judd of Minnesota asked Kennan if "months ago" it was decided to abandon Korea and "this $150,000,000 is just a sop to try and cover our retreat?" When Kennan tried to answer, Judd commented, "I know you cannot say yes." Lawrence W. Smith of Wisconsin told Kennan it was "a strange theme" to "reconcile the position of the State Department toward Korea and that of the department with reference to China." Charles A. Eaton of New Jersey, demonstrating his anger and ignorance, wondered "who was asleep at the switch and who did not have the mailed fist and why did we let them take the industrial-productive half of Korea and leave us with the agricultural section?" Kennan could not satisfy these opponents of policy. He reluctantly admitted that "there is no course open to the United States in Korea which will entirely eliminate the risk of a serious breakdown in the Korean situation." The China-Korea connection would become more important (and interesting) in the immediate period after Chiang fled the mainland in December 1949.[7]

When Acheson appeared before the committee he still had to convince its members to support aid legislation. Republican criticism had taken its toll. Acheson's arguments were weak. Without aid legislation, he told the committee, "you are absolutely certain that Korea will collapse and Korea will fall into the communist area. If you do this, there is a chance that it will not." He suggested that South Korea was a showcase of democracy but could offer no guarantees of the republic's survival. Acheson affirmed that "if the Soviet Union really puts its weight behind it . . . they would take the country over. There is nothing we can do about it."[8]

For a few weeks the matter lay in balance. Few Americans understood that the great issue in Asia was nationalism and not Soviet or Soviet-directed expansion; in Korea and elsewhere, American officials overlooked native nationalists of whatever political inclination and mostly found Asians willing to do, say, and think that which the U.S. government wished. American officials opposed Pak, overlooked Lyuh and Kimm Kiu-sic until it was too late, and reluctantly accepted Rhee. For most Americans, the only issue was Soviet aggression; thus many Congressmen wondered about a stand in South Korea: what made it a better symbol than south China, would the United States enrich the land for the communists to seize? The Republican minority had made telling arguments while House Democratic leaders exerted little pressure on party members to support the administration. Acheson and Under Secretary Webb asked the president to speak out again for aid legislation. At a meeting with congressional leaders on June 20, 1949, Truman repeated arguments for the request. When he voiced a "second urgent appeal" for the approval of the $150 million, political commentators noted that "it put new life in the project which had been heavily beset in the House Foreign Affairs Committee." Meanwhile the State Department continued its lobbying.[9]

The committee voted out the Korean aid bill on June 30, 1949. The vote reflected the increasingly partisan debate over policy. Democrats voted for the measure as a test of party loyalty. Republicans, who failed to bury the legislation, looked to the Rules Committee or the floor vote to defeat the bill.[10] Republican members issued a minority report that condemned a seemingly piecemeal and ineffectual policy in East Asia. They labelled the Korean Assistance Act "a program foredoomed to failure [because] Korea is hopelessly outflanked by the adjacent land mass of China." They saw no logic to a program with a problematical chance of success while the administration ignored the half of China still controlled by the Nationalists. They agreed that Korea was a symbol of American strength of purpose but argued that south China was more critical. Perhaps most important, Republicans wanted the Korean question to serve as an opening for an attack on the administration's China policy.[11]

As the House Committee on Foreign Affairs reported, the Senate began considering the administration's request. The Senate Committee on Foreign Relations would treat witnesses more kindly than its House counterpart, where Republicans had sought to embarrass the Truman administration. Senate Republicans followed the lead of Arthur Vandenberg of Michigan, supporter of bipartisan policy, leader of the internationalist wing of the party. Vandenberg was the key to many of Truman's foreign policies. As debate opened, the outlook for bill S. 2319 looked favorable.

Administration witnesses once again sought to convince a congressional committee that survival of the Republic of Korea would enhance the security of the United States. Webb argued that the ROK had made gains that would continue with American aid and collapse without it. He reminded the Senate committee that since the Moscow Conference of 1945 the United States had accepted an obligation. American prestige was tied to the continued survival of Rhee's government, and Webb sought to convince the committee of Korea's importance as a symbol. The program was a small increase over subsistence relief, yet would demonstrate determination and lead to a time when no more aid would be necessary.[12] As committee members in the Senate questioned witnesses, the situation in China influenced their thinking. Theodore F. Green (D-R.I.) helped Webb to draw a distinction between Nationalist China and South Korea. In a roundabout manner, Webb agreed that the problem with China was government corruption and inefficiency: "One of the real problems in China is that the government for many reasons is not really an effective unit which can take on and carry out a problem." Paul Hoffman, who headed the Economic Cooperation Administration, said that "this government of Korea today does represent the people." It was hopeless in China, but administration witnesses sought to convey the impression—which ran counter to their own estimates—that it was possible to save Korea.[13]

Hoffman and Edgar T. Johnson of ECA pointed out that a strong South Korea would help Japan and further American interests despite the coming debacle in China. It was ironic that four years after Korean-Japanese economic ties were severed, Hoffman explained how the aid program would buy fishing boats for Koreans who would sell their catch to Japan. A democratic and prosperous Japan was important to American security. Hoffman rightly noted that "those two economies are naturally complementary. . . . In helping Korea we are also helping Japan. . . . The Japanese economy needs support from out-side sources and Korea is one of the natural complementary trading areas."[14]

When the Senators considered the administration request, they saw it as the best of many discouraging alternatives. Chairman Tom Connally of Texas commented that Korea "will be a symbol" and Green agreed that "it would be a great disaster to abandon it." Vandenberg spoke out in defense of the bill and provided the means to secure the Republican backing missing in the House. "Korea is the only symbol of any constructive interest on the part of the government of the United States in assisting to contain the communist menace in Asia." He warned Republican colleagues that "to deny a Korean program at this particular moment would have the effect of an atomic bomb in the Far East." With wry humor, Connally and Henry Cabot Lodge, Jr. (R-Mass.) concluded the discussion. "It was pointed out here the other day," Connally noted, "that Korea is the last thing we have in the Far East." Lodge replied that "it isn't much good, but it's ours." The committee voted in favor of the bill.[15] The senators differed from their House colleagues: House Republicans wanted to use the Korean issue to punish the administration for "its loss of China," while Senate Republicans joined with Democrats in accepting the creation of Korea as a vital symbol. The language of the debate gave evidence of widespread acceptance of the rhetoric of containment (a view of containment far different than that advocated by Kennan but popularly associated with him). No senator questioned the need for a Korean symbol; none wondered about the circumstances involved; none desired to see the reality of Korea. They accepted the idea that this once "back-burner" issue had now become a prime agent of the American desire to defend the free world against communism.

Although both committees ultimately approved the Korean aid request, the bill never made it to the House floor. It had to pass the Rules Committee and there it died. Republican committee members argued that aiding Korea made no sense while abandoning south China. In early July, Judge Kee met with State Department officials to report disappointing news. He had few hopes of getting the bill out of the Rules Committee. Democratic leaders had not helped; some Democratic party members were troubled. Representative Edward E. Cox of Georgia had stated, "I'm opposed to spending a dime over there unless our policy towards China is changed." By the end of July, Kee gave up. The Rules Committee postponed a vote until discussion of the forthcoming China White Paper and the Military Assistance Program, surely an acrimonious debate. In mid-August, Sam Rayburn advised the department that the bill was tied up in the Rules Committee. It remained there while Congress debated China policy.[16]

II

While the bill's progress stalled, the State Department faced new problems over the defense of South Korea. As the date for withdrawal neared, Syngman Rhee had become increasingly nervous over a North Korean attack. He wanted vast amounts of weapons. It was a difficult situation, for strategists wanted to provide the infant South Korean army enough weapons for defense but worried at what point might Rhee translate his calls for a "nationalist revolution" into an invasion of the north.

The same day that the House Foreign Affairs Committee reluctantly approved Korean aid legislation, the U.S. Army completed its withdrawal from Korea. When the regimental combat team of seventy-five hundred departed, it left behind nearly $56 million worth of small arms, machine guns, light artillery, jeeps, and light trucks. Army leaders noted that supplies left by the troops were sufficient for the small South Korean army; they did not suggest that Rhee's forces were a match for Kim Il-sung's army.[17]

Army strategists regarded withdrawal as the end of military responsibility for Korea. As the last troops boarded ships in Inchon harbor, the Department of the Army sent the Department of State a memorandum summing up options in case of a North Korean attack. The army could evacuate American forces from Korea (mostly ECA team members); and although it would show lack of faith in the infant republic's ability to provide for foreign nationals, it would "minimize U.S. involvement in a dangerous situation with unknown complexities." Secondly, the State Department could present the problem to the UN Security Council for emergency action as a threat to peace. While such a move would result in a Soviet veto (analysts did not prepare for, nor could imagine, the situation at the UN in late June 1950 during the Soviet walkout over China), it would reaffirm United Nations responsibility for the Republic of Korea, lessen any loss of prestige, and perhaps force the Soviet Union to back down before world opinion. Thirdly, the United States could initiate a police action with UN approval and with troops from member nations. While the army viewed the possiblity as militarily unsound, it did realize that it might be necessary. It wanted the State Department to know that it "would involve a militarily disproportionate expenditure of U.S. manpower, resources, and effort at a time when international relations in Europe are in precarious balance." The fourth course would reconstitute a "U.S. joint task force" in South Korea. It would inspire respect for the United States but the move was fraught with danger. It would commit the nation to the defense of the Republic of Korea; it would compare unfavorably to withdrawal from China and the Philippines; it might cause the Chinese communists to ally with North Koreans in defense of the northern half of the peninsula. It would lead to a long and costly involvement of American forces in an undeclared war. The fifth course envisaged extending the Truman Doctrine to Korea and had nearly the same dangers as the previous options. It would commit the United States to the defense of South Korea, strain the budget, and might force the government to lower military assistance to other, strategically more important nations. The Joint Chiefs agreed with army leaders, including a statement within the army memorandum, noting that South Korea was a strategic liability, regardless of its symbolic importance. It is curious that, given the army's expressed fear of reinvolvement in the peninsula, army leaders did not ask the State Department to reassess the increasing symbolic importance accorded Korea. Apparently, as a symbol, Korea was inviolate.[18]

The army memorandum was consistent with prior military analyses of the Korean and world situation. In a document dated April 29, 1947, the Joint Chiefs of Staff (JCS 1769/1) graded the importance of countries to the nation's security. It noted the continuing paradox: Korea could add little to national security but "to lose this battle would be gravely detrimental to United States prestige, and therefore security." The implication of the document was that, given scarce resources, Korea rated low; however, given the expanding resource commitment implied by NSC 20 (and later NSC 68), military leaders would agree that the United States had much to lose if South Korea collapsed. In early March 1948, George Kennan had traveled to Japan to meet with MacArthur. MacArthur's view of American interests in East Asia recognized the strategic trap of involvement on the Asian mainland. Both men wanted Korea to survive; both men wanted a minimal U.S. presence. No analyst questioned the "why" of Korea.[19]

The army memorandum placed State Department officials in a difficult position. They sympathized with the fear that involvement of armed forces or supplies might invite dangerous repercussions. Other circumstances had made necessary American support for Rhee's government. A strong stand in Korea might help ease the consequences of America's "failure in China" and allow the administration to approach the new rulers in Peking without appearing weak. It might help overcome Republican cries of surrender to communist aggression and would bolster the confidence of America's allies. It would align Japan within the free world orbit. The department hoped somehow to separate political and economic support from military involvement.

However, America's Korean difficulties became even more apparent as Rhee began calling for ever-increasing military assistance. While he had welcomed U.S. withdrawal, perhaps feeling he would have a free hand to invade the north, he soon changed his mind. When he realized he could not delay withdrawal past June 1949, he requested vast amounts of hardware as a sign of a continuing commitment. He wanted weapons for half a million troops (he had sixty-five thousand); he wanted planes, tanks, and a large navy. His demands were clearly exorbitant. Military officers believed he was trying to raise the offensive capability of his army. Rhee vacillated in his attitude toward the communist north. In part his outrageous military requests reflected an irrational fear of the Soviets and their North Korean puppets; in part they would help him reunite the peninsula and make him ruler of all the Korean people.[20]

As the summer months passed, Rhee continued his calls. In mid-July, he instructed his representatives in the United States to call on the secretary of state and ask for an increase in security forces from sixty-five thousand to a hundred thousand men, with the creation of a fifty-thousand-man reserve. He wanted more supplies and public assurance that the United States would "stand by" the Republic of Korea. Rhee told the Associated Press in Seoul that he would propose arming four hundred thousand men as a precaution against rash action by North Korea. Rhee's proposal would have quadrupled his country's military force, giving him twice as many men as Kim Il-sung. State Department officials responded privately that "efforts to put the squeeze on us for military assistance continue to be a source of some irritation." After several more clumsy attempts by his Washington representatives, Rhee wrote to President Truman: "As I sit in my home not much more than thirty miles from positions where soldiers of the Republic are defending with their lives the soil and the people of Korea against savage assaults of Communist armies, my thoughts most naturally turn to our grievous problems of defense." He promised the president that he was not planning war but insisted that he needed more troops, weapons, and other visible signs of support. While U.S. Army officers said that Korea had enough supplies for two months of fighting, Rhee claimed that the supplies would last only two days.[21]

Rhee flirted with Chiang Kai-shek and the idea of a Pacific security pact. When it became apparent that the U.S. government would no longer delay withdrawal, he looked to an Asian equivalent of the North Atlantic Treaty Organization suggested by Chiang and President Elpidio Quirino of the Philippines. Rhee told a press conference in late May 1949, "I think a Pacific pact will be beneficial not only to Asia but to the United States." He envisaged membership by all noncommunist countries bordering the Pacific, including South American nations. The Korean Foreign Ministry began talks with Chinese and Philippine representatives.[22]

Interest in a Pacific pact had begun months earlier, in late February, apparently initially in the Philippines. In mid-March, the American chargé in Manila, Thomas H. Lockett, commenced a steady stream of reports concerning Philippine interest in and calls for a security pact. He believed the idea enjoyed widespread support among government, press, and the people. Quirino expressed uneasiness about the situation in China and equated the pact with "strong moral and economic leadership." Quirino told Lockett that a security pact "might prove the best means of more quickly bringing Japan to her responsibility among nations and relieving the United States of its burden in that country," and Lockett agreed. The American embassy in London warned that including European imperialists in the region "would open us to the accusation that we are underwriting British, French, and Dutch colonial policies." Throughout March and April, the Philippine government appeared alone in its desire for a Pacific pact.[23]

Rhee paid more attention to the Pacific pact when his requests for military assistance failed. In early April, the Korean ambassador, Dr. John M. Chang, raised the idea of a pact in a talk with State Department Far Eastern Division officials. Rhee told a press conference in May that "all democratic nations should not wait, but take definite action and help build up the democratic camp" and "form a defense bloc." By late May, the Seoul government had contacted Philippine officials. Chiang in early July evidenced interest in an anticommunist bloc. No doubt his catastrophic defeat at the battle of the Huai Hai (October 1948-January 1949), the communist crossing of the supposedly easily defendable Yangtze River banks (April 1949), and American abandonment caused Chiang to seek new ways of obtaining U.S. assistance. A security pact might provide the solution. Rhee then invited Chiang and Quirino to Korea in mid-July (Chiang visited Quirino beginning July 10) since, he remarked, all three leaders felt abandoned by the United States. Lockett thought Chiang and Rhee desired that the "Philippines take the lead and pull their chestnuts from the fire." They told Americans they intended to go ahead with the pact, with or without United States approval. Throughout July, a flurry of activity continued in the three Asian capitals to obtain American approval and garner support among Asian and Pacific nations. Rhee told a press conference, "I know that the U.S. will not oppose conclusion of any anti-Communistic alliance in the Far East."[24]

In fact, the State Department sought to discourage this particular anticommunist security pact. Secretary of State Dean Acheson sent a note to eighteen embassies that the pact proposal "is primarily a Chinese Nationalist and Rhee initiative seeking supplementary means to appeal for U.S. military aid and influence U.S. public opinion." The department strongly disapproved of the proposal, but it indicated a desire to see closer ties among Asian nations and peaceful settlement of colonial problems. To make clear to Rhee the department's position, Acheson wrote the embassy in Seoul to "tell Rhee the U.S. is not likely to be moved by maneuvers which appear designed to extract military commitments. . . . It will not have escaped Rhee that the great part of the difficulty of the department's present efforts to secure passage of a Korean aid bill [comes] from a desire of certain members of Congress to tie the Korean problem to the deteriorating situation in China."[25]

What was the impact of Rhee's call for a Pacific version of NATO? It worried American diplomats who were seeking to disengage from Chiang's debacle on the mainland and limit the commitment to Korea to economic assistance. If the Pacific pact became a reality, political pressure at home might force the administration to embrace the three Asian dictators. The pact might encourage Chiang or Rhee into military ventures that could bring about American involvement. It also would divert attention from the pressing domestic problems that had helped bring Chiang's downfall and which threatened Rhee and Quirino. Soviet and Chinese communist leaders no doubt watched the proceedings suspiciously. In duplicating NATO, the pact sought to contain communism, but what did this mean? The three Asian leaders sought some way to secure U.S. assistance and figured that a pact of Western-oriented nations in Asia would prove irresistible. Mao and his fellow guerrillas may have wondered if the pact indicated a return of imperialism to the Asian mainland. It did not seem likely that Rhee would call for it without American approval since he was often considered to be an American creation. Perhaps it signalled a change in the American policy of disengagement from China. Perhaps it meant the U.S. government would commit its resources to "liberate" China from the communists. It was confusing, since evidence suggests the Chinese communists were signalling a desire for accommodation. The Soviets may have worried most, suspecting that the United States was preparing to use the pact nations in an attack on the USSR. Obviously Chiang, Rhee, and Quirino were American puppets. If the government in Washington did not approve of their actions, it would not have permitted them to call for a Pacific pact. Had the pact been formed, had the headlines continued, it might have caused increased tension between the superpowers. As it was, it may have caused the Soviets to look favorably upon an invasion of South Korea to ensure an end to the threat.

Perhaps the high point of the discussion occurred when Chiang visited Korea in early August. Korean officials welcomed the visit, noting it would "bring the much-discussed Pacific Pact nearer realization." Rhee hoped it would result in an anticommunist Pacific Union. For four days (August 5-8), the talks dominated newspaper headlines in the Far East. Compared to publicity surrounding the visit, the joint communiqué at its conclusion was disappointing. Rhee and Chiang agreed that communism was a menace in East Asia and that a Pacific pact was necessary. They called on Quirino to "take all necessary steps to bring about the birth of this proposed union."[26] But within a few days, enthusiasm faded. Twice more Rhee said he was "eager to see this pact develop," but he felt insulted by Chiang's demands for air and naval bases inside Korea for raids against Communist China. Chiang had not given up his view of dominating the small nations about him, even in defeat. By September 1949, the proposed pact was dead.

The State Department managed to surmount each difficulty as it arose, but there was no respite, however brief. By September, Rhee had quieted appeals for military assistance, and the proposed Pacific pact was only a bad memory. The Korean army seemed capable of defending the republic from invasion, according to U.S. Army leaders. The new difficulty concerned the United Nations Commission on Korea. Its term about to expire, the commission returned to New York. The State Department had relied upon its presence along the 38th parallel to help deter a North Korean attack. The moral authority of the United Nations might cause the Soviets to respect the boundary. In late summer, however, a crisis appeared within the commission. Some of its members expected a North Korean invasion by autumn. The North Korean announcement of a nationwide election in September lent credence to the belief that the election would approve the results of such an invasion. Daily reports of clashes along the parallel and frequent accounts of battles between Rhee's security forces and communist guerrillas added to the tension. Commission members deplored rising violence and some feared for their well-being. Several believed the arms race and constant threats of war on the peninsula had frustrated their mission to help unify the former American and Soviet zones. When the Russians stepped up propaganda attacks, other members feared being caught between the superpowers. The atmosphere caused the commission to favor disbanding.[27]

In the weeks before the opening of the United Nations regular session in September, the State Department began gathering arguments urging UNCOK I to return to Korea. Ambassador Muccio, responding to department instruction, cabled a summary of the commission's work and the embassy's recommendation for a new UN commission. With recognition of the Republic of Korea the previous year, he saw no reason for the commission to interfere in internal affairs. Muccio said that the commission's value was to serve as a barrier to communist aggression. He wanted the commission's instructions altered to reflect this task noting increased military activity near the parallel, the need for neutral reporting in case of large-scale hostilities, and the feeling within the commission that it should move on to a new task. The department decided to support the commission's conclusions, although objecting to some of them, to help convince the UN Commission on Korea to continue.[28]

As the General Assembly turned to the question of Korea, it seemed certain that the delegations would support the American position. The UN commission's report noted the warlike atmosphere on the peninsula. It stated that a barbarous civil war appeared inevitable. It found Korea an armed camp and deplored the military posturing throughout the country. It suggested that the situation reflected the state of Soviet-American relations and recommended a change in its terms of reference. Acheson addressed the General Assembly on September 21 and said that the United States wanted the UN to continue its work in Korea. He said the commission had three tasks: to report on the situation along the parallel, to try to avert an outbreak of hostilities based on the influence of the United Nations, and to work for unification of the peninsula. The assembly received his speech favorably.[29]

The General Assembly approved an American-sponsored resolution on UNCOK without difficulty. The U.S. representative, Charles Fahy, introduced the resolution on September 29, 1949. A new UNCOK (several member nations wished to resign) would return to the peninsula and work to preserve the independence of the UN-sanctioned Republic of Korea. It condemned the regime in North Korea for unyielding hostility. Within a month, the Ad Hoc Political Committee of the General Assembly voted 44 to 6, with five abstentions (similar to other UN votes on the Korean situation) to approve. It rejected a Soviet resolution to disband the commission. When the Soviets moved the question to the General Assembly, it rejected the resolution by 42 to 6 (with five abstentions).[30] It was a great victory for the United States, for it kept the United Nations involved in Korea. Perhaps it would even deter a North Korean attack.

III

Success in the United Nations allowed the department to concentrate on the stalled Korean aid bill, a complex issue. Korean assistance was caught up in such larger issues as Sino-American relations and domestic politics. It was an opening for Republicans to continue their criticism of Far Eastern policy or, as they charged, the lack of it. (Perhaps part of their anger derived from the August 1949 release of the China White Paper. Behind a generalization by Acheson that "the communist regime serves not [Chinese] interests but those of Soviet Russia," the documents were a condemnation of Chiang and the policies that led to his collapse.) To members of the China lobby, it was inexplicable to do in Korea what Truman would not do for Chiang. The administration, in part, wanted Korean aid to blunt criticism of its China policy and salvage prestige. Korea was a substitute of sorts for China. Research by Nancy Tucker suggests an interesting reason for the administration's decision to make this substitution. Professor Tucker has shown that the Chinese communists and the Truman administration sought a kind of meeting ground. Mao's forces generally treated American business concerns with respect; Chinese communists dealt evenhandedly with American missionaries (perhaps desiring to use their lobbying power with the U.S. government for economic assistance). Warren W. Tozer has written that the experience of the Shanghai Power Company "substantiates the position of those who believed the Chinese communists desired American aid and cooperation. . . . The PRC [People's Republic of China] not only appeared willing to tolerate American firms for the short term but sought to establish some type of relationship with the U.S. until as late as January or February 1950." Did the executive branch desire the appearance of a strong anticommunist stand in South Korea to allow for negotiations with the new government in Peking without appearing "soft on communism"? Acheson's January 12 speech would fit this hypothesis. The aid bill symbolized America's commitment to defend the free world against aggression. Howard Schonberger offers an interesting perspective, asserting that the post-1948 change in U.S. policy for Japan from reform to rebuilding developed not from a perception of the Soviet threat but from the appearance of a "Japan lobby," the common attitudes of American and Japanese economic interests, and a certain amount of skullduggery. Is it possible that a strong stand in Korea would convince Japan of the Soviet threat, demonstrate American strength of purpose, and bring Japan within the American (economic) umbrella? While available documentation provides little illumination, it seems reasonable to suggest that, given the situation in Northeast Asia and the domestic political scene, the Korean aid bill probably had more than local significance. Of course, the program would substantially help matters in the south. Many problems in Korea, such as runaway inflation, unemployment, and substandard living conditions would ease upon success of the administration's relief and rehabilitation plan.[31]

Korea's need for economic assistance became apparent with each passing day. Government was ineffective; Rhee rewarded loyal but untrained and corrupt supporters. Korean leaders did not understand economics; they expected the United States to save the country from their mistakes. Perhaps they understood the inherent obligation of the U.S. government to protect its symbolism. In October, the American embassy's monthly economic report noted the deteriorating financial situation. The government continued heavy deficit spending; since it made up deficits by printing paper money, the government caused marked rises in consumer prices. A joint State Department-ECA team cabled from Seoul that the deficit would substantially exceed estimates. Unless the government soon adopted sounder policies, uncontrolled inflation could not be postponed. Arthur Bunce, who headed the ECA economic mission in Korea, sought to convince the Korean government of the gravity of the situation. In early December 1949, the Division of Northeast Asian Affairs summarized the situation: "ECA program in Korea and our whole policy in Korea is gravely threatened by mounting inflation." There was a good chance that "the government we are supporting may bring about its own collapse as in Nationalist China by irresponsible financial policies." A few days later, the Office of Intelligence Research analyzed inflationary trends in Korea. "This reads like China in 1948!" it commented, and predicted collapse.[32]

The deteriorating financial situation affected the military and political situation. What was the point of supplying weapons when the Seoul government was pursuing disastrous economic policies? Department officials asked how that government could exhort its people in the name of patriotism when it acted as its own worst enemy, making workers and peasants receptive to communist propaganda. Rhee wanted to increase the army, but the economy could not support the burden. An obvious failure in Korea would not be in American interests; the National Security Council in NSC 48/1 and 48/2 (December 1949) sought a consistent, organized U.S. policy with respect to Asia. To rebuild Korea economically while resisting overt and covert communist pressure would encourage pro-American nationalists to resist the Soviets and their allies elsewhere in Asia.[33]

Department planners pinned their hope on the Korean Assistance Bill. Although House Republicans had tied up the bill in the Rules Committee the previous summer, the changing seasons had altered the situation, or so department planners thought. Perhaps those congressmen who had sought to use the Korean issue to criticize administration China policy would forget their anger and help save South Korea as it tottered on the verge of collapse, threatened from within by its economic folly and without by the communist north. In October, the Senate approved the measure by a vote of 48 to 13 (34 absent). Perhaps House Republicans would join their colleagues in a spirit of bipartisanship. The department had little choice, for, without economic assistance, Korea surely would collapse within a few months. Having announced to the world that Korea was a symbol, the administration was learning the high cost of that exercise. It could not afford to let Korea fall because it had said that the Republic of Korea would survive. At a point which suggested withdrawal (Rhee's economic catastrophe and increasing violence), rhetoric had trapped the administration. It had followed the path of least resistance in Korea, and to quit the peninsula, reversing course, would have important, negative consequences. But it was slow progress. Every three months, Congress passed so-called deficiency appropriation bills that included nearly $30 million for Korea. The department reasoned that Congress was granting $120 million a year by these bills; however, it wanted an additional $30 million. When Congress reconvened, the outlook seemed favorable. Intensive lobbying helped solidify Democratic support.

Prospects improved after a series of congressional junkets to

Korea; six groups travelled to the peninsula. Muccio lobbied for the bill. He convinced visiting representatives that Korea's future (and American prestige) rested on aid, that without aid the Korean government would collapse two days after an attack. While Republicans remained skeptical, wondering whether an additional $30 million miraculously would turn the situation around, most Democrats left Korea willing to vote with the party.[34] The administration was anxious to obtain passage of the legislation. In Korea, inflation spiraled; the troubled economy caused increasing tension; and workers were restive. Rhee sought to divert attention from domestic problems by threatening invasion of the north. Meanwhile, border troops clashed with North Korean units, and ROK security forces battled guerrillas in the countryside. Rhee told Muccio that an invasion was necessary to unify the nation and thought it best to do so while Chinese communists were preoccupied with Nationalist forces in south China.[35]

As Congress prepared to reconsider the aid legislation, Secretary Acheson made a startling pronouncement (surprising to the public but not to officials privy to NSC 48). In a speech in early January 1950, to which historians would attach greater importance than contemporary observers, he described America's defense perimeter in the Pacific. It excluded Korea and Formosa from the line of defense. Although he was repeating MacArthur's earlier statement to a visiting British journalist, it was a case of bad timing. The January 12 speech before the National Press Club in Washington came a few weeks after Chiang's forces fled the mainland for Formosa. Ignoring Formosa, Acheson aroused the ire of Republican critics and the powerful China lobby. After the outbreak of war in Korea in June 1950, some people would blame Acheson for encouraging Soviet and North Korean leaders who felt the United States would allow the south to fall.[36]

What was his purpose? Declassification of the NSC 48 series has shown that the secretary was setting forth American strategic interests in Asia in line with NSC 48/2 as approved by President Truman. Seemingly, he drew a line, behind which the administration would resist vigorously communist actions; he reiterated the government's unwillingness to become involved militarily on the Asian mainland. Most interesting of all, the secretary sought to indicate that the administration wanted friendship of the new Chinese government (announced in Peking on October 1, 1949). Robert R. Simmons in *The Strained Alliance*, writing in advance of public access to NSC 48, correctly suggested that Acheson was seeking to drive a wedge between Moscow and Peking. The "hands off" Formosa policy would help convince Mao of the American desire for friendly relations. Both NSC 48 and Acheson's speech recognized the power of nationalism to resist Soviet domination, even in the case of a communist regime in China. While a policy of friendship, or at least communication, with Chinese communists was an intelligent and potentially powerful policy, it was far ahead of its time in the political atmosphere of January 1950.

The speech had important consequences. Stalin and Kim Il-sung may have reconsidered an invasion of the south. Perhaps they might have been encouraged by the statement of America's defense perimeter; perhaps they feared a Sino-American rapprochement. Mao may have felt that his signalling of reasonable intentions had worked; perhaps he was seeking a bargaining chip with Stalin. Acheson's speech caused politicians devoted to Chiang's cause to seek ways to signal the administration that they wanted an American commitment to assist the defeated Nationalists on Formosa. For the latter, the Korean aid legislation provided an excellent vehicle with which to press the executive branch. Seemingly, it was no major issue. Since the administration regarded Korea as symbolic of American strength of purpose, it might prove willing to barter some gesture to Chiang for Republican support for aid to South Korea. The Truman administration, facing partisan pressure over Acheson's speech and wishing to cut ties with Chiang's bankrupt regime, may have felt greater urgency in maintaining its Korean connection. Korea became hostage to the China lobby's demand for continued support for Chiang Kai-shek.

At this same moment, Alger Hiss was on trial for perjury in a case where emotion overshadowed fact. Hiss had been one of Roosevelt's bright young men in the New Deal days, director of special political affairs in the State Department. He accompanied

Roosevelt to Yalta. He helped arrange the San Francisco Conference of 1945. Whittaker Chambers, a *Time* magazine senior
editor, accused him of passing documents to the Soviets, of having been a member of the Communist party during the 1930s.
Hiss denied the charges; Truman and Acheson (and some prominent Republicans) defended him. Since the statute of limitations
on treason had run out, Hiss was on trial for perjury; it was his
second trial. While Hiss would continue to proclaim his inno-
cence (and historians and interested observers are still engaged
in a lively debate over the matter) the trial had an immediate
impact. As Congress renewed the debate over the Korean aid
bill, such Republican congressmen as Nixon, Judd, and Vorys
used the Hiss trial to attack Truman and his advisers for abandoning Chiang, for selling out to the communists. The trial and
Acheson's "perimeter" speech thus limited the government's room
to maneuver. Truman could refuse to compromise over support
for Chiang, lose passage of the Korean aid legislation, and watch
America's commitment to South Korea collapse. He could give
approval for economic assistance to Formosa, gain Republican
support for Korea, and find himself forced more strongly to
defend the former American zone. It appeared more and more
difficult for the U.S. government to continue a political commitment to the Republic of Korea and deny a military one. While
it is impossible to prove that Truman would intervene in Korea
to silence domestic critics, it is certainly reasonable to suggest
that it may have helped to influence his decision.

As these events swirled about him, President Truman asked
Congress for $111 million for fiscal year 1951 and urged it to
authorize belatedly the appropriations for what remained of FY
1950. He wanted to begin rehabilitation of the Korean economy
to control inflation. "Early enactment of the legislation now
pending," he said, "will . . . hasten the date when our aid can be
concluded."[37] The Senate Foreign Relations Committee reopened hearings on the request for an additional $60 million
for FY 1950. Appearing as chief witness, Acheson spent most of
his time explaining China policy. He described a worldwide communist conspiracy with the Soviets controlling their satellites by
joint economic agreements. He pointed out that in recent years

the Russians had expanded into the Far East: "During the past year the whole western world has suffered a very unfortunate and severe reverse in the communist conquest of China." He reiterated the exclusion of Formosa from America's strategic plans. Connally loyally supported Acheson, stating, "We would have Mr. Chiang Kai-shek on our hands as long as he lived, to support him and wanting more money for armies and equipment and supplies and food for all time to come, as long as he is alive and able to kick." After several days the questioning turned to Korea. Acheson believed South Korea could defend itself from a North Korean attack, but he told the committee that strong Russian or communist Chinese support would overwhelm the south. When Knowland of California asked the secretary about the American response to a Soviet-directed invasion—ironically government officials feared Rhee might act independently and invade north; no one assumed the same sense of independence for Kim—Acheson answered, "We would not undertake to resist it by military force independently. . . . If UN Charter action were taken, we would take our part in that, but probably it would not be taken because they would veto it." Again, many senators wondered why the administration wanted to spend millions in a country it would not defend when it was willing to abandon Chiang and a relatively defensible island and give up hope for recovery of the mainland.[38] Senate Republicans followed a shrewd strategy. They wanted to trade economic assistance for Korea for support for Chiang and Formosa (most parties referred to the island by its Japanese rather than its Chinese name [Taiwan]). They sought their goal by quiet means, in committee rooms and Senate corridors.

As the bill made its way through the Senate, the House began several days of floor debate on January 18, 1950. Department officials had not told House members that the Korean economy was near collapse, nor did they suggest that aid for Korea would allow the government to cut off Chiang and approach Mao, for they feared Congress would then deny aid. Uninformed congressmen wondered why it was wise to send South Korea $150 million in military and economic assistance if invasion seemed certain. Many southern Democrats and Republicans worried over ever-increasing expenditures. As John Rankin (D-Miss.) asked, "If we keep pouring money of the American taxpayers down the ratholes of Europe, Asia, Israel, Africa, and Japan, how long will it be before we will be in economic chaos?" Leo Allen of Illinois and Vorys of Ohio feared an ever-expanding national debt. Robert Chipperfield of Illinois expressed surprise that Acheson wanted money for Korea while he ignored Formosa. Donald L. Jackson of California saw no reason to make Korea a tempting target for the Russians: "If the Congress wills it we shall invest in a gambit of pawns against an opponent whose major pieces are skillfully jockeyed against both south Korea and the U.S. on terrain chosen by our opponent and on terms which he alone will dictate." Christian A. Herter of Massachusetts told his colleagues that money was better spent elsewhere. William Lemke of Nebraska claimed that Far Eastern policy came from Acheson and Hiss "and others who go to bed with Stalin and betray not only our own country but the world." Administration supporters had a difficult time matching the outrage displayed by their opponents as the aid bill became entangled in the events and heated passions of early 1950.[39]

The House narrowly defeated the bill. The vote of 193 to 191 came as a blow to Truman and Acheson. Sixty-one Democrats, mainly southerners, crossed the line to vote with Republicans. Two factors stood out. Southern Democrats and some Republicans did not accept the administration's view of Korea as an important symbol, and Republicans used the vote to signal their position on continued aid to the Nationalists. Truman and Acheson expressed dismay. The president released a statement that criticized his shortsighted opponents. In a letter released by the White House, Acheson told Truman, "This action, if not quickly repaired, will have the most far-reaching effect upon our foreign policy." He expressed concern that the bill's defeat would discourage nations resisting aggression and dependent upon American assistance. Defeat of the aid bill implied that the U.S. was an undependable ally. Acheson wrote his daughter, "This has been a tough day. . . . We now have a long road back."[40]

Despite defeat, a compromise seemed possible. Republican senators approached Acheson to suggest that aid to Korea be linked to continued economic aid for Formosa. They would persuade their fellows in the House to ease opposition. The administration gave in and offered the Far Eastern Economic Assistance Act of 1950 in place of the Korean aid bill.[41] Acheson and Senate Republicans joined to support the new legislation. Knowland said, "Korea will get its help at this session." Acheson's appearance before the Foreign Relations Committee went smoothly. Republican senators explained why Formosa merited continuing economic aid, and Defense Department witnesses made clear that there could be no military ties with the island. The chairman of the Joint Chiefs, General Omar N. Bradley, stated that "in spite of Formosa's strategic importance the disparity between U.S. military strength and our global obligations make it inadvisable to undertake employment of U.S. forces in Formosa." Acheson suggested the compromise: the administration would provide economic assistance for Korea and continue the China Aid Act for Formosa for the balance of the fiscal year. It would not enter into a long-range relationship with Chiang pending what then appeared to be a certain Chinese communist invasion of Formosa.[42]

The new bill fared equally well within the House. The Foreign Affairs Committee passed it the next day "after a strong bipartisan appeal." Judd warned of "the devastating effect inaction would have on 800,000,000 people in Asia not now behind the Iron Curtain." The House debated the bill on February 7. Herter praised the continuance of the old China Aid Act and supported economic assistance for Korea. Jackson of California called the bill a very astute move and ended his opposition. A few days later, the House passed the Far Eastern Economic Assistance Bill by 240 to 134.[43] The bill became law on February 14, 1950. Korea would receive $60 million in addition to money received under deficiency appropriations. Formosa would receive the balance of money granted under the old China Aid Act.

The cost of securing aid legislation had been high and demonstrated some of the problems of symbol creation. To make its stand credible in Korea, the administration altered its planned abandonment of Chiang and allowed the relationship to drag on through remaining appropriations under the China Aid Act. Continued aid to the Nationalists may have caused Mao to feel that his overtures were rejected; continuing aid made subsequent intervention in the straits between Formosa and the mainland more obligatory. Would the administration have had to compromise on China aid had it not wanted Korean aid? Equally important, the administration had implied a commitment to the Republic of Korea. Given its comparison of situations in China and Korea, given the loss of prestige it admitted would follow from the fall of South Korea, and given its overblown rhetoric to secure economic aid, despite the rational analysis of NSC 48/1 and 48/2, the executive branch had backed itself into a corner.

IV

Despite the promise of American aid, the situation continued to worsen in Korea. Border clashes were frequent and bloody; American intelligence officers, dependent upon ROK officers for information, figured that each side shared the blame equally. Perhaps Kim and Rhee were using incidents along the parallel to petition for or force a grant of increased military aid from their benefactors, Stalin and Truman. Perhaps they were attempting to create conditions for an invasion. Months of unit-sized fighting could result in an invasion to end provocations. Kim, of course, might have ordered trouble along the parallel to draw attention away from communist insurgents in the south. North Korean guerrillas passed deep into South Korean territory to foment rebellion. Or the answer to Kim's actions may have come from tension within the North Korean hierarchy. Kim's faction of Soviet-trained Koreans faced a strong challenge from native supporters of Pak Hun-yung. Kim and Pak might have used their respective strengths with the army and southern guerrillas to seek Stalin's favor, win support in North Korea, and appear to be the savior of the Korean people. This could have led naturally to clashes with Rhee's forces. The tangled power relationships between Kim, Pak, and Rhee may help to explain the reasons why the invasion occurred on June 25, 1950; and in addition to the rising level of violence, the economy further deteriorated.

Muccio sought to convince Rhee of the gravity of the situation. In mid-January, he had cabled the department that Rhee would not face up to the coming collapse in Korea. Rhee's "proposed remedies are not related to the magnitude of the overall problem." A few days later, Muccio presented Rhee with a formal note from the U.S. government, expressing "my government's *grave concern* over mounting inflation and recommending a drastic plan of control." He warned that Rhee must act immediately.[44]

The situation did not improve in the weeks after Muccio's talk with Rhee. The embassy in Korea cabled the department that "despite strongest representations ROK does not recognize grave consequences of continued deficit spending." When the downward spiral continued into March, Far Eastern desk officers discussed the problem and concluded Rhee would do nothing to stave off economic collapse. He was convinced that "the United States could not let ROK fall without incurring gravest political repercussions." Passage of Korean aid had denied Washington any leverage with Rhee. He clearly expected the United States to save his regime and concentrated his efforts on an invasion of North Korea. He was learning well how to use certain words and phrases to manipulate his benefactor.[45]

Administration officials decided to stop aid unless the Korean economy showed immediate improvement. Paul Hoffman told Rhee that "further inflation will jeopardize the entire ECA program in Korea." He noted that, as administrator of ECA, "I cannot justify an aid program for Korea . . . unless I am convinced forthright, immediate effort will be made to control inflation in Korea." In April, government officials publicly warned the South Korean leader that they would terminate aid if the economy showed no change.[46] That position appears extreme, for it would have meant reversing a hard-fought policy commitment, established over the previous three years. Had war not occurred when it did, it seems reasonable that the U.S. government would have continued to threaten Rhee, that he would have ignored the warnings, and that economic assistance would have continued.

Discussions and decisions that resulted in NSC 68 did little

to solve paradoxes in Korea. NSC 68 was a comprehensive statement of national security policy that developed from a presidential directive to analyze the world situation and propose an
American response. It affected the Korean situation in two important ways: (1) by suggesting that the West mobilize its moral
and material strength to meet the Soviet challenge, it furthered
the unreality surrounding creation of the Korean symbol; and
(2) by arguing that an expanded commitment to national defense
would not worsen the economy, it implied that the government
would continue Korean assistance despite the problems with
Syngman Rhee. While many historians consider NSC 68 a strategic reassessment, there was no changing perspective on Korea,
just an implied willingness to allocate additional resources to
prop up the ROK government. In fact, NSC 68 barely mentions
Korea, though it is full of catchphrases of the cold war denoting
that the United States would continue on course in Korea, allowing itself to be manipulated increasingly by Rhee and others.
NSC 68 and the people who drafted it (under the direction of
Paul Nitze) belied the insular American perception of the world.

By June 1950, the situation looked bleak in Korea. American
army officers believed the Korean army had enough arms for
defense, but they wondered if Korean soldiers had the will to
fight for a nation in desperate economic straits. The Korean
government seemed powerless to prevent economic collapse.
Rhee had figured correctly that the United States would not cut
off aid. The history of Korea between the wars ended with the
Far Eastern Economic Assistance Act of 1950. Little changed
from February 14 to June 25. The economy continued to deteriorate; the government spent money irrationally; inflation spi-
raled. In March and April, the department publicly warned Rhee
that it would suspend aid unless his government moved to control spending, printing of paper money, corruption, inflation.
There were repeated clashes along the parallel; American intelligence officers and UN observers had difficulty determining
whether North or South Korea had initiated clashes. The embassy expected war each day. Rhee and Kim Il-sung issued bel-
licose statements; each pleaded for more arms and promises of

support when war broke out. Many American officials expected war in the peninsula; they wondered only when it would begin.

Events of January and February 1950, principally the linking of Korea to the China debate, pushed the Truman administration to defend the independence of the Republic of Korea. When North Korean troops crossed the parallel, the administration had little room to maneuver. For months it had restated the symbolic importance of Korea and promised a commitment to its continued survival. As Chiang Kai-shek was defeated on the China mainland and fled to Formosa, as European colonialism declined in Asia and with the tentative American approach to the PRC, the United States needed to make a dramatic stand against communism to reassure worried allies. Pressures were great at home. Alger Hiss's conviction on January 25, 1950, had cast doubt on the bona fides of the nation's diplomatic corps. Had it surrendered Poland at Yalta? Did it give away China? Did it employ communists or communist sympathizers? Republicans attacked the administration. The greatest witchhunt in American history was gathering momentum in the months after a little-known Republican senator from Wisconsin, Joseph R. McCarthy, searching for a reelection issue, had chosen to accuse the administration of harboring communists in the State Department in a speech before the Republican Ladies Club of Wheeling, West Virginia, in February 1950. In Truman's decision to intervene in Korea, scholars must take into account the affect of Korea as a symbol and the process that created it. Future actions in Asia would bear striking resemblance to American action and inaction in and about Korea: policy drift, the subordination of local reality to requirements of the superpower confrontation, the elevation of symbols, a deepening and unwanted commitment, and, finally, a quandary from which there was no escape "with honor" and a minimal loss of prestige.

The tragic result came home when war erupted. The most reasonable explanation of the origins of the Korean War comes from Edmund S. Wehrle and Robert R. Simmons. As they have written, war most likely occurred for reasons contained within the three-sided rivalry of Kim, Pak, and Rhee. While the South Korean economy tottered and workers grew increasingly rebellious, Rhee was moving to strengthen his army. It is possible that by autumn 1950 he might have been in a position to attack the north. Pak watched both rivals uneasily and worried that he might be cut out. Kim controlled the north; Rhee was having success in wiping out southern communists who were the basis of Pak's strength despite his exile in the north. Pak might have forced Kim to invade to save his supporters; Kim might have wanted to invade to seize the mantle of nationalism from Pak. Perhaps Pak overestimated his strength and Rhee's weakness, and promised Kim a fairly easy conquest. Regardless of the war's origins, it underlines the tragedy of American policy. Had the bipolar, confrontationist view not triumphed, had the U.S. government not made Korea into a symbol it could not abandon and instead dealt realistically with the issue, Truman and his advisers might have been able to see that war started not because of a Stalin master plan but to solve problems arising from the end of the Second World War that the superpowers had failed to solve. The United States might not have intervened in the last stages of the Chinese civil war (preventing the communist invasion of Taiwan) and thereby retained chances of a dialogue with the new leadership. Instead, pressed and trapped in a situation of its own making, the Truman administration took the path of least resistance and decided to intervene in Korea. The United States still struggles with the consequences of that decision and the reasoning process which produced it.

Conclusion

THE confusing situation in Korea seemingly cleared as the early morning sun of June 25, 1950, revealed a full-scale North Korean invasion of the Republic of Korea. "Cold warrior" thinking triumphed, and the U.S. government moved to intervene. Many American officials at the time believed that Soviet leaders in Moscow had ordered their Korean puppet, Kim Il-sung, to probe a suspected weak point in American defenses in the western Pacific. Possibly this invasion marked the beginning of a Third World War, a prelude to other Soviet aggression along the Russian border. President Truman reacted almost immediately, ordering military units to help defend South Korea. He would not permit the attack to pass unpunished. The United Nations joined in the defense, and what was then known as the free world showed its determination to resist communist aggression.

This perspective, comforting as it might have been to the Truman administration and cold warriors (then and now), was not a fair assessment. The U.S. government had helped bring about a situation making war nearly inevitable. It interpreted the invasion in a manner that changed the meaning of the Korean civil war, altered the intent of NSC 68, and meant changed relations with the new government in Peking and leftwing nationalists fighting in Southeast Asia. The American government acted on its misperception of events in and about Korea to set forth on twenty-five tragic years of involvement on the Asian mainland, contesting Asian anticolonialism but believing it was resisting Soviet-directed Asian communism.

American foreign policy went through four phases reflecting the changing situation in the Korean peninsula and the development of Korea as symbolic of American determination to defend nations resisting communist aggression. During the Second World War, the government in Washington had made no plans to deal with the situation it would encounter in Korea. Despite discussions about a postwar Korean trusteeship (and the need for radical reform), American diplomats did not study the probable situation after Japan's defeat nor Korea's curious relationship with more important areas. The problem of drift arose. The second period lasted from the end of the war until the winter of 1946-47. The State Department ignored mounting problems and Soviet obstinacy in Korea, let General Hodge flounder about in confusion, and sought an elusive general agreement with the Soviet Union. In Korea, expatriate Koreans came to power, moderates lost out, and the situation deteriorated.

Korea's rise as a symbol marked the beginning of the third phase. Rebuffed by the Soviets, unable to understand the situation in the south, armed with a bipolar worldview and warned by military leaders that Korea was a strategic trap, policymakers agreed that troop withdrawal must wait. American diplomats unilaterally made Korea a symbol of American determination to resist Soviet expansion and pinned the nation's prestige on continued survival of a noncommunist regime in the south. They sought a large economic assistance program, United Nations involvement, and delayed military withdrawal. When this phase ended, the situation continued to deteriorate while the U.S. government remained tied to Rhee's survival. Domestic politics and international events combined during the final stage of American policy to make Korea a litmus test of the Truman administration's resolve. A series of Western reverses, including the collapse of Nationalist China, caused the government to seek a substitute. Domestic pressure from Republican congressmen, upset over the nation's failure in China, made it difficult for diplomats to abandon Korea as they had China. The administration may have sought to use a strong stand in Korea to open relations with Mao and help convince Japan to enter the American orbit. Despite Rhee's disastrous economic situation and his government's suppression of civil liberties, the Truman administration was forced to prop up the Republic of Korea with whatever measures were necessary. Ultimately, and in part because of reasons outside the rise of the Korean symbol, the administration intervened militarily in Korea after the invasion of June 1950.

For many scholars, American policy toward Korea in the latter 1940s became important because of the Korean War; however, it would have been important had war never erupted. Many scholars look to this period solely to answer questions surrounding the outbreak of war; they fail to see that the period had an independent significance. It sheds light on a reasonably "pure" example of cold war diplomacy. There was no sizeable Korean or pro-Korean vote in the United States, and Korea had little or no economic value (no minerals, no valuable resources, no strategic ports, etc.). The lack of domestic importance gave the administration more freedom to act than situations in Poland or the Middle East. But instead of acting in a manner calculated to further the nation's security (and at minimum cost), the administration created a symbol that did little to advance genuine security and potentially could (and did) embroil the United States in no-win situations. American policy toward and about Korea is an interesting case study. It helped establish the pattern for future American policy toward Asian countries caught up in the throes of nationalism amidst the superpower confrontation.

The situation in Korea demonstrated the worst side effects of the cold war and the "containment" philosophy. The United States government became engaged in colossal misperception and simplification to make the world in all its different and unrelated ways fit the bipolar view. Korea was a prime example. As the Second World War drew to a close, Korea was on the verge of collapse. Had there been no cold war, no Soviet "threat," there still would have been difficult times. The United States ignored the internal situation and the need to end Japanese colonialism, satisfy impatient Korean nationalism, and establish a democratic government. Tying resolution of the Korean question to its relationship with the Soviet Union, the U.S. ignored the most important problem. As it would again and again in the decades after the Second World War, the U.S. government concentrated on a bipolar worldview and ignored the social/economic basis for Third World leftwing nationalism. The American government often assumed that native communists were Soviet puppets (as it did in Korea). It assumed that reactionary politicians such as Rhee, who were in fact the cause of peasant distress and often had collaborated with the Japanese, were deserving of American support. American leaders were not evil men, nor did they seek to enslave the world to benefit big business or multinational corporations. They were caught in a world that contained more variables than they could handle. Surface confidence hid fears. Kennan's containment view was comforting, for it enabled diplomats to avoid reality with a comprehensive, manageable outlook. Right or wrong, they could explain and deal with any situation.

The other side of the emergence of containment was the process of symbol creation. The State Department allowed the Korean situation to simmer; within two years after liberation, it was critical. Rather than cut losses and withdraw, the government in Washington began seeking a means to withdraw "gracefully," that is, without the appearance of being forced out. Containment argued that withdrawal from Korea would mean a serious loss of prestige; America's "loss" would be Russia's "gain." The government ignored reality, decided to "save" Korea from Soviet-dominated communism, and elevated the troubled peninsula to symbolic status. Perhaps symbols obey Parkinson's law: their importance and use expands to fill available space. Initially, the symbol hid American weaknesses and the desire to withdraw. As the cost of that initial process increased (i.e., forcing the United Nations into line, pressuring Canada, urging congressional support, contending with Rhee who understood the symbol's manipulative possibilities), the importance and use of the symbol increased. By 1949, the Truman administration sought a fundamental change in American Asian policy to adapt to Mao's victory over Chiang and to contest Soviet expansion. Korea had an important role. It would allow the administration to approach Mao without appearing "soft on communism" and would "buck up" reluctant Japanese leaders. The importance of Korea increased, and American freedom of action decreased as the government followed the path of least resistance. Containment and the symbol process revolutionized American foreign policy, for it meant that certain catchwords, certain ideas, and certain situations would bring a predictable result. By stating anticommunist credentials, by raising the Soviet bogeyman, by claiming to defend American values, by playing up to conservative elements of American policy, Asian leaders could (and did) secure American backing, assistance, and sometimes troops. Policy became hostage to the symbol. The Truman administration lost its independence on the Korea issue. It could not withdraw. It could not threaten Rhee; he knew the threats were empty. It could not easily explain Korea to a skeptical Congress, and the China lobby limited the administration's room to maneuver. The sad legacy of Korean policy is evident today.

When North Korea invaded the south, it made a review of the components of American policy impossible. There will always be some mystery shrouding the outbreak of war, but Truman's decision to intervene made previous policy unalterable. The Simmons-Wehrle hypothesis heightens the unfortunate aspect of American involvement in the conflict. North and South Korea fought for reasons within Korea; the answer lies in the three-sided rivalry between Kim Il-sung, Pak Hun-yung, and Syngman Rhee. In maintaining a divided peninsula, in creating antagonistic regimes in Pyongyang and Seoul, in denying power to native nationalists who deserved the chance to lead their people, the Soviet Union and United States helped create conditions for war. Many Americans would see the Korean conflict as a time when the United States stopped Russian expansion, when the nation defended the free world from communist aggression. It ended any chance for the United States government to understand the dynamics of Asian nationalism, a movement perhaps exploited but not controlled by the Soviet Union, and made difficult any hope for normal relations with the People's Republic of China. Having resisted the Soviets in Korea, the United States would view conflicts in Asian countries as a matter of resisting Chinese communist or Soviet aggression. For twenty-odd years, the United States supported regimes whose values were antithetical to the American system but whose anticommunist credentials were impeccable. It missed the chance to support nationalist though left-leaning revolutionaries; it missed the chance to create strong regional powers all opposed to one another (Vietnam, China, Russia, for example), who might look to the United States for aid. To Asian countries, America would be the distant "barbarian." By unilaterally adopting its particular worldview, by holding to it in the face of minimal support among allies and neutrals, by following its tenets in places such as Korea, the United States opposed legitimate nationalism and allowed the Soviet Union to appear as the defender and friend of anti-colonial movements.

Notes

1. *Department of State Bulletin* 5 (Dec. 13, 1941):519-20; Cordell Hull, *Memoirs of Cordell Hull*, 2 vols. (New York, 1948), 2:1125-26.

2. Robert T. Oliver, *Syngman Rhee: The Man Behind the Myth* (New York, 1955), p. 175; U.S., Department of State, *Foreign Relations of the United States 1942* (Washington, D.C., 1960), 1:858 (hereafter cited as *FR* followed by the appropriate year). Rhee had sent his credentials as early as July 1941, but Under Secretary Welles, in a discussion with Rhee and department officials, recommended caution, 895.00/829, Department of State, Decimal File, Record Group 59, National Archives and Records Service, Washington, D.C. (hereafter cited as NARS following the file number).

3. Oliver, p. 176.

4. *FR 1942*, 1:860-61; 895.01/81, NARS, Gauss to secretary of state, Feb. 28, 1942.

5. *FR 1942*, 1:862-63; 895.01/73, NARS, American embassy London to the secretary of state, Feb. 28, 1942.

6. *FR 1942*, 1:863-64.

7. Oliver, p. 178; 895.01/79, NARS, Langdon to Under Secretary Welles, memorandum, Feb. 20, 1942.

8. Oliver, p. 180; E. Grant Meade, *American Military Government in Korea* (New York, 1951), p. 43. The decision had been reached earlier: 740.00115 PW/1144, NARS, by Dec. 6, 1941 (letter, Legal Adviser to Dept. of Commerce).

9. *FR 1942*, 1:863, 865; Richard C. Allen, *Korea's Syngman Rhee, An Unauthorized Portrait* (Rutland, Vt., 1960), p. 63.

10. Oliver, pp. 181-83.

11. *FR 1942*, China: 730-31.

12. *FR 1942*, 1:870, 872, 869.

13. Ibid., pp. 872-75.

14. Oliver, p. 188; *FR 1943*, 3:1093-94, 1096.

15. *FR 1942*, 1:868-69; the Chinese alternated Russian fears with imperialist dreams; see *FR 1942*, China: 748, 735-36; *FR 1943*, 3:1095.

16. For background on Britain's Indian problem, see *FR 1942*, 1:619-90, passim; LaFeber's article is in the *American Historical Review* 80 (Dec. 1975): 1277-95; see also Christopher Thorne, "Indochina and Anglo-American Relations, 1942-1945," *Pacific Historical Review* 45 (Feb. 1976): 73-96; George C. Herring, "The Truman Adminis-

tration and the Restoration of French Sovereignty in Indochina," *Diplomatic History* 2 (Spring 1977): 97-117; Robert J. McMahon, "Anglo-American Diplomacy and the Reoccupation of the Netherlands East Indies," *Diplomatic History* 2 (Winter 1978): 1-24, for a good starting point for understanding how the American government dealt with the problem of colonial empires and nationalism during the war; *FR 1942*, 1:867, 871.

17.   By April 1, the negotiations had broken down over the limited "dominion status" the British offered the peoples of the Indian subcontinent, *FR 1942*, 1:623; by April 7, the Indian Congress "decided unanimously to reject Cripps's proposals," ibid., pp. 630-31; on April 11, Churchill sent FDR a copy of Cripps's messages: "There is clearly no hope of agreement and I shall start home on Sunday," ibid., p. 632; FDR was disappointed with the Cripps failure, ibid., pp. 633-34; Hull noted "a joint statement of Pacific War aims at this time would raise a number of complex problems relating to the future of many Oriental peoples," ibid., p. 645; *FR 1943*, 3:1091-92; 895.01/100A, NARS, Apr. 11, 1942, memorandum by Pacific War Council to president; 895.01/98-1/2, NARS, Aug. 13, 1942, political adviser to secretary of state.

18.   895.01/232, NARS, Apr. 15, 1943; 895.00/840, NARS, Oct. 10, 1942, memorandum by Division of Far Eastern Affairs; 895.01/363, NARS, July 10, 1943; see also U.S., Congress, House, *Congressional Record*, 77th Cong., 2d sess., 1942, 88, pt. 5:6003; ibid., 78th Cong., 1st sess., 1943, 89, pt. 2:2799; ibid., 78th Cong., 1st sess., 1943, 89, pt. 1:30. The records do not show the origins of and the reasons for the Bloom resolution; presumably it was the result of Rhee's tireless efforts.

19.   Cho Soon-sung, *Korea in World Politics, 1940-1950* (Berkeley, 1967), p. 18; Robert E. Sherwood, *Roosevelt and Hopkins* (New York, 1948), p. 773.

20.   Chang Chi-yun, *Record of the Cairo Conference* (Taipei, Taiwan, 1953), pp. 2, 6, 9-10; Cho, pp. 18, 20; *FR 1943*, Conferences at Cairo and Teheran: 257, 325, 334, 389. Hereafter cited as *FR 1943*, Cairo.

21.   *FR 1943*, Cairo: 434, 449; after Stalin agreed with the communiqué at Teheran, it was issued: ibid., pp. 376, 566.

22.   Hull, 2:1584; the Chinese blamed the British and vice versa: 895.01/335, NARS, Apr. 18, 1944, American embassy China to secretary of state; 895.01/6-2944, NARS, American embassy China to secretary of state.

23.   Meade, p. 44; *FR 1943*, 3:1096; *New York Times*, Dec. 6, 1943, p. 6; 895.01/315, NARS, Dec. 6, 1943, embassy China to secretary of state.

24.   Samuel Eliot Morison, *Strategy and Compromise* (Boston 1958), pp. 88-89.

25.   *FR 1944*, 5:1194, 1225-27, 1291.

26.   Ibid., pp. 1228-29.

27.   Ibid., pp. 1240-41; Harley Notter File, NARS, RG 59, Box 56, PG-4, "Present Trends of Soviet Foreign Policy," Sept. 18, 1943; Box 56, PG-28, "Possible Soviet Attitudes Towards Far Eastern Questions," Oct. 2, 1943. The Notter File is valuable but disappointing. The participants seemingly recognized the probability of Soviet expansion in East Asia but formulated general responses. While some place great emphasis on this file for Korea, these conversations did not lead to any detailed understanding of the relation of Soviet power to Korea. Even the idea of trusteeship lacked details. Seemingly one part of government dealt in theory and another part in reality, ignoring each other.

28.   *FR 1945*, Malta and Yalta: 770; Thomas H. Greer, *What Roosevelt Thought* (East Lansing, Mich., 1958), p. 169; James F. Byrnes, *Speaking Frankly* (New York, 1947), p. 221. For the earlier attempt to arrive at an agreement with the Chinese and British,

see *FR 1944*, 5:1297; 895.01/6-1644, NARS, British embassy to Ballantine; 895.01/7-1744, NARS, memorandum of conversation with Sir George Samson, Ballantine, Stanton, Blakeslee, Notter, Dickover, Borton, McCune; 895.01/7-1844, NARS, draft of oral statement, Samson to Ballantine; 895.01/7-2844, NARS, Gauss to secretary of state.

29. *FR 1945*, Malta and Yalta:358-61; Cho, p. 28; Meade, pp. 45-46; Goodrich, pp. 11-12; Lisle A. Rose, *Roots of Tragedy* (Westport, Conn., 1976), pp. 21-37; Daniel Yergin, *Shattered Peace* (Boston, 1977), pp. 66-68, 138-39, 155-56.

30. Oliver, p. 200. The publicity given this Rhee-State Department pas de deux forced Churchill to answer questions in the House of Commons as to whether there was some substance to Rhee's charges. Churchill said there were no secret agreements on Korea.

31. *FR 1945*, 6:1028.

32. Ibid., pp. 1029-30; 895.01/5-2945, NARS, from Chungking illuminates the KPG statement.

33. *Department of State Bulletin* 12 (June 10, 1945): 1058-59; *New York Times*, June 9, 1945, pp. 1-2; *FR 1945*, 6:1032-36. There is no record of any department reply to this letter. Also, Rhee even charged existence of a "Korean Liberation Committee" in Vladivostok (that Kennan denied). See *FR 1945*, 6:1022-23, 1026; 895.01/7-545, NARS, memorandum of meeting Rhee with officers of Division of Far Eastern Affairs.

34. *FR 1945*, 6:1024-25; ibid., p. 975.

35. Ibid., p. 1025; 740.0011 PW/3-145, NARS, Division of Japanese Affairs to secretary of state, including letter from Kim Koo.

36. *FR 1945*, 2:191, 975, 1242.

37. Ibid., p. 561; Arthur C. Bunce, "The Future of Korea, Part I," *Far Eastern Survey*, Apr. 19, 1944, pp. 67-70 and "The Future of Korea, Part II," *Far Eastern Survey*, May 17, 1944, pp. 85-88.

38. Gregory Henderson, *Korea: The Politics of the Vortex* (Cambridge, Mass., 1968); *FR 1945*, 6:563.

39. Lisle A. Rose, *Dubious Victory: The United States and the End of World War II* (Kent, Ohio, 1973), p. 223; Herbert Feis, *The Atomic Bomb and the End of World War II* (Princeton, N.J., 1966), p. 13; U.S., Department of Defense, *The Entry of the Soviet Union into the War Against Japan: Military Plans, 1941-1945* (Washington, D.C., 1955), pp. 51-52, 70, 78.

40. *FR 1945*, Potsdam, 1:14.

41. Ibid., p. 47.

42. Ibid., pp. 310, 311-14, 927.

43. *FR 1945*, 7:914; Harry S. Truman, *Year of Decisions* (Garden City, N.Y., 1955), pp. 316-17, 433-34; Cho, p. 46; *FR 1945*, Potsdam, 2:631.

44. *FR 1945*, Potsdam, 2:253, 264, 606. Stimson summed up the danger, saying that if the British and French refused to discuss a trusteeship for Indochina (as Stalin suggested), the Russians might forego a trusteeship for Korea and administer it alone.

45. Ibid., p. 351; Feis, p. 97; Truman, p. 383.

46. Roy Appleman, *United States Army in the Korean War* (Washington, D.C., 1961), pp. 2-3; *FR 1945*, 6:1039.

47. John M. Allison, *Ambassador from the Prairie* (Boston, 1973), pp. 116-17; U-Gene Lee, "American Policy Toward Korea, 1942-1947: Formulation and Execution," (Ph.D. diss., Georgetown University, 1973), pp. 58-59.

48. Truman, pp. 317, 444-45; Meade, p. 91.

49. Lee Won-sul, "The Impact of United States Occupation Policy on the Socio-Political Structure of South Korea, 1945-1948," (Ph.D. diss., Western Reserve University, 1961), pp. 44-45; Bruce Cumings, "American Policy and Korean Liberation," in *Without Parallel: The American-Korean Relationship Since 1945*, ed. Frank Baldwin (New York, 1974), p. 46; Cho, p. 51; Truman, pp. 440-44; U-Gene Lee, p. 61.

CHAPTER TWO

1. George M. McCune, "Korea—The First Year of Liberation," *Pacific Affairs* 20 (Mar. 1947): 4. If one may judge from the Harley Notter File, an air of unreality dominated discussion of the Korean issue. Perhaps events moved too swiftly for discussion to have much effect.

2. E. Grant Meade, *American Military Government in Korea* (New York, 1951), pp. 45, 51.

3. U-Gene Lee, "American Policy Toward Korea, 1942-1947: Formulation and Execution," (Ph.D. diss., Georgetown University, 1973), pp. 66, 68; Richard E. Lauterbach, "Hodge's Korea," *Virginia Quarterly Review* 23 (July 1947): 351; Edgar Snow, "We Meet Russia in Korea," *Saturday Evening Post*, Mar. 31, 1946, p. 19; Barbara W. Tuchman, *Stilwell and the American Experience in China, 1941-1945* (New York, 1970), p. 521; Robert T. Oliver, *Syngman Rhee, The Man Behind The Myth* (New York, 1955), p. 202; U.S. Army Center for Military History, "History of United States Armed Forces in Korea" (hereafter "History USAFIK"), vol. 1, chap. 1, p. 1; for more on the situation in north China in 1945-46, see Charles M. Dobbs, "American Marines in North China, 1945-6," *South Atlantic Quarterly* 76 (Summer 1977): 318-31.

4. Gregory Henderson, *Korea: The Politics of the Vortex* (Cambridge, Mass., 1968), pp. 123, 116.

5. Henderson, p. 123.

6. U-Gene Lee, p. 70; Lauterbach, p. 352.

7. Letter, CG XXIV Corps to all Commanders of Units, Aug. 25, 1945, "Indoctrination," Historical Files. Records of the occupation are housed in boxes, without order, at the Records Center at Suitland, Md. As one of many who has tried to find his way through Suitland, I can attest to the difficulty of digging.

8. George M. McCune and Arthur Grey, *Korea Today* (Cambridge, Mass., 1950), pp. 25-26, 37; Bruce Cumings, "American Policy and Korean Liberation," in *Without Parallel: The American-Korean Relationship Since 1945*, ed. Frank Baldwin (New York, 1974), pp. 48-49; George M. McCune, "Occupation Politics in Korea," *Far Eastern Survey*, Feb. 13, 1946, p. 33.

9. Lee Won-sul, "The Impact of United States Occupation Policy on the Socio-Political Structure of South Korea, 1945-1948," (Ph.D. diss., Western Reserve University, 1961), pp. 53-56; U-Gene Lee, pp. 107-8; Robert A. Scalapino and Lee Chong-sik, *Communism in Korea, Part I: The Movement* (Berkeley, 1972), pp. 234-37. Lee Won-sul discusses the occupation and the fate of Korean collaborators with insight. He proves that Rhee's strongest supporters come from that group which never would be punished.

10. Cumings, p. 56; Joyce and Gabriel Kolko, *The Limits of Power* (New York, 1972), p. 280; "History USAFIK," vol. 1, chap. 1, p. 34; chap. 3, p. 9; chap. 8, p. 37; Cho Soon-sung, *Korea in World Politics, 1940-1950* (Berkeley, 1967), pp. 45, 83; Richard E. Lauterbach, *Danger From the East* (New York, 1946), p. 211; Scalapino and Lee, p. 241; Lee Won-sul, p. 54; McCune and Grey, p. 44.

11. Meade, p. 59; Henderson, pp. 114-17; U-Gene Lee, pp. 108-10; Lee Won-sul, pp. 56-60; Scalapino and Lee, pp. 237-40.

12. *New York Times*, Sept. 8, 1945, p. 2; U-Gene Lee, pp. 81, 85.

13. Meade, p. 59; U-Gene Lee, p. 95; *New York Times*, Sept. 6, 1945, p. 2; "History USAFIK," vol. 1, chap. 7, p. 28.

14. Kolko, pp. 280-81; "History USAFIK," vol. 1, chap. 4, p. 18; U-Gene Lee, pp. 128-29; *New York Times*, Sept. 10, 1945, pp. 1, 2; Sept. 11, 1945, pp. 1, 9, 22; Sept. 12, 1945, p. 1; Sept. 13, 1945, p. 8.

15. Henderson, p. 121; Meade, pp. 76, 51; for the extent of relief services by American authorities, see *Summation of Non-Military Activities in Japan and Korea #1-5* (after this, there was a separate issue for Korea), issued by the Supreme Commander, Allied Powers.

16. Meade, p. 8.

17. Cho, p. 68; Meade, pp. 61, 63; U-Gene Lee, p. 167; Scalapino and Lee, p. 246; Donald S. McDonald, "Field Experiences in Military Government," in Carl J. Friedrich and Associates, *American Experiences in Military Government in WWII*, pt. 16, *Military Government in Korea* (New York, 1948), p. 368.

18. "History USAFIK," vol. 1, chap. 4, p. 39; McDonald, pp. 356, 359, 371-72; Lauterbach, p. 354; U-Gene Lee, pp. 88; Meade, p. 47; C. Clyde Mitchell, *Korea: Second Failure in Asia* (Washington, D.C., 1951), p. 16; Nam Koon-woo, *The North Korean Communist Leadership, 1945-1965* (Tuscaloosa, Ala., 1974), p. 26.

19. Benninghoff's conservative beliefs reinforced Hodge's sense of preserving the status quo until some future agreement with the Soviets. Both men meant well; neither was qualified for his near-impossible task. It demonstrates the need for experienced people, if such people existed in 1945 and could be spared for Korea.

20. See Benninghoff's early despatches in U.S., Department of State, *Foreign Relations of the United States 1945* (Washington, D.C., 1969), vol. 6, to demonstrate the cultural baggage he brought with him to Korea. He instinctively sought out the conservatives, overlooked the moderates, and disliked the leftwing nationalists. The *Foreign Relations* series is hereafter cited as *FR* followed by the appropriate date.

21. Meade, p. 76; *FR 1945*, 6:1049-53; Hodge sent a similar message to MacArthur on September 13. Benninghoff called Korea "a powderkeg ready to explode."

22. Henderson, pp. 121-22.

23. *FR 1945*, 6:1049-50, 1073-86; Lauterbach, p. 202.

24. *FR 1945*, 6:1069; Meade, pp. 61-63.

25. Meade, p. 65.

26. *FR 1945*, 6:1061-63.

27. Ibid., pp. 1070-71, 1091-92.

28. For the development of the conflict between Rhee and State Department officials, see chapter 1.

29. Henderson, pp. 126-27; Dickover (Japan) to Vincent, 895.01/9-2445, Department of State, Decimal File, Record Group 59, National Archives and Records Service, Washington, D.C. (hereafter cited as NARS following the file number); Oliver, pp. 210-12.

30. 895.01/9-2145, NARS, Hurley to secretary of state. The Chinese wanted the KPG to return to Korea: 895.01/9-1745, NARS, secretary of state; *FR 1945*, 6:1058, 1060.

31. Given their total lack of guidance from superiors in Washington, it was natural that Benninghoff and Hodge would look to Rhee as a means to help them out of

their plight. Cumings and the Kolkos are mistaken when they suggest that the sad result of American occupation implied evil intentions. Benninghoff and Hodge were in over their heads and no one in Washington truly heeded their call.

32. *New York Times*, Oct. 21, 1945, p. 30.
33. Ibid.; *FR 1945*, 6:1104.
34. Henderson, p. 113.
35. Max Beloff, *Soviet Policy in the Far East, 1944-1951* (New York, 1953), p. 159; "History USAFIK," vol. 2, chap. 4, p. 21; U-Gene Lee, pp. 151-52.
36. Cho, p. 128; U.S., Department of State, *North Korea: A Case Study in the Techniques of Takeover*, Far Eastern Series 103 (Washington, D.C., 1961), pp. 3, 5 (hereafter cited as FES 103); Cho, p. 86; Nam, pp. 15-16; Kolko, p. 293; McCune and Grey, p. 52; Lauterbach, p. 214.
37. FES 103, p. 103; Nam, pp. 19-20; Suh Dae-sook, *The Korean Communist Movement, 1918-1948* (Princeton, N.J., 1967), p. 293; Robert R. Simmons, *The Strained Alliance* (New York, 1975), pp. 23-24.
38. Nam, pp. 14, 26; FES 103, pp. 3, 6.
39. Cho, p. 93; McCune and Grey, pp. 58-60.
40. Cho, p. 93; *FR 1945*, 6:1110-11, 1115-16; Harold R. Isaacs, *No Peace for Asia* (New York, 1947), p. 89.
41. "History USAFIK," vol. 2, chap. 1, p. 36.
42. "History USAFIK," vol. 2, chap. 1, pp. 22-23; chap. 4, pp. 16, 25; *FR 1945*, 6:1055-56, 1059-60, 1106-8; Meade, p. 52; Lauterbach, p. 244. Hodge wrote MacArthur on November 2 that "communistic activities are reaching the point where they may gain control . . . am sure are Russian instigated." At this time Hodge began forwarding rumors the Soviets were dismantling hydroelectric and industrial plants in northern Korea: *FR 1945*, 6:1112-13, 1118-19.
43. *FR 1945*, 6:1091-92, 1112.
44. Ibid., pp. 1113-14.
45. Ibid., pp. 1122-24, 1131-32; U-Gene Lee, pp. 183-84. The War Department pressed the State Department to issue a news release about Korea to inform the American public of the difficulties faced by Hodge and to prepare them in case of an outbreak. Memo, Lt. Gen. Hull, A/C/L, OPD to Col. Vittrup, 10 Nov 45 sub: Immediate Press release on situation in Korea: OPD 336 Korea, RG 218, Records of the Plans and Operations Division, U.S. Army.
46. *FR 1945*, 6:1127.
47. Ibid., p. 1138.

CHAPTER THREE

1. *FDR's Press Conferences*, #636, Apr. 18, 1940, vol. 15, pp. 290-91, as cited in William G. Morris, "The Korean Trusteeship, 1941-1947: The United States, Russia, and the Cold War" (Ph.D. diss., University of Texas, 1974), p. 4; Willard Range, *Franklin D. Roosevelt's World Order* (Athens, Ga., 1959), passim.
2. Walter LaFeber, "Roosevelt, Churchill, and Indochina: 1942-1945," *American Historical Review* 80 (Dec. 1975): 1277-95.
3. Hugh Borton memo, May 23, 1943, T-317, Box 34, Harley Notter File, Record Group 59, National Archives and Records Service, Washington, D.C. (hereafter called as NARS following the file number).

4. 740.00119 Control (Korea)/10-1045, NARS; U.S., Department of State, *Foreign Relations of the United States 1945* (Washington, D.C., 1969), 6:1067-68, 1094, 1099, 1100 (hereafter cited as *FR* followed by the appropriate year); James F. Byrnes, *Speaking Frankly* (New York, 1947), pp. 107-8; U-Gene Lee, "American Foreign Policy Toward Korea, 1942-1947: Formulation and Execution," (Ph.D. diss., Georgetown University, 1973).

5. *FR 1945*, 6:110.

6. Ibid., pp. 1106-9, 1112-13, 1118, 1121-22.

7. Rad, CG USAFIK to SCAP, 100927/1, Nov. 10, 1945, loose messages, Historical Files (records of the occupation), Records Center, Suitland, Md.; *FR 1945*, 6:1120, 1130-31.

8. *New York Times*, Nov. 22, 1945, p. 14; Nov. 25, 1945, p. 8; and intermittently throughout late 1945.

9. Harley Notter File, NARS, "PR" Documents, PR-33 Preliminary, Nov. 29, 1945; *FR 1945*, 6:1137-38; John Paton Davies, *Dragon by the Tail* (New York, 1972), pp. 423-24; 740.00119 Control (Korea)/11-1145, NARS, Blakeslee to John Carter Vincent.

10. WD tele tfymg 459, Dec. 14, 1945, clear transmission of garbled department 740.00119 Control (Korea)/12-1145, Historical Files, Suitland; *FR 1945*, 6:1140-44.

11. See *FR 1945*, 2:560-86. In preparing for this conference, the Korean issue seemed surprisingly unimportant.

12. Ibid., pp. 587-88, 617, 611-21, 627, 629.

13. Ibid., pp. 639, 641-43.

14. Ibid., pp. 696-98, 699-700.

15. Ibid., pp. 699-700; see also ibid., pp. 716-17, 721.

16. Ibid., p. 820.

17. George F. Kennan, *Memoirs (1925-1950)* (Boston, 1967), pp. 287-88; Harry S. Truman, *Year of Decisions* (Garden City, N.Y., 1955), pp. 600-606; idem, *Years of Trial and Hope* (Garden City, N.Y., 1956), p. 96; Dean Acheson, *Present at the Creation* (New York, 1969), pp. 135-36; James F. Byrnes, *All in One Lifetime* (New York, 1958), p. 402. For a good explanation of that confusing January 1946 meeting between Truman and Byrnes, see George Curry's sketch of Byrnes in *The American Secretaries of State and Their Diplomacy*, ed. Samuel Bemis and Robert Ferrell, vol. 14 (New York, 1965).

18. 740.00119 Council/12-3145, NARS, American embassy London to secretary of state; *New York Times*, Dec. 28, 1945, pp. 1, 4, 14; Dec. 29, 1945, p. 12; Jan. 4, 1946; p. 20; *Manchester Guardian*, Dec. 31, 1945; and *Izvestia*, Jan. 12, 1946, quoted in Max Beloff, *Soviet Policy in the Far East, 1944-1951* (New York, 1953), p. 16.

19. Supreme Comander, Allied Powers, *Summation of Non-Military Activities in Japan and Korea #3*, Dec. 1945, p. 189; U-Gene Lee, p. 237; "Korean Guinea Pig," *The Voice of Korea*, Jan. 10, 1946; Cho Soon-sung, *Korea in World Politics, 1940-1950* (Berkeley, 1967), p. 105; George M. McCune, "Korea—The First Year of Liberation," *Pacific Affairs* 20 (Mar. 1947): 6; Byrnes, *Speaking Frankly*, p. 222.

20. Rad, CA56471, CG USAFIK to SCAP, date unknown, Historical Files, Suitland; *FR 1945*, 6:1152-53, 1154; *New York Times*, Dec. 31, 1945, pp. 1-2; Cho, p. 79; Robert A. Scalapino and Lee Chong-sik, *Communism in Korea, Part I: The Movement* (Berkeley, 1972), p. 277.

21. *New York Times*, Dec. 28, 1945, pp. 1, 5; U-Gene Lee, p. 236.

22. Rad, CG USAFIK to SCAP, 021512/2, Jan. 2, 1946, Historical Files, Suitland; TFGCG 206 to SCAP from USAFIK and TFGBI 99, from CG XXIV Corps through CINCAFPAC Adv to War Dept., both dated Dec. 30, 1945, Historical Files, Suitland;

New York Times, Jan. 11, 1946, p. 4; Rad, CG USAFIK to SCAP (personal to General MacArthur) TFGCG 262, Jan. 28, 1946, loose messages, Historical Files, Suitland.

23. U.S. Army, Center for Military History, "History of United States Armed Forces in Korea" (hereafter "History USAFIK"), vol. 1, pp. 241-43.

24. "History USAFIK," vol. 2, chap. 1, p. 24; Cho, pp. 123-24; Scalapino and Lee, p. 278.

25. *FR 1946*, 7:617-19, 622; U-Gene Lee, pp. 245-47; *New York Times*, Jan. 23, 1946, p. 18; USSR, Ministry of Foreign Affairs, *The Soviet Union and the Korean Question* (Moscow, 1948), pp. 7-10.

26. Rad, CG USAFIK to SCAP (personal to General MacArthur), TFGCG 262, Jan. 28, 1946, loose messages, Historical Files, Suitland; "report of inquiry," Jan. 29, 1946, Historical Files, Suitland.

27. "History USAFIK," vol. 2, chap. 2, pp. 89-92.

28. Rad, CG USAFIK to SCAP (personal to General MacArthur), TFGCG 262, Jan. 28, 1946, loose messages, Historical Files, Suitland.

29. Memo for JCS, Sub: Need for Promptness in Political Guidance for Korea, JCS 1483/27, by Lincoln, Feb. 13, 1946; this letter sent to State Department, Mar. 18, see U-Gene Lee, p. 255.

30. *FR 1946*, 8:654-56.

31. U-Gene Lee, pp. 190-93; directive given to General Lerch on Jan. 18, 1946, to prepare for such action, Historical Files, Suitland; Rhee sought to convince American officials that "they" in Washington were against "we" in Korea.

32. Cho, p. 35; U-Gene Lee, p. 195.

33. 740.00119 Control (Korea)/2-2846, NARS, Far Eastern Affairs to Langdon and Hodge; *FR 1946*, 8:646; Carl Berger, *The Korea Knot*, rev. ed. (Philadelphia, 1964), pp. 66-67.

34. *FR 1946*, 8:688-89; Richard C. Allen, *Korea's Syngman Rhee* (Rutland, Vt., 1960), pp. 80-81; George M. McCune and Arthur Grey, *Korea Today* (Cambridge, Mass., 1950), p. 66; *FR 1946*, 8:658-59; "History USAFIK," vol. 2, chap. 4, p. 38.

35. "History USAFIK," vol. 2, chap. 1, pp. 63-65; John C. Caldwell, *The Korea Story* (Chicago, 1952), pp. 8, 12; *New York Times*, Mar. 5, 1946, p. 15; Mar. 6, 1946, p. 7; Major Robert K. Sawyer, *Military Advisers in Korea: KMAG in Peace and War* (Washington, D.C., 1962) discusses the point system and replacement of troops at this time in Korea, p. 20; A. Wigfall Green, *The Epic of Korea* (Washington, D.C., 1950) sets out the prostitution problem and the struggle between army doctors and chaplains over the issue of venereal disease and its control.

36. CG USAFIK to SCAP, 211647/L, Jan. 21, 1946, Historical Files, Suitland; CG USAFIK to SCAP, Tfgct 161600, Jan. 16, 1946, Historical Files, Suitland; U-Gene Lee, pp. 266-67; RG 218, CCAC:014, Korea (8-28-45), sec. 2, radiogram OPD to CIN-CAFPAC Advance Tokyo, Dec. 29, 1945, Historical Files, Suitland.

37. *FR 1946*, 8:621, 634; Rad Tfgbi 179, 3120221, CG USAFIK to SCAP, Jan. 31, 1946, MacArthur Library, Norfolk, Va.; Rad, CG USAFIK to SCAP, 211647/L, Jan. 21, 1946, Historical Files, Suitland.

38. *FR 1946*, 8:620, 635-36; U-Gene Lee, pp. 274-75; Rad Hodge to Marshall (SCAP), Tfgbi 261, Jan. 17, 1946, Historical Files, Suitland.

39. *FR 1946*, 8:632, 640-41; U-Gene Lee, pp. 195-96.

40. Kennan, pp. 313, 583-98.

41. *FR 1946*, 8:619-20.

42. Ibid., pp. 623-27.

43. Ibid., pp. 632-33.
44. Ibid., p. 653; *New York Times*, Mar. 21, 1946, p. 1; SWNCC 176/18, Jan. 22, 1946: ABC 014 Japan sec. 17-B, Historical Files, Suitland.
45. 501.BB Korea/4-1246, NARS; *FR 1946*, 8:657, 659.
46. *FR 1946*, 8:660; *Summation of Non-Military Activities #7*, Apr. 1946.
47. *FR 1946*, 8:666, 669-70.
48. Ibid., pp. 680, 681-82, 686.
49. Ibid., pp. 697-99, 718-19.
50. 740.00119 Control (Korea)/6-2846, NARS; "Korea—Policy and Information Statement," n.d., James F. Byrnes Collection, Clemson Library, South Carolina; "Current US Policy Toward the Soviet Union," May 15, 1946, Papers of Clark M. Clifford, Harry S. Truman Library, Independence, Mo.; Box 15-Russia (folders 1 and 3), Papers of Clark M. Clifford, Harry S. Truman Library.

CHAPTER FOUR

1. Hilldring to OPD, 740.00119 Control (Korea)/6-646, State Department, Decimal File, National Archives and Records Service, Washington, D.C. (hereafter cited as NARS following the file number); 740.00119 Control (Korea)/6-1246, Langdon to secretary of state; 740.00119 Control (Korea)/7-1646, meeting among Far Eastern specialists, Washington; U-Gene Lee, "American Policy Toward Korea, 1942-1947: Formulation and Execution," (Ph.D. diss., Georgetown University, 1973), p. 204; Cho Soon-sung, *Korea in World Politics, 1940-1950* (Berkeley, 1967), p. 133.
2. U. S. Army, Center for Military History, "History of the United States Armed Forces in Korea" (hereafter "History USAFIK"), vol. 2, chap. 2, pp. 333-34; U-Gene Lee, p. 201. Adding to General Hodge's suspicion of native communists under Pak was the report of President Truman's personal ambassador on reparations, California oilman Edwin W. Pauley. The former Democratic party national committee treasurer had traveled through Manchuria and north Korea in May and June 1946. Closely guarded by Soviet political cadres, Pauley's party visited a few selected sites and later concluded that the 38th parallel had become a temporary truce line between hostile forces. Pauley compared the Soviets in Manchuria and north Korea. In Manchuria the Soviets had stripped the provinces of all transportable wealth and Pauley figured that meant the Russians intended to withdraw. There was no comparable rape of northern Korea, and Pauley concluded that it indicated a permanent Soviet presence. Pauley wrote the president in June 1946 that "Korea is not receiving the attention and consideration it should" and warned that communist subversion threatened the American zone. His report and warning fell on largely deaf ears, though temporarily he must have improved Hodge's spirits with his support of Hodge's adversary views of the issues in Korea. See Edwin W. Pauley, *Report on Japanese Assets in Soviet-Occupied Korea* (report to the president), June 1946, Washington, D.C.; U.S., Department of State, *Foreign Relations of the United States 1946* (Washington, D.C., 1971), 7:706, 708, 713 (hereafter cited as *FR* followed by the appropriate year); 740.00119 Control (Korea)/6-2246, NARS.
3. *FR 1946*, 7:215; Hodge stated: "The American command fully endorses and supports in every way possible the efforts of Dr. Kim and Mr. Lyuh." Special press release, June 30, 1946, HG USAMGIK, Dept. of Public Information, Historical Files,

Suitland; Benjamin Weems, "Behind the Korean Elections," *Far Eastern Survey*, June 23, 1948, pp. 142-47.

4. Lee Won-sul, "The Impact of United States Occupation Policy on the Socio-Political Structure of South Korea, 1945-1948," (Ph.D. diss., Western Reserve University, 1961), pp. 196-97. Lee brilliantly explains the political alliance of Rhee, who wanted power, and Korean collaborators who saw in the expatriate their only chance to escape the punishment they richly deserved. It may well have been the military government's greatest fault—failure to punish the collaborators as the Russians did immediately after occupying the north; Bertram D. Sarafan, "Military Government: Korea," *Far Eastern Survey*, Nov. 20, 1946, p. 357; C. Clyde Mitchell, *Korea: Second Failure in Asia* (Washington, D.C., 1951), p. 17; U.S., Department of State, *Korea, 1945*, Far Eastern Series #28 (Washington, D.C., 1948), p. 31.

5. Rhee represented the "haves" and Kimm the "have-nots" of the Korean right; see 740.00119 Control (Korea)/7-346, NARS; 740.00119 Control (Korea)/5-1647, NARS; Mark Gayn, *Japan Diary* (New York, 1948), pp. 353, 434.

6. 740.00119 Control (Korea)/5-1647, NARS; *FR 1946*, 7:720; Nam Koon-woo, *The North Korean Communist Leadership, 1945-1965* (Tuscaloosa, Ala., 1974), p. 81; Robert A. Scalapino and Lee Chong-sik, *Communism in Korea, Part I: The Movement* (Berkely, 1972), p. 301.

7. 740.00119 Control (Korea)/8-846, NARS, Hilldring to Acheson; "History USAFIK," vol. 2, chap. 2, p. 119; Lee Won-sul, pp. 175-76; George M. McCune and Arthur Grey, *Korea Today* (Cambridge, Mass., 1950), p. 86.

8. "History USAFIK," vol. 2, chap. 2, pp. 141-42; *FR 1946*, 7:753-55, 741-42, 757-58; Nam, pp. 75-76; Gayn, passim; U.S. Army Forces, Pacific, *Summation of U.S. Army Military Government Activities in Korea #12* (hereafter *Summation*), Sept. 1946, pp. 12-14, 23-25.

9. Gayn, p. 430; McCune, p. 85; Sarafan, p. 352; *FR 1946*, 7:750.

10. *Summation #12*, pp. 115-16; Cho, pp. 132-33; Gregory Henderson, *Korea: The Politics of the Vortex* (Cambridge, Mass., 1968), p. 154. Henderson's is the best scholarly account of events in the American zone.

11. *Summation #13*, Oct. 1946, pp. 11-13.

12. *FR 1946*, 7:772, 776-78, 786; *FR 1947*, 6:598-99, 604-5; Will Hamlin (pseudonym), "Korea: An American Tragedy," *The Nation*, Mar. 1, 1947, pp. 245-46.

13. *Department of State Bulletin* 16 (Jan. 19, 1947): 128; U-Gene Lee, p. 372; *FR 1947*, 6:596; *Summation #16*, Jan. 1947, pp. 22-23.

14. 895.00/2-2447, NARS, Bunce to Martin (personal letter); *Department of State Bulletin* 16 (Feb. 2, 1947): 210.

15. 740.00119 Control (Korea)/1-1347, NARS, memorandum by Dr. James Shoemaker, chairman, National Economic Board, USAMGIK; Calvin Joyner, director, Dept. of Commerce, USAMGIK; and Hugh Borton, Japanese Affairs, State Department.

16. 740.00119 Control (Korea)/1-1347, NARS; Henderson, p. 167; *FR 1947*, 6:601.

17. *FR 1947*, 6:601; see 740.00119 Control (Korea)/1-647, NARS, Gross to Borton, for a discussion of the problems with Korea.

18. 740.00119 Control (Korea)/1-2447, NARS, Martin to Bunce; *New York Times*, Jan. 30, 1957, letter, John Carter Vincent to the editor; *FR 1947*, 6:603, 608-18.

19. *New York Times*, Jan. 30, 1957; *FR 1947*, 6:609.

20. *FR 1947*, 6:603, 609, 618-19.

21. *New York Times*, Jan. 30, 1957, Vincent to editor; 740.00119 Control (Korea)/2-2447, NARS, Noce to Hilldring.

22. For brief but complete explanations of the Greek-Turkish crisis, see John Lewis Gaddis, *The Origins of the Cold War, 1941-1947*; Daniel Yergin, *Shattered Peace*; and other related monographs. For a recent study of the British origins of the Truman Doctrine, see Terry Anderson's unpublished Ph.D. dissertation, Indiana University, 1978. For contrasting points of view about the significance of the Truman Doctrine and Kennan's influence, see: John Lewis Gaddis, "Reconsiderations: Was The Truman Doctrine a Real Turning Point?" *Foreign Affairs* 52 (Jan. 1974): 386-402; John Lewis Gaddis, "Reconsiderations: Containment: A Reassessment," *Foreign Affairs* 55 (July 1977): 873-87; and Eduard Mark, "The Question of Containment: A Reply to John Lewis Gaddis," *Foreign Affairs* 56 (Jan. 1978): 430-41.

23. *FR 1947*, 6:620; Rhee had earlier knowledge of the aid program: see 740.00119 Control (Korea)/2-2847, NARS, Robert Oliver to Hilldring; Dean Acheson informed the embassy in Moscow that the department still recommended a three-year aid program for Korea but with reduction of overall cost estimate and of first year estimate to ease congressional qualms about funding expensive aid programs, 740.00119 Council/3-1447, NARS; 740.00119 Control (Korea)/3-2247, NARS, Douglas, American embassy London to secretary of state; *New York Times*, Mar. 2, 1947, sec. 4, p. 4.

24. U.S., Congress, Senate, *Congressional Record*, 80th Cong., 1st sess., 1947, 93, pt. 3:3297, 3774; U.S., Congress, House, *Congressional Record*, 80th Cong., 1st sess., 1947, 93, pt. 4:5244-45, 5276; *New York Times*, Mar. 21, 1947, p. 12; Joseph M. Jones, *The Fifteen Weeks* (New York, 1955), pp. 190-93; Council on Foreign Relations, *The United States in World Affairs, 1947-1948* (New York, 1948), p. 174.

25. *Department of State Bulletin* 16 (Mar. 23, 1947): 544-46; 740.00119 Control (Korea)/3-2747, NARS, Vincent to Hilldring; 740.00119 Control (Korea)/3-3147, NARS, Martin to Wood; *FR 1947*, 6:621-22; RG 353, Box 86, Decimal File 334, SANACC, Interdepartmental Korea, Mar. 31, 1947, p. 16.

26. 740.00119 Control (Korea)/5-1547, NARS, John Peurifoy, assistant secretary of state, to James E. Webb, director, Bureau of the Budget; 895.50 Korea/6-1247, NARS, memorandum of legal adviser; 895.01/6-1347, NARS, State Department to Jacobs (Polad); 740.00119 Control (Korea)/6-2547, NARS, Martin to Bunce.

27. 895.50 Recovery/7-847, NARS, Fahy to Sandifer on aid legislation; 740.00119 Control (Korea)/6-2547, NARS, Martin to Bunce, personal letter; 740.00119 Control (Korea)/6-2747, NARS, Acheson to Hilldring.

28. 895.00/3-1047, NARS, Langdon to secretary of state; Mitchell, p. 18; *FR 1947*, 6:607-8; 740.00119 Control (Korea)/4-347, NARS, Vincent to secretary of state; *FR 1947*, 6:623-25; *Department of State Bulletin* 16 (Apr. 20, 1947): 716-17.

29. *FR 1947*, 6:632-35, 638-43; CG USAFIK to CINCFE, Mar. 1, 1947, Box 46, MacArthur Archives, Norfolk, Va.

30. *FR 1947*, 6:645, 646, 647; *New York Times*, May 20, 1947, p. 24.

31. 740.00119 Control (Korea)/5-2647, NARS, Jacobs to Hilldring; *FR 1947*, 6:650, 649-74 passim; Cho, pp. 139-40; *Summation #20*, May 1947, p. 19.

32. In the meantime, the State Department had sent Joseph E. Jacobs, the long-awaited high-level diplomat who replaced Langdon. Langdon continued in his other, permanent position as consul-general.

33. *FR 1947*, 6:679-80, 681.

34. 740.00119 Control (Korea)/6-2847, NARS, Marshall (JNA) to Polad, Seoul;

740.00119 Control (Korea)/6-2847, NARS, Smith, American embassy Moscow, to Marshall; *FR 1947*, 6:683-84.

35.   740.00119 Control (Korea)/7-1247, NARS, Jacobs to secretary of state; *FR 1947*, 6:686-87, 688-89, 691, 691-92, 696, 698; *Summation #22*, July 1947.

36.   Hodge's public relations campaign ran into difficulties when Lt. Gen. Albert C. Wedemeyer arrived in Korea on the tail end of a six-week, whirlwind visit to China. Wedemeyer was on a fact-finding mission, but to Koreans, schooled in a different culture, his coming was evidence of offical disapproval of Hodge and his subordinates in Washington. Many Koreans would assume—incorrectly at this time—that Hodge was on his way out; even communists agreed with Rhee's claim that Wedemeyer came to reaffirm a secret understanding with Rhee. Hodge used the visit to complain bitterly over his predicament, caught between the Soviets, Korean factions, and low-quality troops. Although it damaged Hodge's prestige, the visit was for naught because by the time Wedemeyer could submit his report, the government in Washington had decided to take the Korean issue to the United Nations. See records of the Wedemeyer Mission to China, NARS: Box 2, Hodge Briefing—Korea; Box 4, Korea—USAF in Korea (B); Box 3, Political Notes on Korea; and Wedemeyer, *Report to the President: Korea, September 1947*. The deletions were later printed in *FR 1947*, vol. 6. See also *Wedemeyer Reports!*

37.   See *Summation #23*, Aug. 1947, pp. 182-85 for Brown's proposals and pp. 190-93 for Shtikov's reply.

38.   *FR 1947*, 6:748-49, 771-74.

CHAPTER FIVE

1.   895.01/2-2547, State Department, Decimal File, National Archives and Records Service, Washington, D.C. (hereafter cited as NARS following the file number); U.S., Department of State, *Foreign Relations of the United States 1947* (Washington, D.C., 1972), 6:70 (hereafter cited as *FR* followed by the appropriate year).

2.   895.00/2-2447, NARS, Bunce to Martin (personal letter); 740.00119 Control (Korea)/2-?-47, NARS, the date of Allison's (proposal) paper not noted on document.

3.   FE Files, NARS, Lot 244, Box 7946 (see *FR 1947*, 6:713-14), Allison proposal to SWNCC of July 25, 1947.

4.   *FR 1947*, 6:734, 734-36; SWNCC 176/30 (SWNCC Files), NARS; 740.00119 Control (Korea)/8-647, NARS, Hilldring memorandum on letter to Marshall.

5.   *FR 1947*, 6:748-49.

6.   "Korea—Notes and Memoranda, 1947," John Foster Dulles Collection, Princeton University Library, Princeton, N.J.; Leland M. Goodrich, *Korea: A Study of U.S. Policy in the United Nations* (New York, 1956), pp. 36-37; Wainhouse (USUN) to Rusk, Sept. 28, 1947, Record Group 84 (Records of the U.S. Mission at the United Nations), Box 84, NARS; 895.00/8-1747, NARS, Lovett (acting secretary) to Jacobs.

7.   *FR 1947*, 6:771-74.

8.   740.00119 Control (Korea)/8-2847, NARS, Embassy Nanking to secretary of state; 740.00119 Control (Korea)/9-847, NARS, Embassy London to secretary of state.

9.   *FR 1947*, 6:779-81.

10.   Ibid., pp. 781, 784-85; 740.00119 Control (Korea)/9-547, NARS; 740.00119 Control (Korea)/9-947, NARS, Jacobs and Langdon to secretary of state; NARS, RG 84, Box 84, Korea—1947, Sayre to Marshall, Sept. 22, 1947.

11. *FR 1947*, 6:790.

12. Ibid., 1:762-63. The deputy director of the Office of European Affairs, John Hickerson, wrote his director, Matthews, that there is "no other alternative than to assume that the USSR has aggressive intentions." He added there can be "no question of 'deals or arrangements.' " Ibid., pp. 715-16.

13. Goodrich, pp. 29-30; *New York Times*, Sept. 18, 1947, p. 24. It is sad that, given the seeming importance of Korea to the United States at this session of the United Nations, that the material is so meager. The RG 84, Box 84 files are rather thin, the papers at the Dulles Collection relatively few, and none of the participants left records for scholars to peruse.

14. *New York Times*, Sept. 18, 1947, p. 24; United Nations, General Assembly, *Official Records*, 2d sess., vol. 1, 84th Plenary Meeting, Sept. 17, 1947 (hereafter cited as UNGA followed by appropriate meeting and date).

15. UNGA, 84th Plenary Meeting, Sept. 17, 1947; *New York Times*, Sept. 18, 1947, p. 24.

16. UNGA, 84th Plenary Meeting, Sept. 17, 1947; Goodrich, pp. 30, 36-37; Leon Gordenker, *The United Nations and the Peaceful Unification of Korea* (The Hague, 1959), p. 15.

17. UNGA, 91st Plenary Meeting, Sept. 23, 1947.

18. *New York Times*, Sept. 27, 1947; *FR 1947*, 6:816-17; Cho Soon-sung, *Korea in World Politics, 1940-1950* (Berkeley, 1967), p. 173.

19. *FR 1947*, 1:191; NARS, RG 84, Box 84, Korea—1947, Popper to Sandifer, Sept. 26, 1947; Wainhouse (USUN) to Rusk, Sept. 28, 1947; 501.BB Korea/10-147, NARS, Butterworth to Lovett.

20. 740.00119 Control (Korea)/9-2747, NARS; *FR 1947*, 6:822, 826-27.

21. UNGA, 88th First Committee Meeting, Oct. 28, 1947; 91st First Committee Meeting, Oct. 30, 1947.

22. UNGA, 88th First Committee Meeting, Oct. 28, 1947; 91st First Committee Meeting, Oct. 30, 1947.

23. UNGA, 111th Plenary Meeting, Nov. 13, 1947; *United Nations Weekly Bulletin* [the name would change during this period to *United Nations Bulletin*] 3 (Nov. 11, 1947): 638.

24. UNGA, 112th Plenary Meeting, Nov. 14, 1947.

25. See UNGA, 112th and 113th Plenary Meetings, Nov. 14 and 15, 1947.

26. Surprising as it appears in retrospect, it seems that, according to records of the U.S. Mission to the United Nations, the list of nominees for the Korean commission was compiled in an offhand fashion and with the assumption that all of the nominated member nations would agree to serve. Perhaps the U.S. delegation should have investigated the motives of the seven nations to avoid future difficulties in Korea.

27. 501.BB Korea/12-3047, NARS, memorandum by Daniels; *FR 1947*, 6:888; copies were sent to all seven embassies.

28. Robert A. Spencer, *Canada in World Affairs, From UN to NATO, 1946-1949* (Toronto, 1959), pp. 76, 84; Denis Stairs, *The Diplomacy of Constraint: Canada, The Korean War, and the United States* (Toronto, 1974), p. 8; Dale Thomson, *Louis St. Laurent* (New York, 1968), p. 215; J. W. Pickersgill, *My Years with Louis St. Laurent: A Political Memoir* (Toronto, 1975), pp. 40-41; J. W. Pickersgill and D. F. Forster, *The Mackenzie King Record, Volume 4, 1947-1948* (Toronto, 1970), pp. 133-55 passim. Although the matter of the Korean commission nearly caused senior members of the Canadian government to resign en masse, and most important biographies and/or memoirs include long

passages about the crisis from the Canadian side, there are few records at such common American sources as the National Archives, the Truman Library, etc. Seemingly it mattered little to American diplomats; perhaps it is indicative of how lightly they treated Canadian sensitivities.

29. Stairs, p. 9; Thomson, pp. 217, 220-21; Lester B. Pearson, *Mike: The Memoirs of the Right Honorable Lester B. Pearson, Volume 2, 1948-1957* (Toronto, 1973), p. 136; Pickersgill and Forster, pp. 133-34.

30. Thomson, pp. 216-17, 221; Stairs, pp. 9-10; Pickersgill and Forster, pp. 135-36.

31. Thomson, p. 222; Spencer, p. 106.

32. Stairs, pp. 12-13; Pickersgill, p. 42.

33. Stairs, p. 13; *FR 1947*, 6:880-81, 881-82; Pickersgill and Forster, pp. 141-43.

34. *FR 1947*, 6:887; 740.00119 Control (Korea)/12-3047, NARS.

35. *FR 1947*, 6:883-86; 740.00119 Control (Korea)/12-3047, NARS.

36. Stairs, pp. 14, 15, 16; Pearson, p. 140; Pickersgill and Forster, pp. 144-45.

37. Pearson, pp. 140-41; *FR 1948*, 6:1079-81.

38. *FR 1948*, 6:1082; 740.00119 Control (Korea)/1-547 and earlier drafts, NARS.

39. Stairs, pp. 16-17; Thomson, pp. 224-25.

40. Stairs, p. 18.

41. *FR 1948*, 6:1084.

CHAPTER SIX

1. United Nations, General Assembly, Interim Committee of the General Assembly, "Problems of the Independence of Korea," (A/AC. 18/28), Feb. 19, 1948 (hereafter cited as UNGA, IC); Leon Gordenker, *The United Nations and the Peaceful Unification of Korea* (The Hague, 1959), p. 52.

2. United Nations, General Assembly, *Official Records*, 3d sess., 1948, Report of UNTCOK, pt. 1, vol. 2, pp. 8, 41 (hereafter cited as UNTCOK); 501.BB Korea/1-2848, State Department, Decimal File, National Archives and Records Service, Washington, D.C. (hereafter cited as NARS following the file number); U.S., Department of State, *Foreign Relations of the United States 1948* (Washington, D.C., 1974), 6:1088 (hereafter cited as *FR* followed by the appropriate year). See also Gordenker, p. 53.

3. 895.00/1-348, NARS, Hodge and Jacobs to secretary of state; 740.00119 Control (Korea)/1-2048, NARS, Langdon to secretary of state; 501.BB Korea/1-3148, NARS, Jacobs to secretary of state; CG USAFIK (Hodge sends for Jacobs), 290720 Z #31 and 290721 Z #30, Jan. 1948, Box 48, MacArthur Archives, Norfolk, Va.; Gordenker, p. 68.

4. 501.BB Korea/1-3148, NARS, Jacobs to secretary of state; *FR 1948*, 6:1083; Gordenker, p. 57.

5. 501.BB Korea/1-3048, NARS, Jacobs to secretary of state.

6. 501.BB Korea/1-2948, NARS, secretary of state (JNA) to Mitchell, Seoul; *New York Times*, Jan. 22, 1948; 501.BB Korea/2-648, 2-1048, 2-1348, and 2-2548, NARS, secretary of state (JNA) to Mitchell.

7. UNGA, IC, "Problem of the Independence of Korea."

8. *FR 1948*, 1, pt. 2:524-26; ibid., 6:1115; NARS, RG 84, Feb. 10, 1948, memorandum of conversation by Jessup; Feb. 11, 1948, Gordon Knox with M. Pierre Ordonneau, France; Feb. 12, 1948, Jessup with Nasrollah Entezam, Iran; Feb. 13, 1948, Knox with George Ignatieff, Canada; Feb. 16, 1948, Knox with Lawford, G. B.; NARS, RG 84, Box 84, Korea—1948, Feb. 10, 1948, Jessup with Van Longenhoue (Belgium)

and Stolk (Venezuela); Feb. 21, 1948, Dorothy Fosdick to Jessup; Feb. 23, 1948, Jessup and Ambassador Selim Sarper, Turkey; Feb. 25, 1948, Fosdick memorandum; and Feb. 26, 1948, Knox with Ralph Harry, Australia.

There was a problem with Canada. Ignatieff told American officials that Canada opposed the UN-observed elections in the south for it did not want the world organization to take sides in the Soviet-American confrontation. Pearson argued that the Interim Committee did not have the power to change the commission's terms of reference (to observe elections in the south only). He "condemned the USSR for preventing the objective of a free-united, and democratic Korea," but he would not support a UN-sanctioned permanent division of the peninsula. See Denis Stairs, *The Diplomacy of Constraint: Canada, the Korean War and the United States* (Toronto, 1974), pp. 21-22.

9. UNTCOK, pt. 1, vol. 1, p. 41; Gordenker, p. 71; *New York Times*, Feb. 27, 1948.

10. Hodge later remarked that he had thought the State Department had cleared the election date with the commission—another example of the lack of communication between occupation officials in Seoul and officials in Washington. UNTCOK, pt. 1, vol. 1, pp. 28-30.

11. *FR 1948*, 6:1153; *New York Times*, Mar. 9, 1948, p. 12.

12. 501.BB Korea/3-1148, NARS, secretary of state [Butterworth] to Seoul; 501.BB Korea/3-948, NARS, Bond to Butterworth; 501.BB Korea/3-2548, NARS, Saltzman to Marshall; *FR 1948*, 6:1145.

13. 501.BB Korea/3-2448, NARS, Jacobs to secretary of state; 501.BB Korea/3-948, NARS, Saltzman to Marshall.

14. 501.BB Korea/3-1148, NARS, Atherton to secretary of state; pressure on the Canadian cabinet was intense: see 501.BB Korea/3-2348, NARS, Harrington, American embassy Ottawa, to secretary of state.

15. 895.00/4-148, NARS, Jacobs to secretary of state; John Kie-chang Oh, *Korea: Democracy on Trial* (Ithaca, N.Y., 1968), p. 8.

16. 740.00119 Control (Korea)/4-1448, NARS, Bunce (Seoul) to Martin, chief, Division of Occupied Areas; Oh, p. 8.

17. 501.BB Korea/4-1648, NARS, Jacobs to secretary of state; *FR 1948*, 6:1179-84.

18. *FR 1948*, 6:1164-69; ibid., 1, pt. 2:545-50; Robert Jervis, *Perceptions and Misperceptions in International Politics* (Princeton, N.J., 1976), esp. pp. 321-23 and idem, "Hypothesis on Misperception," *World Politics* 20 (Apr. 1968): 454-79.

19. 501.BB Korea/4-948, NARS; *FR 1948*, 6:1170-71.

20. The Kims had tried to visit with moderate politicians they had known before the occupation (prior to 1945), but North Korean authorities had refused them permission to see so-called enemies of the people.

21. *Department of State Bulletin* 18 (May 30, 1948): 700; Oh, p. 12; John C. Caldwell, *The Korea Story* (Chicago, 1952), p. 29.

22. Leland M. Goodrich, *Korea: A Study of U.S. Policy in the United Nations* (New York, 1956), p. 58.

23. UNTCOK, pt. 1, vol. 1, p. 37; ibid., vol. 2, pp. 64-67; Kim Yongjeung, "The Cold War Korean Elections," *Far Eastern Survey*, May 5, 1948, p. 102.

24. Gregory Henderson, *Korea: The Politics of the Vortex* (Cambridge, Mass., 1968), p. 157; Gordenker, p. 107; Goodrich, pp. 43, 58, 59; Benjamin Weems, "Behind the Korean Elections," *Far Eastern Survey*, June 23, 1948, p. 142; UNTCOK, pt. 1, vol. 2, p. 43.

25. *FR 1948*, 6:1219-22, 1229; Oh, p. 9; Gordenker, p. 68; UNTCOK, pt. 1, vol. 1, pp. 46-47; UNTCOK, pt. 2, vol. 1, p. 1.

26. 895.6463/10-2847, NARS, Seoul to secretary of state; 895.51/3-2048, NARS, Langdon to secretary of state; 895.6463/3-2847, NARS, Hodge to secretary of state; 895.6463/4-1648, NARS, Bunce to secretary of state.

27. 895.51/3-2048, NARS; 895.6463/4-1648, NARS; 895.6463/4-1948, NARS, Bunce to secretary of state.

28. For the latest, most detailed study of the Berlin crisis, see Daniel F. Harrington, "American Policy in the Berlin Crisis of 1948-49," (Ph.D. diss., Indiana University, 1979); 501.BB Korea/9-2448, NARS, American embassy Warsaw to secretary of state; 740.00119 Control (Korea)/9-2448, NARS, American embassy Vienna to secreatary of state; 895.00/1-1349, NARS.

29. Alex George, "Nothing Happens in Russia By Accident," *International Studies Quarterly* 13 (1969): 204-5; Adam Ulam, *Stalin: The Man and His Era* (New York, 1973), p. 549.

30. *FR 1948*, 1, pt. 2: 583-84, 585-88.

31. 895.6463/5-748, NARS, Jacobs to secretary of state; 895.6463/5-1248, NARS, Bunce to secretary of state; MacArthur Archives, CG USAFIK to State Department, Seoul (Polad), #323, May 7, 1948.

32. 501.BB Korea/6-1048, NARS, Smith, American embassy Moscow, to secretary of state; Hodge had replied that his command had paid 35 percent and another 40 percent waited in depots in the south: MacArthur Archives, DA/WCL May 1948, Box 41, May 14, 1948, CSPID to CINCFE, WCL 23361.

33. 895.6463/5-1448, NARS, Draper to Saltzman; *FR 1948*, 6:1198-99.

34. 501.BB Korea/6-248, NARS, Marshall to American embassy Moscow; *FR 1948*, 6:1227-28.

35. *FR 1948*, 6:1252-53.

36. Ibid., pp. 1024, 1214, 1232; *Department of State Bulletin* 19 (July 11, 1948): 50-51 and (Aug. 1, 1948): 147-48.

37. 501.BB Korea/6-1248, NARS, Jacobs to secretary of state; 501.BB Korea/7-1348, NARS, Jacobs to secretary of state.

38. *FR 1948*, 6:1204-6, 1211-13, 1213, 1217.

39. Ibid., pp. 1236-37; see also 501.BB Korea/7-1048, NARS, secretary of state (JNA) to American embassy London.

40. 895.01/7-2348, NARS, conversation between Sprouse of Chinese Affairs and Tsui Tswen-ling, counselor, Chinese embassy; *FR 1948*, 6:1238-40, 1241, 1242, 1246, 1247-48, 1265.

41. *FR 1948*, 6:1249-51.

42. 501.BB Korea/7-1048, NARS, secretary of state (JNA) to American embassy London; *FR 1948*, 6:1248, 1255-57.

43. 895.01/8-1548, NARS, Rhee's inaugural address; 895.01/8-1648, NARS, Seoul to secretary of state; 895.01/8-1348, NARS, Jacobs to secretary of state; 895.01/8-1548, NARS, Jacobs to secretary of state.

44. *Department of State Bulletin* 19 (Aug. 22, 1948): 242; 895.01/8-1848, NARS, Lockett, American embassy Manila, to secretary of state.

45. 895.01/9-348, NARS, Truman to Hodge; Truman to Hodge, Aug. 15, 1948, Official File, Papers of Harry S. Truman, Harry S. Truman Library, Independence, Mo.; *FR 1948*, 6:1225-26, 1235.

46. *FR 1948*, 1, pt. 2:589-93, 599-600, 609-11, 617-19, 620-22, 623.

47. 740.00119 Control (Korea)/6-2448, NARS, Lovett to Secretary Royall; *FR 1948*, 6:1225-26, 1235.

48. 740.00119 Control (Korea)/8-648, NARS, Allison and Bond to Butterworth; 895.00/8-1948, NARS, conversation between Rusk and Draper; *FR 1948*, 6:1278.

49. 895.01/9-148, NARS, secretary of state to political adviser, Seoul.

50. *New York Times*, Sept. 20, 1948, pp. 1, 7; 740.00119 Control (Korea)/9-2248, NARS; 740.00119 Control (Korea)/9-2448, NARS, American embassy Vienna to secretary of state; 740.00119 Control (Korea)/9-3048, NARS, Kohler, American embassy Moscow, to secretary of state; 501.BB Korea/9-2448, NARS, American embassy Warsaw to secretary of state.

51. *FR 1948*, 6:1299, 1319, 1341-43; 501.BB Korea/10-2948, NARS, Claxton to Saltzman.

52. 501.BB Korea/5-2948, NARS, Jacobs to secretary of state; 501.BB Korea/7-1848, NARS, Jacobs to secretary of state.

53. 501.BB Korea/7-1848, NARS, Jacobs to secretary of state; 895.50/9-1848, NARS, Muccio to secretary of state; Kyung-cho Chung, *New Korea: New Land of the Morning Calm* (New York, 1962), p. 16.

54. 895.00/10-2148, NARS, Muccio to Bond; 895.001/10-3048, NARS, Muccio to Bond; 740.00119 Control (Korea)/11-1248, NARS, Muccio to secretary of state; 501.BB Korea/12-2048, NARS, Muccio to secretary of state.

55. Goodrich, pp. 63, 76; *FR 1948*, 6:1234.

56. 740.00119 Control (Korea)/7-2348, NARS, Saltzman, Butterworth, et al. to Lovett; 895.50 Recovery/8-1248, NARS, meeting with Frank Pace, Jr. of Budget, Hoffman of ECA, Lovett, Draper, etc.; *FR 1948*, 6:1288.

57. *FR 1948*, 6:1294-96, 1296-98; 895.50 Recovery/9-1648, NARS, Saltzman to Lovett.

58. *FR 1948*, 6:1313; U.S., Department of State, *The Record on Korean Unification, 1943-1960*, Far Eastern Series 101, (Washington, D.C., 1960), p. 14 (hereafter cited as FES 101).

59. *FR 1948*, 6:1299-1300.

60. 501.BB Korea/9-1148, NARS, Dickover (London) to secretary of state; 501.BB Korea/10-1248, NARS, Donovan (New Delhi) to secretary of state; 501.BB Korea/10-2248, NARS, Jacobs (in Paris) to Butterworth and Bond; *FR 1948*, 6:1302.

61. United Nations, General Assembly, *Official Records*, 3d sess., 1948, First Committee, 229th and 230th meetings, Dec. 6, 1948; 231st meeting, Dec. 7, 1948 (hereafter cited as UNGA).

62. UNGA, First Committee, 231st meeting, Dec. 7, 1948; 233d meeting, Dec. 8, 1948; *New York Times*, Dec. 8, 1948, p. 22; Goodrich, pp. 69, 74; FES 101, p. 76; *Department of State Bulletin* 19 (Dec. 12, 1948): 729.

CHAPTER SEVEN

1. Untitled position paper, 895.00/1-149, State Department, Decimal File, National Archives and Records Service, Washington, D.C. (hereafter cited as NARS following the file number); 895.00/1-1349, NARS, Perry Laukoff (Division of Central European Affairs) noted "increasing Soviet propaganda on parallels between Korea and Germany." Edgar A. J. Johnson of the ECA called Korea "our last lodgment of

democracy in Asia," *Times-Herald* (Washington, D.C.), Feb. 5, 1949, in the Papers of Edgar A. J. Johnson, Harry S. Truman Library, Independence, Mo.

2. U.S., Department of State, *Foreign Relations of the United States 1948* (Washington, D.C., 1974), 1, pt. 2:589-92, 663-69 (hereafter cited as *FR* followed by the appropriate year); *FR 1949*, 7, pt. 2:969-78.

3. 895.50/2-2449, NARS, Sipes to Marcy; 895.50 Recovery/1-1349, NARS, Whitman to Thorp; 895.50 Recovery/3-2249, NARS, Butterworth to secretary of state; 895.24/5-1249, NARS, Muccio to Butterworth; 895.50 Recovery/5-1949, NARS, Butterworth to Webb; *New York Times*, Jan. 7, 1949, p. 5; *FR 1947*, 7, pt. 2:1024-29.

4. *New York Times*, June 9, 1949, p. 18; *Department of State Bulletin* 20 (June 19, 1949): 782-83; U.S., Department of State, *The Record on Korean Unification, 1943-1960*, Far Eastern Series 101 (Washington, D.C., 1960), pp. 80-81 (hereafter cited as FES 101); 895.50/6-349, NARS, Webb to president.

5. U.S., Congress, House, Committee on International Relations, *Selected Executive Session Hearings of the Committee, 1943-1950*, vol. 7, pt. 2, pp. 46, 47, 50-51, 55, 57-58 (hereafter cited as *Korea Assistance Acts*); *Department of State Bulletin* 20 (June 19, 1949): 783-86.

6. *Korea Assistance Acts*, pp. 59, 82-83.

7. Ibid., pp. 50-100.

8. Ibid., pp. 237-38; U.S., Congress, House, Committee on Foreign Affairs, *Hearings on H. R. 5330*, 81st Cong., 1st sess., 1949, p. 192; *New York Times*, June 4, 1949, p. 2.

9. 895.50 Recovery/6-1849, NARS, Webb to President Truman; *New York Times*, June 21, 1949, p. 13; *Time* magazine, June 20, 1949, "Korea: Temporary Roof."

10. *New York Times*, July 1, 1949, p. 6.

11. U.S., Congress, House, Committee on Foreign Affairs, *Aid to Korea*, 81st Cong., 1st sess., 1949, pt. 2, p. 1.

12. U.S., Senate, Committee on Foreign Relations, *Economic Assistance to China and Korea, 1949-1950. Hearings Held in Executive Session Before Committee on Foreign Relations*, 81st Cong., 1st and 2d sess., 1974, pp. 110-19.

13. Ibid., pp. 120, 129.

14. Ibid., pp. 126, 127, 133-34.

15. Ibid., pp. 157, 164-65, 181, 185-86.

16. *New York Times*, July 2, 1949, p. 1; 895.50 Recovery/7-849, NARS, Ernest Gross to secretary of state; *New York Times*, July 28, 1949, p. 4; 895.50 Recovery/7-2849, NARS, Ben Brown to secretary of state; 895.50 Recovery/8-1649, NARS, Gross to secretary of state on talk with Sam Rayburn.

17. There has been some argument concerning the value of goods left behind by departing troops. How did the army arrive at its $56 million estimate? Whether it was high or low, there were enough arms for the Korean army to use effectively for defense.

18. *FR 1949*, 7, pt. 2:1046-57.

19. See *FR 1947*, 1:738-50 and *FR 1948*, 6:700-702.

20. *FR 1949*, 7, pt. 2:1058-59; 895.24/7-1149, NARS, discussion, Special Representative Chough of Korea and Chang, ambassador of Korea, with Acheson, Bond.

21. 895.24/7-1349, NARS, Muccio to secretary of state; *FR 1949*, 7, pt. 2:1974-76.

22. *FR 1949*, 7, pt. 2:1144, 1145-46.

23. Ibid., pp. 1123-24, 1125, 1126-27, 1127-28, 1133-34.

24. Ibid., pp. 1141-42, 1144-45, 1145-46, 1151-52, 1152-53, 1154, 1157-58, 1159, 1160-66, 1168, 1169, 1178; 890.20/7-1549, NARS, Muccio to secretary of state. See *FR 1949*, 7, pt. 2:1143 for May 18 press release by secretary of state on proposed Pacific pact: "U.S. not currently considering participation in any further special collective defense arrangements other than North Atlantic Treaty."

25. *FR 1949*, 7, pt. 2:1170-71, 1172, 1177-78. See p. 1176 for British view: "combination of discredited former Chinese president, Philippine politician with not too good reputation, and head of an insecure Korean state as nucleus of a Pacific Union is to reduce whole thing to absurdity." See pp. 1180-81 for report by the American embassy China on communist Chinese reaction: "This criminal act not only aims at opposing the Chinese people, but also aims at opposing peoples in Philippines, Korea and other Far Eastern countries."

26. Ibid., pp. 1177, 1184; 501.BB Korea/8-2794, NARS, Muccio to secretary of state; 895.001 RHEE/8-1249, NARS, Muccio to Department of State; Tsou Tang, *America's Failure in China, 1941-1950* (Chicago, 1963), p. 507.

27. 501.BB Korea/7-1149, NARS, American embassy Manila to secretary of state; 501.BB Korea/7-1449, NARS, embassy Seoul to secretary of state; 501.BB Korea/7-1849, NARS, Dr. Hector David Castro, ambassador of El Salvador, with department officials; 501.BB Korea/7-2149, NARS, Muccio to secretary of state; 501.BB Korea/7-2249, NARS, embassy El Salvador to secretary of state; 501.BB Korea/7-2849, NARS, Bruce in Paris to secretary of state; 501.BB Korea/8-1349, NARS, Kirk, embassy Moscow, to secretary of state; 501.BB Korea/8-2049, NARS, Muccio to secretary of state; *FR 1949*, 7, pt. 2:1063-64.

28. *FR 1949*, 7, pt. 2:1068-74; 501.BB Korea/9-1349, NARS, Department of State to American embassy Moscow.

29. *New York Times*, Sept. 9, 1949, p. 1; *Department of State Bulletin* 21 (Oct. 3, 1949): 490; (Oct. 24, 1949): 625-26.

30. *FR 1949*, 7, pt. 2:1090-92; *Department of State Bulletin* 21 (Nov. 7, 1949): 694.

31. See Nancy Bernkopf Tucker, "An Unlikely Peace: American Missionaries and the Chinese Communists, 1948-1950," *Pacific Historical Review* 45 (Feb. 1976): 97-116 and idem, "American Business and the Chinese Communists: Dilemmas of 1949-1950" (Paper delivered at the New England Conference of the Association for Asian Studies, 1979 Annual Meeting); Warren W. Tozer, "Last Bridge to China: The Shanghai Power Company, the Truman Administration, and the Chinese Communists," *Diplomatic History* 1 (Winter 1977): 64-78; Howard Schonberger, "The Japan Lobby in American Diplomacy, 1947-1952," *Pacific Historical Review* 46 (Aug. 1977): 327-59 and idem, "Of Arms and Men: Harry F. Kern and the American Corruption of Postwar Japan" (Paper delivered at the New England Conference of the Association for Asian Studies, 1979 Annual Meeting).

32. 895.50/10-1749, NARS, American embassy Seoul to secretary of state; 895.51/10-2949, NARS, State-ECA despatch; *FR 1949*, 7, pt. 2:1097; 895.50 Recovery/12-949, NARS, Doherty to Butterworth and Allison; 895.51/12-1349, NARS, Butterworth (personal) to Muccio.

33. See U.S., Department of Defense, *United States-Vietnam Relations, 1945-1967* (Washington, D.C., 1971), 8:226-64, 265-72; also in the Declassified Documents Reference Catalog, 75, 269B, NSC.

34. 895.00/12-549, NARS, Muccio for Bond; 895.00/12-1049, NARS, Muccio to secretary of state; Harry S. Truman Library, Oral History Interview with John J. Muccio, p. 28.

35. 895.00/11-149, NARS, Muccio to Butterworth; 895.00/11-749, NARS, American embassy Seoul to Department of State; 895.00 RHEE/11-2549, NARS, Muccio to State Department; *New York Times*, Jan. 4, 1950, p. 74.

36. In later years Acheson would complain that his speech repeated what military leaders had been saying—publicly and privately—for years. He was right.

37. *New York Times*, Jan. 10, 1950, pp. 1, 20.

38. U.S., Congress, Senate, Committee on Foreign Relations, *Reviews of the World Situation: 1949-1950, Hearings Held in Executive Session before the Committee on Foreign Relations*, 81st Cong., 1st and 2d sess., 1974, pp. 108, 109, 130, 163, 183-84, 191 (hereafter cited as *Reviews of the World Situation*).

39. U.S., Congress, House, *Congressional Record*, 81st Cong., 2d sess., 1950, 96, pt. 1:572, 663-64, 639-40, 644, 649. See Sabath of Illinois, Javits of New York, and Burnside of West Virginia for a defense of the administration bill: ibid., pp. 632, 636, 640-41, 655.

40. Dean Acheson, *Present at the Creation* (New York, 1969), p. 358; Athan Theoharis, "The Rhetoric of Politics: Foreign Policy, Internal Security, and Domestic Politics in The Truman Era, 1945-1950," in *Politics and Policies of the Truman Administration*, ed. Barton Bernstein (Chicago, 1970), pp. 221-22; John Foster Dulles, *War or Peace* (New York, 1950), p. 181; Schnabel, p. 31; *New York Times*, Jan. 20, 1950, p. 2.

41. Schonhaut, pp. 90-91; *New York Times*, Jan. 21, 1950, p. 1; Jan. 31, 1950, p. 2.

42. *Reviews of the World Situation*, pp. 232, 233, 239-40, 242; *New York Times*, Jan. 21, 1950, p. 1; Jan. 31, 1950, p. 2.

43. *Korea Assistance Acts*, pp. 406-7; *New York Times*, Feb. 15, 1950.

44. *FR 1950*, 7:8-11. Emphasis in original.

45. Ibid., p. 26.

46. Ibid., pp. 36-37.

47. For NSC 68, see ibid., 1:237-92.

Bibliographical Essay

Although literature on the Korean War is extensive, the period between the Second World War and the Korean War deserves more attention from participants and scholars alike than it heretofore has received. As American officials have ignored many problems in Korea, so scholars have tended to overlook this period in their writings.

Primary materials on Korea admittedly are often disappointingly thin. Many officials seem not to have put their feelings on paper. At the National Archives and Records Service in Washington, the diplomatic division holds decimal files and several special collections of records concerning Korea. The decimal files in Record Group 59 (the main State Department holdings) contain the largest group of records on Korea. Documents in the 740.00119 Control (Korea) group are of the occupation; they describe relations between Washington and authorities in Korea, Hodge and the Koreans, the Soviets in the north and the military government in the south, and the problems of trusteeship. When Rhee assumed the presidency of the Republic of Korea in 1948, the occupation ended and the file closed. File 501.BB Korea covers United Nations involvement in Korea beginning in 1947 and continuing in 1950. While the file contains extensive records of successive UN commissions on Korea, it is most important for materials during the UN debates of 1947 and the elections of 1948 in Korea. Relations with Korea after Rhee's inauguration and economic matters are in decimal files numbered around 895.00. No file is large, and the system seems confusing, but the documents detail increasing economic problems in Korea and attempts by the Truman administration to secure economic aid from a reluctant Congress. The Harley Notter File has wartime discussions on trusteeship; there are many documents, but the discussions were increasingly irrelevant as the situation in Korea changed. Records of the State-War-Navy Coordinating Committee (SWNCC), later changed to State-Army-Navy-Air Force Coordinating Committee (SANACC), help make clear differences between diplomatic and military views on the importance of Korea. Lt. Gen. Albert Wedemeyer undertook a whirlwind fact-finding tour to China and Korea (in all of six weeks in 1947!). Records of the Wedemeyer mission to China and Korea include a briefing paper from

Hodge to Wedemeyer, minutes of discussions between Wedemeyer and Hodge's staff, and a few press clippings. Records of the U.S. Mission to the United Nations represent one of the most important new groups of material to become available at the archives. For many years the records remained in New York City, and in the past few years archivists have taken them to Washington and opened them for scholarly research. The folders on Korea are slim, but the memorandums of conversations help prove the importance of the Korean question to policymakers. The Modern Military Division of the archives has records of the occupation, army strategy, and other matters. The filing system is not as clear as that of the Diplomatic Division, but archivists can always find requested materials. War Department materials have indexes totalling eighty-one pages which are necessary to find items in the files. For the Second World War, the ABC Files contain papers on American-British conversations for planning and policy on Korea. The CAD Files, prepared by the Civilian Affairs Division of the War Department, help illuminate problems the occupation encountered with Koreans and the workings of military government. The OPD Files represent the work of the Operations and Planning Division and are important to understanding differences between diplomats and the military. Records now are open through 1951.

Records of day-to-day events of the occupation are stored in the National Records Center in Suitland, Maryland, but these records are stored haphazardly in boxes without organization or indexes. Records show General Hodge's increasing concerns as the situation worsened, provide much material about the daily routine of military government, and help make clear the views of American officers in Korea.

The U.S. Army's Center for Military History, presently housed in the Forrestal Building (it has moved several times in past years), has two multipart manuscripts on the Korean occupation. Titled "History of United States Armed Forces in Korea" and "History of United States Army Military Government in Korea," they consist of several volumes each. Apparently written in the early 1950s by an army officer in Japan, they are based on records in Suitland. More than a thousand pages long, they help organize material found in the Suitland depository.

In addition to the Washington area primary resources, several other depositories have holdings on Korea. The Franklin D. Roosevelt Library at Hyde Park has a few slim folders on Korea reflecting the minimal attention paid Korea by the wartime president and his advisers. The Harry S. Truman Library in Independence, Missouri has little on Korea before the outbreak of war. The papers of Clark M. Clifford contain discussions by presidential advisers on Russian intentions in 1946. There are few items of interest in the president's personal file, secretary file, and official file not duplicated by State Department records. See the papers of Edgar A. J. Johnson for information about the ECA in Korea. There are a few interviews of interest in the Oral History Collection, including those of former ambassador John J. Muccio and several Korean officials. The library also has a file of discussions held at Princeton University by Dean Acheson after he left office in January 1953, a series of meetings attended by key officials who had served under him when he was secretary of state. Also there are some papers of Acheson's of importance for prewar Korean relations. These all helped Acheson prepare his memoirs. The Library of Congress Manuscript Division holds papers of such people involved in Korea as former ambassador Philip C. Jessup and Senator Tom Connally of Texas. Neither set of papers has any reference to Korea.

Private collections also are disappointing. The MacArthur Archives in Norfolk, Virginia are worth a trip, for MacArthur was General Hodge's superior and communications between Seoul and Washington passed through his command. Many of the documents in Norfolk are copies of papers in the National Archives. There is a file of letters from Syngman Rhee to MacArthur that obscures as much as it illuminates. The Hoover Institution on War, Revolution, and Peace at Stanford University holds papers of Stanley K. Hornbeck, Preston Goodfellow, and Joseph E. Jacobs. The Hornbeck Collection is large, but documents on Korea mostly are duplicates of papers in the National Archives. Goodfellow was an adviser to Rhee, and the file holds letters from the period when Rhee sought American recognition as exile leader. Jacobs was Hodge's first high-level political adviser, but he went on to more important assignments and his file reflects his progress. As he advanced in the department, he left more records. The John Foster Dulles Collection in the Princeton University Library has a few items of interest. Dulles helped argue the Korean question before the United Nations, but the slim file of his notes from 1947 does little to help fill in gaps in the records of the U.S. Mission. The Oral History Collection at Princeton has interviews with former Korean officials and several minor State Department officers. Recollections are interesting but too general. Clemson University holds the James F. Byrnes Collection; the former secretary of state's papers on Korea consist of a briefing book for the Moscow Conference of December 1945. Inexplicably not in the department's records, it is worth reading. The Hull Papers at the University of Tennessee have little of relevance on Korea, for Korea was of little importance during Hull's secretaryship. The George C. Marshall Papers at Virginia Military Institute in Lexington may have papers of great value for the period when Marshall was secretary of state; the opening of the collection, however, is tied to publication of Forrest Pogue's books on Marshall, which have not yet reached the period of his secretaryship. Other participants in the Korean question have not left records. Perhaps use of the telephone cut down written communications; few officials had Hull's habit of dictating the sense of telephone conversations to record them for history. Knowledge of this period would be greater if such people as John Carter Vincent, General John R. Hodge, Ambassador John J. Muccio and such others as Butterworth, Bond, Jacobs, and Allison had left papers or diaries.

In addition to holdings of archives and libraries, there are a great many published documents. The Department of State has published a small portion of its papers. As Korea increased in importance, so did the number of documents. Indispensable for historians is the department's *Foreign Relations of the United States* series. This ongoing series is the greatest of its kind in the world. The following volumes have materials on Korea: *1942, Vol. I: General, The British Commonwealth, The Far East* (Washington, 1960); *1943, Vol. III: The British Commonwealth, Eastern Europe, The Far East* (Washington, 1963); *1944, Vol. V: The Near East, South Asia, and Africa, The Far East* (Washington, 1965); *1945, Vol. II: General, Political and Economic Matters* (Washington, 1967); *1945, Vol. VI: The British Commonwealth, The Far East* (Washington, 1969); *1946, Vol. VII: The Far East* (Washington, 1971); *1947, Vol. I: General, The United Nations* (Washington, 1973); *1947, Vol. VI: The Far East* (Washington, 1972); *1948, Vol I: General, The United Nations* (Washington, 1974); *1948, Vol VI: The Far East, Australia* (Washington, 1974); *1949, Vol. I, National Security Affairs, Foreign Economic Policy* (Washington, 1976); *1949, Vol. VII: The Far East, Australasia*, part two (Washington, 1976); *1950, Vol. I: National Security Affairs, Foreign Economic Policy* (Washington, 1977); *1950, Vol. VII: Korea* (Washington, 1977); *The Conferences at Cairo and Teheran, 1943* (Washington, 1961); *The Conferences at Malta and Yalta, 1945* (Washington, 1955); *The Conference of Berlin (Potsdam), 1945,* two volumes (Washington, 1960). Owing to space limitations in the series and the increasing number of documents, volumes often had to leave out whole areas; the Korean aid bill of 1947 is one such area.

The department has issued collections of documents in the Far Eastern Series. Many issues contain selections dealt with in more detail in volumes of the *Foreign Relations* series. Several issues concern Korea: #18, *Korea's Independence* (Washington, 1947); #28, *Korea, 1945-1948* (Washington, 1948); #61, *Armistice in Korea: Selected Statements and Documents* (Washington, 1953); #101, *The Record on Korean Unification, 1943-1960* (Washington, 1960); #103, *North Korea: A Case Study in the Techniques of Takeover* (Washington, 1961). The last issue contains documents seized in Pyongyang when UN forces advanced up the peninsula.

The *Department of State Bulletin* has items of interest. The *Bulletin* sometimes reproduced speeches of department personnel.

Congress has released material concerning Korea, and recently committees of the House and Senate have published hearings held in executive session during the 1940s. The hearings help make clear the domestic pressures that faced the Truman administration over Korea and other issues. The *Congressional Record* has statements by southern Democrats and Republicans reflecting concern with increased spending, failure of the China policy, government deficits, and, occasionally, Korea. The House Committee on Foreign Affairs has printed hearings on Korea, but oftentimes key exchanges were held in "executive session." See *Korean Aid, 81st Congress, First Session, Hearings on House Report 5330* (Washington, 1949); *Aid to Korea, 81st Congress, First Session, Report of the Committee on Foreign Affairs, House Report #962*, two parts

(Washington, 1949) [part two is *Aid to Korea: Minority Views*]; *Background Information on Korea, House Report #2495, Report of the Committee on Foreign Affairs Pursuant to House Resolution 206, 81st Congress, Second Session* (Washington, 1950); *Economic Assistance to Certain Areas in the Far East, 81st Congress, Second Session; House Report 1571* (Washington, 1950). The record shows the administration's attempt to make Korea a symbol before the House. The House Committee on International Relations (successor to the Committee on Foreign Affairs) recently declassified and released *Selected Executive Session Hearings of the Committee, 1943-1950*. See volume 7, *United States Policy in the Far East*, part 2, *Korean Assistance Acts* (Washington, 1976). The series helps delineate the administration's problems with Congress in 1949 and 1950. The Senate also has published material on Korea. Contemporary releases include *Aid to the Republic of Korea, 81st Congress, First Session, Senate Report 748* (Washington, 1949); Armed Services Committee and Foreign Relations Committee, *Military Situation in the Far East*, five parts (Washington, 1951) [Prof. John Wiltz was instrumental in declassifying and obtaining material deleted from the published hearings]; *The United States and the Korean Problem, Documents, 1943-1953, 83d Congress, First Session, Document #74* (Washington, 1953). Recently the Senate Committee on Foreign Relations has declassified and released hearings held in executive session. See: Committee on Foreign Relations, *Economic Assistance to China and Korea, 1949-1950, Hearings Held in Executive Session Before the Committee on Foreign Relations, 81st Congress, First and Second Sessions* (Washington, 1974) and Committee on Foreign Relations, *Historical Series, Reviews of the World Situation, 1949-1950* (Washington, 1974). The hearings help illuminate the uses and abuses of the Korean symbol in domestic politics.

There are a goodly number of publications by the Government Printing Office. Edwin W. Pauley, Truman's personal ambassador on reparations, went to Korea and Manchuria in 1946. His *Report on Japanese Assets in Soviet-Occupied Korea (To the President of the United States)*, June 1946, declassified and printed in 1949, contained recommendations about Korean policy. The administration largely ignored his report, and a few years later he appeared before a Senate committee to explain his report, its reception, and his observations. See: *Hearings on Statement by Edwin W. Pauley with Reference to the Korean Situation, Committee on Armed Services, 81st Congress, Second Session* (Washington, 1950). In 1947, Lt. Gen. A. C. Wedemeyer embarked on a six-week fact-finding mission to China and Korea. Although the department ignored his report as it prepared to submit the Korean question to the UN, the report contains attitudes and opinions of military officials in Korea. Wedemeyer seemed to grasp the fundamentals of the situation. See his *Report to the President, Korea, September, 1947* (Washington, 1951). The New Korea Company, the large U.S.-run holding company for Japanese assets in Korea, should have been the centerpiece of Korea's economic reconstruction, but events went differently. See: C. Clyde Mitchell, director, New Korea Company, Ltd., *Final Report and History of the New Korea Company, Limited*, U.S. Army Military Government in

Korea, National Land Administration, 1948. To understand the economy's collapse and the U.S. government's hope for its regeneration, see Economic Cooperation Administration, *Economic Guides of Republic of Korea*, January 1950. Lastly, for press conferences and occasional presidential speeches, see Harry S. Truman, *Papers of the President of the United States, 1945-1950* (Washington, 1965).

The U.S. Army Center of Military History has published several important studies for Korea, among them Harry L. Coles and Albert K. Weinberg, *The United States Army in World War II, Civil Affairs: Soldiers Become Governors* (Washington, 1964). This generally perceptive work is a good beginning point for studying postwar occupations even though it does not deal with Korea in great detail. There is an important chapter ("Case History: Planning the End of the War Against Japan") in Ray S. Cline, *The United States Army in World War II, Washington Command Post: The Operations Division* (Washington, 1951). Major Robert K. Sawyer, *Military Advisers in Korea: KMAG in Peace and War* (Washington, 1962), has several chapters on the military situation in 1949 and 1950. He details the development of Korean armed forces, levels of American military aid, and strategic estimates of the situation. Sawyer shows army strategists were confident that the ROK Army could resist a North Korean attack. Roy E. Appleman, *United States Army in the Korean War: South to the Naktong, North to the Yalu* (Washington, 1961), and James F. Schnabel, *United States Army in the Korean War, Policy and Direction: The First Year* (Washington, 1972), although concentrating on wartime, have introductory chapters on the situation before June 25, 1950. They agree that the ROK Army was prepared for war. Interested scholars may consult Department of Defense, *The Entry of the Soviet Union into the War Against Japan: Military Plans, 1941-1945* (Washington, 1955), to help explain the situation in the closing days of the Pacific war. For a convenient gathering of important government documents on microfiche cards, see the *Declassified Documents Reference System*. For a reproduction of NSC 68 and examples of the sort of thinking that made Korea an unreal symbol, see Department of Defense, *United States-Vietnam Relations, 1945-1967* (Washington, 1971).

No other nation opens its diplomatic record as does the United States, and foreign documentary sources on Korea reflect the matter. The Soviet Union has issued one set of documents on Korea: Ministere des Affaires Etrangeres de l'U.R.S.S., *L'Union Sovietique et la Question Coreene (Documents)* (Moscow, 1948). It contains speeches and public documents but does not reveal the thought processes of Soviet leaders on Korea. British sources are meager: Secretary of State for Foreign Affairs, *Summary of Events Relating to Korea, 1950* (London, 1950) [Command Paper CMD 8078]. The material concentrates on reasons for British involvement in Korea after June 1950. Canadian material does not reflect the importance of Korea within Canadian politics and Canadian-American relations. See: Department of External Affairs, *Canada and the United Nations, Conference Series 1948, No. 1* (Ottawa, 1949);

Canada and the Korean Crisis (Ottawa, 1951); and *Documents on the Korean Crisis* (Ottawa, 1951).

The United Nations releases minutes of General Assembly and Security Council meetings. The Korean question deeply affected the UN, and the discussions are important. See: UNGA, *Official Records,* Second Session, vol. 1, Plenary Meetings; UNGA, *Official Records,* Second Session, First Committee; UNGA, *Official Records,* Third Session, first part of the Report of UNTCOK, vol. 1, Supplement #9, A/575 (1948); UNGA, *Official Records,* Third Session, first part of the Report of UNTCOK, vol. 2, annexes I-VIII, Supplement #9, A/575, add 1 (1948); UNGA, *Official Records,* Third Session, first part of the Report of UNTCOK, vol. 3, annexes IX-XII, Supplement #9, A/575 (1948); UNGA, *Official Records,* Third Session, second part of the Report of UNTCOK, vol. 1, Supplement #9, A/575, add 3 (1948); UNGA, *Official Records,* Third Session, First Part, First Committee (1948). *The United Nations Weekly Bulletin* (changed to *United Nations Bulletin* in 1948), vols. 3-5, 1947-49, published some of the most important speeches on the Korean question.

Newspapers are a good source of contemporary views and detail. The *New York Times* is the best reference source with its annual indexes and broad coverage. The *Times* often editorialized about Korea, and its Seoul correspondent, Richard J. H. Johnston, reported throughout the latter 1940s. The *Washington Post* and other major newspapers responded to crises in Korea. The *Christian Science Monitor* occasionally analzyed conditions in Korea. *The Voice of Korea* represented Korean exile opinion in the United States. Some Soviet newspaper articles on Korea appear in English-language journals and translation services discussed later.

Secondary sources on Korea include memoirs and autobiographies, biographies, contemporary writings, historical accounts.

Major participants in the Korean issue have written memoirs. Harry S. Truman, *Year of Decisions* (Garden City, N.Y.: Doubleday, 1955) and *Years of Trial and Hope* (Garden City, N.Y.: Doubleday, 1956) are useful. Even if the historical record casts doubt on their objectivity and accuracy, they may be the best memoirs by a contemporary American political leader for explaining perceptions of the president and his chief advisers. Although Truman has little to say about Korea before the outbreak of war, it is clear he accepted the symbolism and bipolarity which produced it. Dean Acheson, *Present at the Creation* (New York: W. W. Norton, 1969) discusses his dismay in January 1950 over defeat of the Korean Assistance Act but says little else about Korea. An account of the Moscow Conference appears in James F. Byrnes, *Speaking Frankly* (New York: Harper, 1947). One can sense the tension between Byrnes and Truman. Cordell Hull gives his view on the Cairo Conference of 1943 in *The Memoirs of Cordell Hull,* 2 vols. (New York: Macmillan, 1948). John M. Allison's *Ambassador from the Prairie or Allison Wonderland* (Boston: Houghton, Mifflin, 1973) is a delightful retelling of years in the State Department, recalling changes as the department greatly expanded in the mid-1940s. Allison recalls little about Korea, and a letter to him could not elicit more information. James Forrestal, *The Forrestal Diaries* (New York: Viking, 1951) helps illuminate one of the more tragic figures of the period but adds little on Korea. Korea occasionally appears in William J. Sebald, *With MacArthur in Japan, A Personal History of the Occupation* (New York: W. W. Norton, 1965). Since the Canadian government records remain closed (or in the process of opening), Lester B. Pearson, *Mike: The Memoirs of the Right Honorable Lester B. Pearson, Volume 2, 1948-1957* (Toronto: University of Toronto Press, 1973) is must reading as Pearson provides information.on Canadian-American relations and the Korean question.

There are not enough biographies of key persons in the Korean question. Two books detail Syngman Rhee's life. Robert T. Oliver, a former Rhee adviser, writes sympathetically in *Syngman Rhee: The Man Behind the Myth* (New York: Dodd, Mead, 1955). Oliver concentrates on Rhee as longtime battler for and savior of Korean independence. His uncritical account is balanced by Richard C. Allen, *Korea's Syngman Rhee, An Unauthorized Portrait* (Rutland, Vt.: C. E. Tuttle, 1960). Allen punctures the aura about Rhee, but at times his account is petty (about Rhee's German-born wife and other matters). Along with Pearson's memoirs, Dale C. Thomson, *Louis St. Laurent: Canadian* (New York: St. Martin's Press, 1974), explains Canadian concern over Korea and the cabinet crisis. Equally helpful is J. W. Pickersgill and D. F. Forster, *The Mackenzie King Record, Volume 4, 1947-1948* (Toronto: University of Toronto Press, 1970), especially chapter 4, "The Crisis over Korea, Palestine, and North Atlantic Security." The authors have organized and annotated King's diary. Also see J. W. Pickersgill, *My Years with Louis St. Laurent: A Political Memoir* (Toronto: University of Toronto Press, 1975). Pickersgill walks a fine line between St. Laurent and King, empathizing with both men and their respective viewpoints. An account of Stilwell's brief tenure as commander of the Korean occupation is in Barbara Tuchman, *Stilwell and the American Experience in China, 1911-1945* (New York: Macmillan, 1970). Arthur H. Vandenberg, Jr., *The Private Papers of Senator Vandenberg* (Boston: Houghton, Mifflin, 1952), details in diary form the special relation between Vandenberg and the Truman administration.

Korea was one among many crises in American foreign policy in the 1940s. In recent years historians have settled on several ways of viewing the origins of the cold war. John Lewis Gaddis, *The United States and the Origins of the Cold War, 1941-1947* (New York: Columbia University Press, 1972), is a basic, moderate, and award-winning approach in the vast historiography on the cold war. Gaddis believes that the U.S. had more power and fewer options and the USSR more options and less power. Unfortunately, he overlooks East Asia, which certainly mattered to the Soviet Union. Perhaps the most controversial work is Daniel Yergin, *Shattered Peace, The Origins of the Cold War and the National Security State* (Boston: Houghton, Mifflin, 1978). Yergin divides policymakers into those favoring cooperation with the Soviet Union ("Yalta") and those favoring confrontation ("Riga"). Byrnes's tenure marks the high point of the "Yalta" faction while the Truman Doctrine and rising influence of Kennan and Bohlen mark ascendancy of the "Riga" faction on whom Yergin lays blame for the cold war. (For a combative review of Yergin's work, see Daniel F. Harrington's essay in *Diplomatic History*, 1978). Thomas G. Paterson, *On Every Front, The Making of the Cold War* (New York: W. W. Norton, 1979) is a brilliant attempt to cast the origins of the cold war in an intellectual light. An admitted apologist for American foreign policy, Lisle A. Rose has written several volumes on this period. See *Dubious Victory: The United States and the End of World War II* (Kent, Ohio: Kent State University Press, 1973). Rose writes principally to correct what he claims are misimpressions of New Left historians. The late Herbert Feis was a strong defender of the U.S. government and wrote a great many monographs; see: *The Atomic Bomb and the End of World War II* (Princeton: Princeton University Press, 1960); *Between War and Peace: The Potsdam Conference* (Princeton: Princeton University Press, 1960); *The China Tangle: The American Effort in China from Pearl Harbor to the Marshall Mission* (Princeton: Princeton University Press, 1953); *From Trust to Terror: The Onset of the Cold War, 1945-1950* (New York: W. W. Norton, 1970), and many others. Feis's works are curiousity pieces biased by his pro-American stand. Other works in praise of American conduct during early cold war years are Dean Acheson, *The Pattern of Responsibility* (Boston: Houghton, Mifflin, 1952) and John Foster Dulles, *War or Peace* (New York: Macmillan, 1950). New Left historians have written much about this period in American diplomacy. Perhaps "hardest" of the New Leftists are Joyce and Gabriel Kolko, *The Limits of Power: The World and United States Foreign Policy, 1945-54* (New York: Harper & Row, 1972) and Gabriel Kolko, *The Politics of War* (New York: Random House, 1968). This ambitious work is marred by errors. Chapters on Korea misuse information, ignore what is bothersome, and overlook reality. The authors, for instance, quote an administration source for a crucial point; the footnote attributes the quotation to Edwin W. Pauley. By no stretch of the imagination, however, was Pauley representative of, or a spokesperson for the Truman administration. The Kolkos used him because it suited their purposes. Lynn H. Miller and Ronald W. Pruessen, *Reflections on the Cold War, A Quarter Century of American Foreign Policy* (Philadelphia: Temple University Press, 1974), employ a cavalier treatment of facts and the tortuous logic of the ideologically committed scholar. It is "presentism" rather than history. Solid research, sound reasoning, and a welcome emphasis on economic diplomacy characterize Walter LaFeber, *America, Russia, and the Cold War, 1945-1975* (New York: John Wiley, 1976), and Thomas G. Paterson, *Soviet-American Confrontation* (Baltimore: Johns Hopkins University Press, 1974). For particular conferences, see Diane Shaver Clemens, *Yalta* (New York: Oxford University Press, 1970) and Patricia Dawson Ward, *The Threat of Peace: James F. Byrnes and the Council of Foreign Ministers, 1945-1946* (Kent, Ohio: Kent State University Press, 1979). To see how the United States misperceived reality in situations similar to Korea, see Bruce Kuniholm, *The Origins of the Cold War in the Near East* (Princeton: Princeton University Press, 1979) and David Green, *The Containment of Latin America* (Chicago: Quadrangle, 1971). For an interesting view of Stalin and the dynamics of Soviet foreign policy (though difficult to prove), see William O. McCagg, Jr., *Stalin Embattled, 1943-1948* (Detroit: Wayne State University Press, 1978). McCagg believes Stalin acted as he did owing to domestic political struggles!

There are many studies of Far Eastern diplomacy in the 1940s, and some more recent works attempt to explain the complex and confusing situation. Richard Lauterbach, *Danger From the East* (New York: Harper and Bros., 1946), warns of Soviet expansion and American indecisiveness. Lauterbach lacks perspective, for he ignores Soviet security interests, postwar Asian nationalism, and American attitudes toward emerging Asian nationalism. Owen Lattimore, *The Situation in Asia* (Boston: Little, Brown, 1949), is another perceptive work from a famous China historian who understands intercultural blendings. Lattimore explains relations between Asian nationalism and great-power politics. Max Beloff, *Soviet Policy in the Far East, 1944-1951* (New York: Oxford University Press, 1953), remains a reasonable explanation of Soviet politics despite its age and lack of access to Soviet documents. Few other works of that period make a positive impression. See Harold M. Vinacke, *Far Eastern Politics in the Postwar Period* (New York: Appleton-Century-Crofts, 1956); David J. Dallin, *Soviet Russia and the Far East* (New Haven, Conn.: Yale University Press, 1948); Harold R. Isaacs, *No Peace for Asia* (New York: Macmillan, 1947); Kenneth S. Latourette, *The American Record in the Far East, 1945-1951* (New York: Macmillan, 1952); Harriet L. Moore, *Soviet Far Eastern Policy, 1931-1945* (Princeton: Princeton University Press, 1945); and Ralph N. Clough, *East Asia and U.S. Security* (Washington, D.C.: The Brookings Institution, 1975); and William Mandel, *Soviet Source Materials on the U.S.S.R.'s Relations with East Asia, 1945-1950* (New York: International Secretariat, Institute of Pacific Relations, 1950). Several recent works demonstrate a variety of views on postwar Asia and the cold war. Lisle A. Rose, *Roots of Tragedy: The United States and the Struggle for Asia, 1945-1953* (Westport, Conn.: Greenwood Press, 1975), is another work by a master stylist. Rose cannot stand aside from his defense of America and has no chapters on Korea during the key period 1947-50 when the symbol emerged. Perhaps he attempts to cover too much territory in too little space. Regardless, this will remain the standard monograph until something new replaces it. More provocative is Akira Iriye, *The Cold War in Asia* (Englewood Cliffs, N.J.: Prentice-Hall, 1974). Iriye is a brilliant and perceptive diplomatic historian whose earlier works concentrate on the theme of order; however, he grants too much logic and order in the development of the cold war in East Asia. This lengthy essay seems to overlook the confusion that marked American policy and possibly Soviet deliberations. He forgets the dramatic increase in size of the State Department, the vast new concerns concomitant with great power status, and the insular nature of many American diplomats. Rather than order, confusion and misperception make a better framework for understanding American policy in Asia. Robert R. Simmons has engaged in a noteworthy hypothesis in *The Strained Alliance: Peking, Pyong-yang, Moscow, and the Politics of the Korean Civil War* (New York: Free Press, 1975). To Simmons, war came about because of tension in the North Korean hierarchy between Kim Il-Sung and Pak Hun-yung. Perhaps his work is overly ambitious, but it is a stimulating and brilliant explanation. Yonosuke Nagai and Akira Iriye, editors, *The Origins of the Cold War in Asia* (New York: Columbia University Press, 1977), have produced a provocative set of essays. The quality of articles varies from Robert M. Slusser, "Soviet Far Eastern Policy, 1945-1950: Stalin's Goals in Korea," which has little to recommend it, to such excellent contributions as John Lewis Gaddis, "Korea in American Politics, Strategy, and Diplomacy, 1945-1950" (a good, general introduction to the topic) and George McT. Kahin, "The United States and the Anticolonial Revolutions in Southeast Asia, 1945-1950."

Given the intertwining of China and Korea in late 1949 to early 1950, it is important to understand American policy during the Chinese civil war. The standard work, Tsou Tang, *America's Failure in China, 1941-1950* (Chicago: University of Chicago Press, 1963), shows the passage of time. It predated the opening of archives, has an outdated framework, and is somewhat simplistic. Much more compelling are two recent works. Michael Schaller, *The U.S. Crusade in China, 1938-1945* (New York: Columbia University Press, 1979), combines careful scholarship and sound analysis. Schaller proves an early commitment to Chiang (by 1938) and thus possibly dates the beginnings of American misperceptions over Asia. More challenging though less satisfying is Lewis McCarroll Purifoy, *Harry Truman's China Policy, McCarthyism and the Diplomacy of Hysteria, 1947-1951* (New York: New Viewpoints, 1976). Purifoy argues that by Acheson's address of January 12, 1950, the administration had negotiated disengagement from the Asian mainland, perhaps in order to approach Mao. McCarthyism and the China lobby forced the administration back into Asia and confrontation with the PRC. If Purifoy is correct, it is a damning and incisive account. Just published is an exciting set of essays in Dorothy Borg and Waldo Heinrichs, editors, *Uncertain Years: Chinese-American Relations, 1947-1950* (New York: Columbia University Press, 1980). Several essays may help explain matters in Korea and the administration's use of Korea to ease its China difficulties. See Warren I. Cohen, "Acheson, His Advisers, and China, 1949-1950," which argues Acheson lacked widespread State Department support for a rapprochement with Chinese communists. Nancy Bernkopf Tucker, "Nationalist China's Decline and its Impact on Sino-American Relations, 1949-1950," argues that Chinese Nationalist ineptitude and disarray helped the C.C.P.-U.S.A. rapprochement. Also see Michael H. Hunt, "Mao Tse-tung and the Issue of Accommodation with the United States, 1948-1950."

From more general works, the literature increases as it turns to Korea. Aleksandr Ilich Gitovich and B. Bursov, *North of the 38th Parallel* (Shanghai:

Epoch Publishing, 1948), present the Soviet view of the North Korean paradise. Interestingly, they compare the situation in Germany and Korea—was Korea a signal of Soviet intentions for Germany? In *The Epic of Korea* (Washington, D.C.: Public Affairs Press, 1950), A. Wigfall Green recounts his experience in Korea and the lot of American troops in the south. Leland M. Goodrich, *Korea: A Study of US Policy in the United Nations* (New York: Council on Foreign Relations, 1956), concentrates on American actions at the UN, while Leon Gordenker, *The United Nations and the Peaceful Unification of Korea: The Politics of Field Operations, 1947-1950* (The Hague: M. Nijhoff, 1959), concentrates on the UN commissions in Korea. As opposite halves of the same question, they should be read together. Of course, these works lack access to State Department records and could use updating. Allen Guttman, *Korea: Cold War and Limited War*, second edition (New York: D. C. Heath, 1972), is a good sampling of writing on the war. The most perceptive work on the situation in Korea is Gregory Henderson, *Korea: The Politics of the Vortex* (Cambridge, Mass.: Harvard University Press, 1968). He describes a society that had undergone tremendous, almost unacceptable, change during the period of Japanese rule and which tottered on the brink of collapse. When the Americans failed to rule harshly, Korean society and polity disintegrated. It is a clear and convincing account. Koh Byung-chul, *The Foreign Policy of North Korea* (New York: Praeger, 1969), attempts to explain thought processes behind North Korean diplomacy, but his use of jargon often obscures points. Lee Chong-sik makes modern Korean nationalism come alive in *The Politics of Korean Nationalism* (Berkeley: University of California Press, 1965). Lee serves as an able introduction to Simmon's hypothesis and provides valuable background on major figures in Korea. A former official in the State Department, George M. McCune, wrote a great deal about Korea after he retired. In *Korea Today* (Cambridge, Mass.: Harvard University Press, 1950), McCune and Arthur Grey describe never-ending errors in Korea and Washington and decry the lack of attention Korea received. C. Clyde Mitchell noted similarities to the debacle in China in *Second Failure in Asia* (Washington, D.C.: Public Affairs Institute, 1951). Concentrating on economic matters, Mitchell, former director of the New Korea Company, presents a strong critique of America's failure to create a sound Korean economy and institute needed reforms. Until 1951, native communists under Pak and Soviet Koreans under Kim divided power in the north. The struggle for control dominates early chapters of Nam Koon-woo, *The North Korean Communist Leadership, 1945-1965, A Study of Factionalism and Political Consolidation* (Tuscaloosa, Ala.: University of Alabama Press, 1974). Nam's monograph is another argument that the critical issue in Korea was competing nationalist figures and not the superpower confrontation. John Kie-chang Oh, *Korea: Democracy on Trial* (Ithaca, N.Y.: Cornell University Press, 1968), details the increasing repression of Rhee's government during the 1940s. Oh tends to blame Rhee for most developments. Robert A. Scalapino's *North Korea Today* (New York: Praeger, 1963) and his monumental study (with Lee Chong-sik), *Communism in Korea, Part I: The Movement* and *Part II: The Society* (Berkeley: University of California Press, 1972), uses many North Korean sources captured when American forces occupied Pyongyang in the race to the Yalu. This work will remain the standard one on North Korean society and the guerrilla movement in the south. Shih-chieh Chih-shih, *A Chronicle of Principal Events Relating to the Korean Question, 1945-1954* (Peking: [World Culture], 1954), is the Chinese communist story of the situation in Korea. It paints the invasion as a response to cries for help from oppressed Korean patriots in the south and blames American imperialist aggressors for saving the renegade, reactionary Rhee from people's justice. Given the hostility in Sino-American relations in the mid-1950s, the work is characteristic of Chinese communist attitudes toward the United States. I. F. Stone engages in imaginative flights of fancy in *The Hidden History of the Korean War* (New York: Monthly Review Press, 1952 [reissued 1970]). Stone writes an interesting but not convincing account of a clever charade in Korea. Rhee and MacArthur (possibly with connivance of John Foster Dulles) planned to trick North Korea into a punitive border raid, describe it as a major invasion, have the ROK Army retreat, and cry out for U.S. intervention. It is plausible but can only appeal to those who see conspiracies everywhere. The history of the native communist movement is in Suh Dae-sook, *The Korean Communist Movement, 1918-1948* (Princeton: Princeton University Press, 1967). Significantly, Suh ends his account when Pak flees north, again arguing that the major issue in Korea was competing nationalisms and not superpower confrontation.

There are several works on American-Korean relations, but all are found wanting in critical areas. For many years the standard work was Cho Soon-sung, *Korea in World Politics, 1940-1950, An Evaluation of American Responsibility* (Berkeley: University of California Press, 1967). Cho wants to assess American "blame" for the peninsula's permanent division; he overlooks many other issues. Also, he wrote his monograph years in advance of the publication of pertinent *Foreign Relations* volumes and the opening of State Department archives. Cho's work replaced two earlier monographs on American-Korean policy: John C. Caldwell, *The Korea Story* (Chicago: H. Regnery, 1952), and Carl Berger, *The Korea Knot* (Philadelphia: University of Pennsylvania Press, 1964). These early accounts make the Korean issue in American diplomacy too simple; they do not see the many ways Korea affected other, more important, situations. The most recent work, Frank Baldwin, editor, *Without Parallel: The Korean-American Relationship Since 1945* (New York: Pantheon, 1974), is the most controversial. It is a New Left critique born out of anger at current conditions in southern Korea. The contributors share a similar premise: the current political-economic-social situation came about because of *deliberate* American actions. Bruce Cumings writes passionately of the denial of Korean nationalism in the weeks and months after the end of war. His description of conditions in Korea is moving, his understanding of policy somewhat shallow. He underestimates Washington's confusion and divides the south into radical left and collaborationist right without a middle. Jon Halliday attempts to discuss the period when the U.S. involved the UN in Korea. He seeks to fit facts into a preconceived mold and uses evidence as he wills. He notes "as with most of the UN discussions over Korea, the vast mass of speeches and maneuvers can be ingored" (p. 113). His flaws are those of the ideologically committed scholar. Other articles, while not dealing with the time period 1945-50, all introduce material with the same preconceived notions. They force evidence to fit the concept of a deliberate American attempt to seek a base in Korea to threaten the PRC and USSR and deny the Korean people their destiny. William W. Stueck, Jr., *The Road to Confrontation* (Chapel Hill, N.C.: University of North Carolina Press, 1980), seeks to explain the intricacies of American policy toward China and Korea in less than three hundred pages. It is too brief, overlooks such matters as the Pacific pact, and finds the U.S. government wanted to confront communism rather than the fact that the situation helped control American policy.

Historians have written several works about the occupation in Korea. Hajo Holborn, *American Military Government, Its Organization and Policies* (Washington, D.C.: Infantry Journal Press, 1947), and Carl J. Friedrich and Associates, *American Experiences in Military Government in World War II* (New York: Rhinehart, 1948), contain chapters on Korea. These works concentrate on technical matters pertaining to organizing and implementing a military occupation. They help explain circumstances from which the Korean occupation developed, for most planning concerned defeated enemies rather than possibly friendly peoples as in Korea. E. Grant Meade, *American Military Government in Korea* (New York: King's Crown Press, 1951), is a stinging critique of the occupation from 1945 to its end in 1948. Meade, a former officer in the occupation, understood the differing perceptions of Koreans and occupiers.

Korea affected American politics and vice versa, and there are a few monographs that examine the relationship. The initial Korean aid bill of 1947 receives notice in Joseph M. Jones, *The Fifteen Weeks* (New York: Viking Press, 1955), which discusses the origins of the Truman Doctrine. Jones's monograph would benefit from a further opening of the archives. In *The Korean War and American Politics: The Republican Party as a Case Study* (Philadelphia: University of Pennsylvania Press, 1968), Ronald Caridi details the change from bipartisan to partisan foreign policy that made congressional support of Korean aid almost impossible. He helps delineate the relationship between Korea and China from 1949 to 1950. Another important monograph is H. Bradford Westerfield, *Foreign Policy and Party Politics, Pearl Harbor to Korea* (New Haven, Conn.: Yale University Press, 1955). Westerfield shows the change in Republican party attitudes on foreign policy after Vandenberg's decline. Richard H. Rovere and Arthur Schlesinger, Jr., discuss the situation during the Korean War in *The Truman-MacArthur Controversy and American Foreign Policy* (New York: Farrar, Strauss and Giroux, 1965).

There are a few works on Canadian diplomacy, and as the Canadian government opens it records, there should be many more. Stephen Clarkson, editor, *An Independent Foreign Policy for Canada* (Toronto: McClelland and Stewart, 1968), bemoans Canada's giant neighbor to the south and its attempt to dominate Canadian foreign policy. Robert A. Spencer, *Canada in World Affairs, From UN to NATO, 1946-1949* (Toronto: Oxford University Press, 1959), shows the change in Canadian foreign policy from the isolationism of Prime Minister King to the internationalism of Louis St. Laurent and Lester Pearson. Denis Stairs, *The Diplomacy of Constraint: Canada, The Korean War, and the United States* (Toronto: University of Toronto Press, 1974), is an outstanding work. Benefiting from several long interviews with Lester Pearson and admirable use of available sources, Stairs delineates the tremendous pressure brought to bear on the Canadian government and the ways it affected Canadian politics.

The 1940s saw a flood of articles on the Korean situation. Most articles decried American policy in Korea as innocently mistaken and deliberately reactionary, causing war. Few have importance for the quality of analysis, but they are significant indicators of concern over the situation in Korea. See: William N. Angus and Sunoo Hagwon, "American Policy in Korea: Two Views," *Far Eastern Survey*, July 31, 1946, pp. 228-31; Roger N. Baldwin, "Our Blunder in Korea," *The Nation*, Aug. 2, 1947, pp. 119-21; Hugh Borton, "Occupation Politics in Japan and Korea," *Annals of the Academy of Political and Social Science* 255 (Jan. 1948): 146-55; J. P. Brinton, III, "Small Korea is a Big Test," *The New Republic*, Mar. 14, 1949, pp. 19-22; Arthur C. Bunce, "The Future of Korea: Part I," *Far Eastern Survey*, Apr. 19, 1944, pp. 67-70 and "The Future of Korea: Part II," *Far Eastern Survey*, May 17, 1944, pp. 85-88; Dean Hugh, "The Death of Lyuh Woon-hyung," *The Nation*, Sept. 6, 1947, pp. 228-29; Tyler Dennet, "In Due Course," *Far Eastern Survey*, Jan. 17, 1945, pp. 1-4; F. L. Eversull, "Korea: Russia and the United States in the Orient," *Vital Speeches*, Feb. 15, 1948, p. 273; J. Earnest Fisher, "Korea Today," *The Far Eastern Quarterly* 15 (May 1946): 261-71; Mark Gayn, "Cold War: Two Police States in Korea," *The New Republic*, Sept. 15, 1947, pp. 15-16; Andrew J. Grajdanzev, "Korea Divided," *Far Eastern Survey*, Oct. 10, 1945, pp. 281-83; Will Hamlin (pseudonym), "Korea: An American Tragedy," *The Nation*, Mar. 1, 1947, pp. 245-47; Kim Yong-jeung, "The Cold War and Korean Elections," *Far Eastern Survey*, May 5, 1948, pp. 101-2; Owen Lattimore, "Rebuilding Our Policy in Asia," *The Atlantic Monthly*, Jan. 1950, pp. 21-23; Richard E. Lauterbach, "Hodge's Korea," *Virginia Quarterly Review* 23 (July 1947): 349-68; Liem Channing, "United States Rule in Korea," *Far Eastern Survey*, Apr. 6, 1949, pp. 77-80; George M. McCune, "Korea—the First Year of Liberation," *Pacific Affairs* 20 (Mar. 1947): 3-17; George M. McCune, "Occupation Politics in Korea," *Far Eastern Survey*, Feb. 13, 1946, pp. 33-37; George M. McCune, "Postwar Government and Politics in Korea," *Journal of Politics*, Nov. 1947, pp. 605-23; Shannon McCune, "Physical Basis for Korean Boundaries," *The Far Eastern Quarterly* 15 (May 1946): 272-88; C. Clyde Mitchell, "Land Reform in South Korea," *Pacific Affairs* 22 (June 1949): 144-54; Brainard Prescott, "How We Built the South Korean Republic," *Reporter*, Sept. 26, 1950, pp. 11-14; Andrew Roth, "Crossfire in Korea," *The Nation*, Feb. 23, 1946, pp. 220-22; Andrew Roth, "Korea's Impending Explosion," *The Nation*, Aug. 13, 1949, pp. 151-53; Bertram D. Sarafan, "Military Government: Korea," *Far Eastern Survey*, Nov. 20, 1946, pp. 349-52; Edgar Snow, "We Meet Russia in Korea," *Saturday Evening Post*, Mar. 31, 1946, pp. 18-19; Maxwell S. Stewart, "Blunder in Korea," *The Nation*, May 22, 1948, pp. 569-71; Irene B. Taeuber, "Potential Population of Postwar Korea," *The Far Eastern Quarterly* 15 (May 1946): 289-307; John N. Washburn, "Russia Looks at Northern Korea," *Pacific Affairs* 20 (June 1947): 152-60; John N. Washburn, "The Soviet Press Views North Korea," *Pacific Affairs* 22 (Mar. 1949): 53-59; Benjamin Weems, "Behind the Korean Election," *Far Eastern Survey*, June 23, 1948, pp. 142-47; "Korea—A Desperate Situation," *Intelligence Digest*, Dec. 1, 1948, pp. 16-17; "Korea Heads for the Shoals," *Business Week*, Sept. 17, 1949, pp. 116-18; "Our Record in Korea in the Light of Increasing Hostility of the Korean People to Our Military Government," *Amerasia*, Nov. 1946; "Soviets Pin Down US in Korea," *Business Week*, Oct. 4, 1947, pp. 109-12; "US Decision to Quit Korea," *US News and World Report*, May 5, 1948, pp. 19-20; "US Policy Act II: Korea," *The New Republic*, May 5, 1947, pp. 24-27; "World Policy and Bipartisanship," *US News and World Report*, May 5, 1950, pp. 28-31.

In the past few years good articles have appeared using recently opened archival collections; hopefully this heralds forthcoming monographs. Russell D. Buhite gives a good overview of East Asian diplomacy in "Major Interests: American Policy Toward China, Taiwan, and Korea, 1945-1950," *Pacific Historical Review* 47 (Aug. 1978): 425-51; Russell D. Buhite, "Soviet-American Relations and the Repatriation of Prisoners of War, 1945," *The Historian* 35 (May 1973): 384-97; another area of lost opportunity is described in Evelyn Colbert, "Reconsiderations: The Road Not Taken, Decolonization and Independence in Indonesia and Indochina," *Foreign Affairs* 51 (Apr. 1973): 608-28; Senator Vandenberg seemingly occupied the middle ground in the China debate between the China lobby and the administration as decribed in James Fetzer, "Senator Vandenberg and the American Commitment to China, 1945-1950," *The Historian* 36 (Feb. 1974): 283-303; in recent years there has been a debate over Kennan and the meaning of containment, see John Lewis Gaddis, "Reconsiderations: Containment: A Reassessment," *Foreign Affairs* 55 (July 1977): 873-87 and the response by Eduard Mark, "The Question of Containment: A Reply to John Lewis Gaddis," in *Foreign Affairs* 56 (Jan. 1978): 430-41; for a view of the Truman Doctrine and its importance see John Lewis Gaddis, "Reconsiderations: Was the Truman Doctrine a Real Turning Point?" *Foreign Affairs* 52 (Jan. 1974): 386-402; George Ginsburg,

"The U.S.S.R. and the Issue of Reunification," International Conference on the Problems of Korean Unification, *Report* (Seoul: Asiatic Research Center, Korea University, 1971); George C. Herring, "The Truman Administration and the Restoration of French Sovereignty in Indochina," *Diplomatic History* 1 (Spring 1977): 97-117; Robert J. McMahon, "Anglo-American Diplomacy and the Reoccupation of the Netherlands East Indies," *Diplomatic History* 2 (Winter 1978): 1-24; George T. Mazuzan, "America's U.N. Commitment, 1945-1953," *The Historian* 40 (Feb. 1978): 309-30; Robert L. Messer, "Paths Not Taken: the U.S. Department of State and Alternatives to Containment, 1945-1946," *Diplomatic History* 1 (Fall 1977): 297-320; Edward T. Rowe, "The United States, the United Nations, and the Cold War," *International Organization* 25 (Winter 1971): 59-78; John J. Sbrega, "The Japanese Surrender: Some Unexpected Consequences in Southeast Asia," *Asian Affairs* 7 (Sept.-Oct., 1979): 45-63; Mark J. Scher, "US Policy in Korea 1945-1948: A Neocolonial Policy Takes Shape," *Bulletin of Concerned Asian Scholars* 5 (Dec. 1973): 17-27; Howard Schonberger, "The Japan Lobby in American Diplomacy, 1947-1952," *Pacific Historical Review* 46 (Aug. 1977): 327-59; Christopher Thorne, "Indochina and Anglo-American Relations, 1942-1945," *Pacific Historical Review* 45 (Feb. 1976): 73-96; Warren W. Tozer, "Last Bridge to China: The Shanghai Power Company, the Truman Administration, and the Chinese Communists," *Diplomatic History* 1 (Winter 1977): 64-78; Nancy Bernkopf Tucker, "An Unlikely Peace: American Missionaries and the Chinese Communists, 1948-1950," *Pacific Historical Review* 45 (Feb. 1976): 97-116; Wesley T. Wooley, "The Quest for Permanent Peace—American Supranationalism, 1945-1947," *The Historian* 35 (Nov. 1972): 18-31; Paul J. Zingg, "The Cold War in North Africa: American Foreign Policy and Postwar Muslim Nationalism, 1945-1962," *The Historian* 39 (Nov. 1976): 40-61.

In recent years Korean scholars have written on this period; possibly many of the articles had to pass censorship and thus reflect current Korean politics rather than historical scholarship. See Hong Chong-hyuk, "The Historical Background of Korea's Division," *Koreana Quarterly*, Autumn 1972, pp. 10-32; B. C. Koh, "Dilemma of Korean Unification," *Asian Survey*, May 1971, pp. 47-96; Chan Kwon, "The Leadership of Syngman Rhee," *Koreana Quarterly*, Spring 1971, pp. 31-48; Lee Chong-sik, "Kim Il-sung of North Korea," *Asian Survey*, June 1967, pp. 274-82; Lhee Ho-joh, "Diplomatic Activities and Proposals of Rhee Syngman following withdrawal of US Armed Forces in 1949," *Korea Observer*, July 1970, pp. 22-48; Moon Hwanchoi, "A Review of Korea's Land Reform," *Koreana Quarterly*, Spring 1960, pp. 55-63; Ro Kwang-ane, "The United Nations and the Founding of the Republic of Korea: A Reappraisal," *Koreana Quarterly*, Spring 1968, pp. 65-74; Tai Yon-han, "Impact of Western Democracy on Modern Korea," *Koreana Quarterly*, Spring 1960, pp. 11-21; Tom Won-lee, "How the United Nations Failed in Korea," *Koreana Quarterly*, Summer 1961, pp. 28-41; Wan Hyok-pu, "The History of American Aid to Korea," *Koreana Quarterly*, Summer 1961, pp. 71-96; Young Kyo-yoon,

"United Nations Participation in Korean Affairs, 1947-1951," *Koreana Quarterly*, Spring 1960, pp. 22-54.

In 1973 an interesting exchange appeared, based on letters between Rhee and MacArthur housed at the MacArthur Archives in Norfolk, Virginia, in the November issue of *Pacific Historical Review*: William Stueck, "Cold War Revisionism and the Origins of the Korean Conflict: The Kolko Thesis," pp. 537-60; and Joyce and Gabriel Kolko, "To Root Out Those Among Them—A Response," pp. 560-66.

Official Soviet records of Korea are not available, but during the 1940s many Soviet journalists, probably reflecting the official position, wrote about Korea in the Soviet English-language publications, *New Times* and *Soviet Press Translations*. *New Times* articles included M. Markov, "The Soviet Union and the Korean Question," Dec. 15, 1948, pp. 7-10; M. Markov, "True and False Friends of the Korean People," May 1, 1947, pp. 27-29; M. Tarasov, "What We Saw in Japan and Korea," May 30, 1947, pp. 20-23; A. Volochayesvsky, "In South Korea (Travel Notes)," Aug. 18, 1948, pp. 18-21; I. Yermashev, "American Policy Towards Korea: An Historical Retrospect," Oct. 22, 1947, pp. 13-15; "The Soviet Union and Korea," Oct. 20, 1948, pp. 4-5.

Soviet Press Translations included articles from Soviet magazines and also reflects the official view. See: V. Kovizhenko, "What American 'Aid' Means to Southern Korea," *Trud*, Jan. 8, 1949 (in *SPT*, Apr. 15, 1949, pp. 235-37); P. Krainov, "The Struggle of the Korean People for a United, Independent, Democratic Korea," *Bolshevik*, June 15, 1949 (in *SPT*, Oct. 15, 1949, pp. 549-58); R. Moran, "The Position of the Korean Pretender," *Izvestia*, Dec. 24, 1946 (in *SPT*, Mar. 31, 1947, p. 23); N. Pakhonov, "The Colonial Regime in Southern Korea," *Izvestia*, Feb. 5, 1949 (in *SPT*, Apr. 1, 1949, pp. 201-3); V. Perlin, "On Both Sides of the 38th Parallel," *Trud*, Aug. 20, 1947 (in *SPT*, Nov. 1, 1947, pp. 191-93); V. Smolensky, "The American Plan for the Dismemberment of Korea in Action," *Pravda*, Mar. 18, 1948 (in *SPT*, Apr. 15, 1948, pp. 227-29); V. Smolensky, "The Situation in Korea," *Pravda*, Nov. 16, 1946 (in *SPT*, Mar. 15, 1947, pp. 8-11); Y. Viktorov, "American 'Bearers of Democracy' in Southern Korea," *Pravda*, Sept. 6, 1947 (in *SPT*, Oct. 15, 1947, pp. 158-59); Y. Viktorov, "The Situation in the Joint Soviet-American Commission on Korea," *Pravda*, Sept. 1, 1947 (in *SPT*, Oct. 1, 1947, pp. 123-27); "The American Democrats Reveal Their True Colors in Korea," *Izvestia*, Oct. 2, 1947 (in *SPT*, Dec. 15, 1947, pp. 290-91); "Appeal of the Korean Supreme People's Assembly to the Governments of the U.S.A. and the Soviet Union," *Pravda*, Sept. 14, 1948 (in *SPT*, Nov. 1, 1948, pp. 581-82); "The Korean People Speak Out Against Separate Elections in South Korea," *Izvestia*, Apr. 16, 1948 (in *SPT*, June 16, 1948, pp. 364-66); "The Korean People Welcome the Soviet Government's Decision," *Izvestia*, Sept. 25, 1948 (in *SPT*, Nov. 1, 1948, pp. 584-85).

Also of significance are N. Pakhomov, "The Colonial Regime in Southern Korea," *Izvestia*, Feb. 5, 1949, in *The Current Digest of the Soviet Press*, vol. 1, issue 6, p. 39 (1949) and E. F. Kovalev, "A New Step in the Study of Sino-Soviet Relations Between 1945 and 1970," *Voprosy Istorii* (1972) in *Soviet Studies in History* 12 (Winter 1973-74): 71-87.

There are a steadily increasing number of unpublished dissertations on Korea. Philip L. Gridgham, "American Policy Toward Korean Independence, 1866-1920," (Ph.D. dissertation, Tufts University [Fletcher School of Law and Diplomacy], 1952) lacks a theme but has a wealth of detail on early American diplomacy. Kwang S. Kim, "The Failure of U.S. Policy Toward Korea, 1945-1950," (M.A. thesis, Columbia University, 1964) shows the author's Korean nationalism. Kim seeks to blame the U.S. government for the present division of his homeland. U-Gene Lee, "American Policy Toward Korea, 1942-1947: Formulation and Execution," (Ph.D. dissertation, Georgetown University, 1973) cites Korean language sources and makes abundant use of U.S. military records. Lee has no central theme and seeks to apportion blame for Korea's divided status. Lee Won-sul, "The Impact of United States Occupation Policy on the Socio-Political Structure of South Korea, 1945-1948," (Ph.D. dissertation, Western Reserve University, 1961) is first-rate. Lee explains the key role played by former collaborators in Rhee's consolidation of power in the south. Lee believes that the collaborators controlled Rhee's drive to power, had strong influence with the military occupation, and successfully avoided the just retribution of the Korean people. Beatrice May Schonhaut, "Secretary Acheson's China Policy, January 1949-June 1950," (Ph.D. dissertation, Ohio State University, 1965) uses mostly secondary sources. More recent are the following: Kang Han-mu, "The United States Military Government in Korea," (Ph.D. dissertation, University of Cincinnati, 1970); Bruce Cumings, "The Politics of Liberation: Korea, 1945-1947," (Ph.D. dissertation, Columbia University, 1975); John Barry Kotch, "United States Security Policy Toward Korea, 1945-1953: The Origins and Evolution of American Involvement and the Emergence of a National Security Commitment," (Ph.D. dissertation, Columbia University, 1976); James I. Matray, "The Reluctant Crusade: American Foreign Policy in Korea, 1941-1950," (Ph.D. dissertation, University of Virginia, 1977); William W. Stueck, Jr., "American Policy Toward China and Korea, 1947-1950," (Ph.D. dissertation, Brown University, 1977); Charles M. Dobbs, "American Foreign Policy, the Cold War, and Korea: 1942-1950," (Ph.D. dissertation, Indiana University, 1978); and Kenneth R. Mauck, "The Formation of American Foreign Policy in Korea, 1945-1953," (Ph.D. dissertation, University of Oklahoma, 1979).

Index

Charles M. Dobbs earned his doctorate at Indiana University and now teaches modern history at Metropolitan State College in Denver.